On the Way to the Sky

Photo by Dennis J. Williams, courtesy of the Bob Brookmeyer Special Collection, Sibley Music Library, Eastman School of Music, University of Rochester, NY.

On the Way to the Sky
Remembering Bob Brookmeyer

Michael Stephans

Number 20 in the North Texas Lives of Musicians Series

University of North Texas Press
Denton, Texas

© 2025 Michael Stephans

All rights reserved.
Printed in the United States of America.
10 9 8 7 6 5 4 3 2 1

Permissions:
University of North Texas Press
1155 Union Circle #311336
Denton, TX 76203-5017

The paper used in this book meets the minimum requirements of the American National Standard for Permanence of Paper for Printed Library Materials, z39.48.1984. Binding materials have been chosen for durability.

Library of Congress Cataloging-in-Publication Data

Names: Stephans, Michael author
Title: On the way to the sky: remembering Bob Brookmeyer / Michael Stephans.
Other titles: North Texas lives of musicians series no. 20.
Description: Denton, Texas : University of North Texas Press, [2025] | Series: Number 20 in the North Texas lives of musicians series | Includes bibliographical references and index.
Identifiers: LCCN 2025019224 (print) | LCCN 2025019225 (ebook) | ISBN 9781574419696 cloth | ISBN 9781574419771 ebook
Subjects: LCSH: Brookmeyer, Bob, 1929-2011 | Composers--United States--Biography | Jazz musicians--United States--Biography | Jazz--United States--History and criticism | BISAC: MUSIC / Genres & Styles / Jazz | BIOGRAPHY & AUTOBIOGRAPHY / Music | LCGFT: Biographies
Classification: LCC ML410.B8585 S74 2025 (print) | LCC ML410.B8585 (ebook) | DDC 781.65092--dc23/eng/20250417
LC record available at https://lccn.loc.gov/2025019224
LC ebook record available at https://lccn.loc.gov/2025019225

On the Way to the Sky is Number 20 in the North Texas Lives of Musicians Series.

The electronic edition of this book was made possible by the support of the Vick Family Foundation.

Typeset by vPrompt eServices.

Contents

Preface: Dreams and Realities vii

Chapter 1 Brookmeyer 101 1

Chapter 2 Awakenings Along the Way 21

Chapter 3 For the Record I 47

Chapter 4 For the Record II 67

Chapter 5 For the Record III 107

Chapter 6 Inside Voices, Shining Lights 149

Chapter 7 . . . And Other Bright Moments 199

Chapter 8 Goodbye World 229

Selected Discography 235

Acknowledgments 239

In Memoriam 241

Endnotes 243

Bibliography 249

Index 253

Bob in our home in California (late '70s). Photo from author's collection.

Preface
Dreams and Realities

Dreams

As a child growing up in South Florida, I remember being deeply affected by the song "When You Wish upon a Star" from the 1940 Disney movie, *Pinocchio*. I remember most the opening lyrics:

> When you wish upon a star,
> Makes no difference who you are.
> Anything your heart desires,
> Will come to you.[1]

Now many of us hope that our dreams and wishes come true, but as we get older, we discover much to our disappointment that the Universe has other plans for us, and that not all of our wishes are granted. However, if we pay attention as the years roll by, we may see that some of our dreams—small or large, or both—do become realities. I experienced a number of such instances in my years on the planet that are, indeed, beyond my comprehension or any rational explanation.

I think that Shakespeare was one of the first people I read who, in effect, reaffirmed what I've been thinking with one of his most profound and endearing statements from *Hamlet* whereupon Hamlet responds in conversation with the philosopher Horatio: "There are more things in heaven and earth, Horatio / Than are dreamt of in your philosophy."[2]

I think the gist of Hamlet's comment is that when there are occurrences in each of our lives that seem to be more than just everyday coincidences, we would do well to understand *and accept* the fact that these phenomena often cannot be explained away by some philosophical treatise or logical explanation; they may only be classified as unexplainable. If we accept that notion, then the world may well become a much more interesting and unpredictable place.

It would take me years to begin to really understand Hamlet's belief. My early exposure to Brookmeyer's music was the first inkling I had that something special was happening in my young life—a path that I was compelled to follow for reasons I could not codify.

Realities: Who Could Care?

When I first approached a fellow author about the possibility of a book about valve trombonist / pianist / composer / arranger / NEA Jazz Master Bob Brookmeyer, he cautioned me that it might be a hard sell. I had already written a book about the late Ornette Coleman, preceded by another called *Experiencing Jazz: A Listener's Companion*. I responded by saying that I would not be deterred and would write about a genius who, unlike Louis Armstrong, Duke Ellington, Lester Young, Charlie Parker, and Ornette, did not change the face of jazz; however, he was a unique man who played a unique brass instrument and piano, and was one of the major improvisors, composers, and arrangers of jazz music—a man who pushed the boundaries of both jazz and classical music and has been revered by award-winning protégés, musical colleagues, writers, former students, and jazz aficionados.

Throughout the book I discuss many of Bob's songs and albums. I strongly recommend that, where possible, readers listen to and experience this music for themselves. Most of Bob's music can be found by visiting the "Discography" section of his website, https://www.bobbrookmeyer.com/discography. There you will find links to where the music can be either purchased or streamed online through sites like Amazon, iTunes, Spotify, and Apple Music, among others.

Bob Brookmeyer first became an integral part of my own existence via his recordings some sixty years ago. He literally changed the trajectory of my life. Now that may sound rather trite and overly dramatic to you, dear reader; however, the dream that began as a teenage boy's infatuation with the music and persona of one of modern jazz's most distinct and original voices evolved ultimately into a deeply endearing personal and musical relationship that pointed to the notion that in life, maybe mysterious things like this happen for unidentifiable reasons. Just ask Shakespeare and Jiminy Cricket! How often does that happen? Maybe dreams *can* come true, if a higher power intervenes and gives us the opportunity to follow our hearts, helping us along the way to make a dream into a reality. Maybe. Who knows? All I know is that it happened to me, and now you have this book—and the words of all of the wonderful and talented folks who contributed to it—that celebrates the life and music of Bob Brookmeyer.

What follows is not an analytical biography of my close friend and *honorarius frater major*, Bob Brookmeyer, but rather a hybrid work—a sort of gumbo that consists of relevant biographical information, a number of key interviews and personal narratives, chronological descriptions of pivotal recordings, a selected discography and videography, a bibliography, and a collection of tributes, accolades, and anecdotes from many of Bob's musical collaborators, students, family members, and fans.

All of these voices deliver insightful portraits of who Bob Brookmeyer was—a creative artist and teacher and a man of great intellect, razor-sharp perception, and a spot-on sardonic sense of humor. My memoir, which flows through *On the Way to the Sky*, hopefully offers some endearing windows into our unique thirty-five-year friendship. I hope that by focusing upon this uniqueness, as well as on the expansive quality of our relationship, I have offered an inspiring and deeply personal look at who Bob Brookmeyer was and who he ultimately became, both in performance in concerts and clubs and around the dinner table with family and friends. And I'm positive that my colleagues and Bob's family, whose words also grace these pages, feel much the same way.

Hopefully, this book will also provide musicians and new and seasoned jazz fans alike a glimpse into the life and art of one of the most brilliant and individualistic jazz musicians in the history of the music.

Actually, to call Bob Brookmeyer a "jazz musician" is too easy and doesn't really do him justice. Bob was much more than that. In the latter half of his life, he became a dedicated and ever-evolving composer and arranger who studied conducting and wrote contemporary music for large and small ensembles in both the jazz and classical genres. And the minute he put the valve trombone to his lips, he became one of jazz's great and most beloved storytellers.

I also believe that *On the Way to the Sky: Remembering Bob Brookmeyer* sits nicely in the middle of a triptych of excellent Brookmeyer books: One is by Dave Rivello of the Eastman School of Music, based upon ten hours of discussions with Bob regarding his approaches to composition, conducting, and much more; and the other is note-for note-transcriptions and annotations of selected Brookmeyer recorded solos, collected and annotated by trombonist and Carnegie Hall archivist Rob Hudson.

One of Bob's early compositions, "Who Could Care," is both a wistful statement and a question; wistful in that Bob faced some hard times growing up. Many of us who knew and loved Brookmeyer as a musical icon, an inspiration, and a warm and compassionate human being know the answer to that question. *We* cared—and still do. Although he is gone from us, Bob's presence—and especially his music—lives on.

So, borrowing the title of another of Bob's compositions, "Step Right Up" and join us here on these pages! As Bob would often say at the beginning of a gig, "We're glad we're here and glad you're here too."

—Michael Stephans

Bob and me after a Lake Tahoe concert (2000).
Photo from author's collection.

Chapter 1

Brookmeyer 101

Bob *Who*-Meyer?

Right about now, many of you may be asking the question: Bob *Who*-meyer? Actually, I think that readers of this book fall into four categories. The first is jazz musicians who knew and performed with Brookmeyer in urban centers in New York, California, and elsewhere, including in Europe. Category two is made up of musicians and fans who love jazz and know Bob through both his own records and performances with high-profile jazz artists like Gerry Mulligan, Stan Getz, and Clark Terry. Category three includes new jazz listeners who are curious about a widely respected guy who, while not as famous as say Mulligan or Getz, plays a weird-looking trombone and, as a Google search shows, seems to have been on a lot of jazz recordings from the '50s through the new millennium. And the remaining category of potential readers is the prospective reader and listener who sees this book for the first time online or in the music section of a local bookshop and decides to take the plunge and give *On the Way to the Sky* a whirl.

While there may be a variety of hypotheses as to why Bob Brookmeyer never achieved the elevated status of a Stan Getz or a

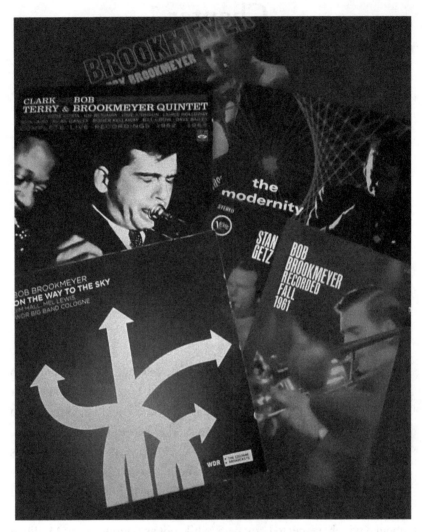

Collage created by author.

Gerry Mulligan, my guess is that he played alongside these artists as a sideman, rather than as an equally billed co-leader. Initially, Brookmeyer was associated with Getz and Mulligan and received exposure as a member of their groups. So it would not have been unusual to hear someone say, "Oh, Bob Brookmeyer. He played a lot with Stan Getz, right?"

Years ago I expressed my frustration to Bob of not being well-known enough in the jazz world: "Always a bridesmaid, never a bride."

He looked at me for a moment, then said something like. "Now you know how I feel."

Stunned, I said, "You? A bridesmaid? Come on! You're Bob Brookmeyer! Famous the world over." He just patted me on the shoulder and told me not to waste my time and energy fretting about things like that. In retrospect, I realize I was hoping that his retort to my exhortation would've been something like "Yeah? Tell that to Stanley [Getz]."

Live and learn . . .

One of the aims of this book, then, is to introduce a new generation of listeners to Bob Brookmeyer and another is to reaffirm Bob's stature as one of the greatest soloists and composers in jazz—a completely unique improviser who played both valve trombone and piano with equal skill, and an iconoclastic composer whose musical palette was all his own.

Just Plain 'Meyer: A Bit of Brookmeyer History

Bob Brookmeyer was born on December 19, 1929, in Kansas City, Missouri. His first musical instrument was the clarinet, even though his first impulse was to play the drums. He describes that experience this way: "When I was eight years old, my father brought home a clarinet. . . . I got better so I bought a wooden clarinet and began to study with my clarinet teacher who lived across the street. He didn't pay much attention to my practice habits, so I learned to sightread very well at an early age because I was practicing Benny Goodman's [book] *Hot Licks*."[1]

At age 13 Bob's teeth and his bite changed, and he was forced to abandon the clarinet. His next instrument of choice was the trumpet; however, his band director had other ideas and Bob ended up being the sixth trombonist in the junior high school band.

His first trombone teacher also happened to be a composer—primarily of marches—and had quite a few handwritten pages of music lying around the room. Bob found that very inspiring, not so much for the marches themselves as for the calligraphy. Seeing those pieces of original music written out so beautifully led to Bob's interest in writing arrangements—that is, music for each musician in the brass, woodwind, and rhythm sections of a big band. He said that he became a bona fide commercial arranger at the tender age of 14.

Bob also began studying the piano, which may have been because of his interest in being an arranger. By learning to play the keyboard, Bob began to understand how to combine notes happening simultaneously from different instruments in order to create layers of sound, much as a painter would combine various colors to create some visual mood.

While he continued to play the slide trombone, Bob ultimately gravitated to the valve trombone. As he explained it: "I wasn't happy with [being sixth trombonist], so I learned how to finger trumpet, which was my second choice [after clarinet]. After watching the trumpet players, I began to cop baritone horns out of the music room. Finally got a series of really bad valve trombones and in 1948, I got a brand-new Reynolds."[2]

Ultimately, when the Reynolds valve trombone found its way into his hands, the love affair with the instrument began. Even so, he continued his piano studies and played both instruments in large and small group settings. The piano continued to become an indispensable tool to Bob as he began honing his craft as both a composer and an arranger—and eventually as a soloist on the piano and the valve horn.

Bob's ensuing rise to national prominence in the jazz world has been well-documented in many jazz books and magazines. Even so, after playing and recording with jazz stars like Gerry Mulligan, Stan Getz, Clark Terry, Jim Hall, and Bill Evans, and after having a sizable output of his own recordings as a leader and co-leader, national recognition on the part of the listening public was slow in coming. He would often be recognized as "the guy who played on a Stan Getz record." It's my opinion that the problem might've been due to little or no marketing on the part of record companies whenever a new Brookmeyer-led recording surfaced. And he was featured on only a few television shows that focused on the art of jazz. For example, Bob was a major soloist with Gerry Mulligan's Quartet and Concert Jazz Band, and with the Thad Jones/Mel Lewis Jazz Orchestra on Ralph J. Gleason's two widely televised *Jazz Casual* television shows (see the videography). Bob had no such opportunities as bandleader. And yet in the face of all that, he continued to grow and blossom as an improvising musician, composer, and arranger.

Accidental Music: Improvisation

> If you are playing jazz, you have to play what comes out at any moment—something that you have never said before!
> —John Coltrane, *About John Coltrane*

> You have to . . . be able to tell a story, tell how you're feeling, and make a sound—a sound that is expressive and that says what you want to say, rather than a series of notes that don't say anything.
> —Bob Brookmeyer, *Evolution: The Improvisational Style of Bob Brookmeyer*

Improvisation is one of the quintessential elements that characterizes jazz. It is the music's heart and soul; it's lingua franca, if you will. In other words, it's the extemporaneous language—the act of instant creation—that connects musical communities with one another and, most importantly, with their audiences.

Brookmeyer helped me get to that realization years earlier. Here are two of the ways it manifested itself:

In the summer of 2000, while we were recording *Stay Out of the Sun*, Bob suggested that, rather than play a song, we should just start a four-way "conversation" and see where it goes. So the track that Bob ultimately titled "Bruise" begins with Bob, guitarist Larry Koonse, bassist Tom Warrington, and me playing out of tempo very sparsely, introducing our "voices" to one another and to the listener. After this bit of abstract noodling, Bob sets a medium tempo and plays some blues, which we all fall into for several choruses before Larry takes the lead and offers a solo that builds intensely, with Bob playing repeated rhythmic figures underneath him, until a spontaneous fade-out leads to a drum solo that moves from sparseness into complexity until settling back into the original tempo. Bob and Larry duet briefly, and the piece winds down slowly as Bob repeats a one-note figure with counterpoint from Larry, who ends the track with single notes that seem to evaporate into the ether—a good example of an eight-minute spontaneous invention.

Another example:

At the beginning of a performance one night in 2008 at the Deer Head Inn here in Pennsylvania, I announced that our trio (guitarist Vic Juris and bassist Francois Moutin) was going to create music on the spot. We had no idea what we were going to play; still, we set out to stay "in the moment" and jump into the deep end of the pool, allowing the music to unwind and go in whatever direction it took us. Before we began I invited the audience to travel along with us on the path we were creating. After a bit of silence, we began: no road map, no written music. What followed was fifteen to twenty minutes of interplay between guitar, bass, and drums, in and out of tempo. It was like an extemporaneous conversation among three people. In short, the audience really liked what they heard. Best of all, our improvisation was an example of what I call "heart-music"—namely, that which has never been heard before and will never be heard again. There was no past, no future—only the present.

Bob Brookmeyer was a great teacher for me in that his gifts as a skilled and imaginative improvisor are well-known globally among many musicians and listeners; yet in certain ways, he stands alone. Writer/musician Rob Hudson, in the introduction to his excellent book, *Evolution: The Improvisational Style of Bob Brookmeyer*, explains, "Bob Brookmeyer defies categorization. Critics and historians love to push jazz music and musicians into one camp or another: East Coast or West Coast, Bebop or Traditional, Hard Bop or Cool, and so on. Consider Brookmeyer's path: a Kansas City native weaned on midwestern swing and [classical composer Anton] Webern! He apprenticed among the likes of Coleman Hawkins, Ben Webster, Dizzy Gillespie, and Charles Mingus."[3]

Bob talked about his unique approach to improvisation (circa 1957) this way: "My style is composed of everything I've heard that I've liked, and even, I'm afraid, some things I haven't liked. There's also a big folk influence in what I've been doing. . . . By folk [song], I mean old blues and spirituals, including Homer Rodeheaver and Jimmy Rushing."[4]

At that time Bob indicated that while he was attracted to early forms of jazz, blues, and spirituals, he had little interest in being a traditionalist. However, he defended his interest in early genres, by saying, "Music can be like love and painting. Just because a song and spirit have been around for a while doesn't mean it's diminished in value."[5]

One of a Kind: Sounds and Stories

There are two distinct characteristics that support the notion that Bob was unique as a player and improvisor.

1. Although he could play the conventional slide trombone, Brookmeyer chose the **valve trombone** as his instrument of choice, although he was equally at home as a pianist. The valve horn is unique in that it articulates notes in a manner similar to a trumpet. In fact, someone once said that with the exception of Brookmeyer and one or two others, most valve trombonists sounded like trumpet players who sometimes doubled on valve trombone.

   In a story related by writer Nat Hentoff when Bob was interviewed in 1957 by *Melody Maker* writer Steve Voce, he spoke about his choice of the valve trombone rather than the more popular slide trombone: "I found the slide instrument lacked the passion of the valve. And it's easier to say the things I want to say with trumpet fingering . . . and this way, I can play what I like without having doubts about finding the technique to say it."[6]

Valve trombone. Stock photo.

2. Bob's trombone sound was unique and certainly different than many of the fine jazz trombonists playing during the bebop era. Unlike the smooth-as-silk sound of the virtuosic J. J. Johnson, for example, Bob explored the entire range of his horn, from deep rumbling in the lower register up into the highest register—and he did so utilizing the three valves to the fullest extent. The results were often sounds that were startlingly humanlike. He didn't use these sounds consciously as "gimmickry" to entertain listeners. His tone was never acrid or nasally; to the contrary, it was a warm and smooth sound that never smacked you in the face.

I know from our conversations and from spending much of my life listening to his recordings beginning in the late '50s that Bob wanted to explore all the possible sounds the valve trombone had to offer. That he did so in such an original fashion set him apart from many other jazz musicians. Along with Charles Mingus, Eric Dolphy, Clark Terry, Bennie Maupin, Roswell Rudd, and others from even earlier generations, Brookmeyer's valve trombone "voice" was very close to approximating the human voice, with its growls, cries, smears, and yawns, as well as its genuine warmth and wistfulness. Once in his later years, Bob and I talked about the evolution of his trombone voice, and when I asked why he abandoned that unique vocalized style in favor of a more harmonically complex and linear approach to his solos, he responded in his typically oblique way: "I stopped being angry."

I couldn't think of anything in the way of a response that would make any sense. Maybe because those human sounds, visceral as they were, reached down into a listener and woke up something primordial, something that wordlessly mirrored aspects of the human condition: the joy, the melancholy, the humor, and even the anger, to name a few. I think that writer Nat Hentoff inadvertently nails Bob's observations perfectly: "Of all sophisticated forms of music, jazz is the most self revealing, the music where there is the least room for the performer to hide who he or she is."[7]

As does legendary saxophonist, Charlie "Bird" Parker: "Music is your own experience, your thoughts, your wisdom. If you don't live it, it won't come out of your horn."[8]

Sing, Sang, Sung: Brookmeyer and Lyricism

The term *lyricism* is nearly impossible to place comfortably into a single universal definition and, as such, it falls into the abyss of conceptual words like *liberty*, *freedom*, and *beauty*. If you look up *lyrical* in a thesaurus, you'll see all sorts of descriptive synonyms like *emotional*, *deeply felt*, *subjective*, *passionate*, and *expressive*. It's been my experience that some musicians and ardent listeners might say that a particular jazz solo was quite lyrical, and when asked to elaborate on their comment, they might point out that the solo was beautifully melodic and expressive, or that it was (pick one or two of the other similar terms above). At the end of the day, there isn't much agreement when it comes to a universal definition of *lyricism*. A few years ago, when I asked a fellow musician to describe briefly what lyricism was, he responded by saying, "I can't really come up with a solid definition for that word; you just know when someone is playing lyrically. You can really feel it!"

Let me elaborate on the last part of my friend's response. Sometimes in jazz, when we believe that a soloist is playing lyrically, it may be because they are embellishing the original melody of the song in such a way as to create their own improvised variation of it while maintaining its recognizability, or at least the feeling of it. In other less arcane words: as a listener, you might still hear some phrases in the soloist's improvisation that allude either to the song's melody or perhaps to the feeling it produces *in you*. Such is the case in a song like "Blue in Green," a lovely Bill Evans ballad made famous by Miles Davis on his immortal recording, *Kind of Blue*. The solos by Evans, Miles, and John Coltrane are all considered to be quite lyrical. But why would they be considered as such?

Formulate your own perception of lyricism. Listen to the song and see how it makes you *feel*.

I tried an experiment in one of my Pasadena City College jazz appreciation classes to see if Miles's "Blue in Green" had any emotional effect on my students. I dimmed the lights in the room and asked for complete silence. All in the room complied. From the beginning of Bill Evans's solo piano intro through the closing notes of Paul Chambers's bowed bass, the listeners were attentive. When I brought the lights back up, I asked for volunteers to talk about what they just heard. For many the song was a diving board into feelings of love and loss; however, a number of them found the solos to be expressions of pure beauty, as though Miles and Coltrane were singing through their instruments.

So how does all of this conjecturing about lyricism relate to Bob Brookmeyer? Like others who came before him, Bob believed in knowing a song inside and out, and improvising in a manner that would both embellish the song's melody and spontaneously create a new and wholly original interpretation—that is, a completely improvised song sung by the trombone, layered atop the harmonic/chordal structure of the original melody.

Another personal example: On the recording session for our *Stay out of the Sun* project, I asked Bob to play "Blue in Green" with the brilliant guitarist Larry Koonse, just the two of them. No rehearsal. It was pure intuitive expression. I had hoped to capture both the creative intimacy that marked the best duo performances and to showcase Bob's great ballad playing on one of jazz's most unforgettable ballads.

I was not disappointed. Bob and Larry wrapped their musical lines around each other and created a rich tapestry of sound that, still to this day, sounds and feels purely magical. Bob caressed the melody, moving gently in and out of its simple statement with instantaneous songlike variations that, throughout his solo, found their way back to the theme, as Larry's sensitive layering and understated soloing helped to fashion the delicate intimacy of the track. Larry describes this magical experience later, in chapter 7.

Bob's solo was indeed lyrical in that it moved around and through the melody, and did so in a way that "sang" the song and created simple melodic variations that actually seemed at times to be a logical extension of Bill Evans's original melody.

Style and Substance: Four Songs Described

There is a wealth of recorded examples of Bob's lyrical solo flights to be found on the majority of his recordings. While the few solos that I refer to here are some that are well-known by other musicians (and Brookmeyer fans) there are many, many others—wonderful examples of a brilliant mind in the act of spontaneous composition. If you take a deep dive into Bob's improvisations, you will begin to hear and feel the uniqueness of his spontaneous melodic inventions, much like those that Johann Sebastian Bach created. Farfetched? Not really.

"On the Sunny Side of the Street"

In mid-June 1960 Bob recorded what was to become one of his greatest early achievements as a soloist. The album was called *The Blues Hot and Cold* (Verve Records) and featured Bob with a very simpatico rhythm section. In Bob's hands the valve trombone seemed to have a life of its own, and the album's opening track, "On the Sunny Side of the Street," placed Bob in the pantheon of the most original jazz soloists of all time. As opposed to the usual medium tempo strut it was known for, "Sunny Side" was played by Bob and company at a much slower tempo. If you know this old

1930 chestnut, you can easily sing the lyrics along with Bob's opening statement of the melody. If you've never heard the song before, listen to an early version of it, print out the words, and follow the lyrics as Bob states his version of the melody. When you get to the middle section of the song (musicians call this the bridge), it sounds quite literally like Bob is throwing an enormous kiss to the listener: "mmmmWWWWHAHHH!"! This is not silly gimmickry; that is, it was not performed as part of the arrangement with the idea being that it would make listeners laugh. On the contrary, it is spur-of-the-moment stuff from Brookmeyer's inventive imagination directly to our ears. That's the joyful essence of this highly accessible recording. From the first track to the last, Bob's raucous, all-too-human playing throughout continues not only to be one of the highlights of this recording but is also one of the finest examples of what the cornetist Ruby Braff called "the adoration of the melody." Bob honors the song's lyrics yet makes them his own through the voice of his valve trombone.

"Old Man River"

First, some background: The year 1960 also saw the release of Columbia Records's *The New Jazz Sounds of Showboat*, which was essentially jazz versions of songs made famous as part of that venerable Broadway show. Johnny Carisi, composer of the oft-played jazz tune "Israel" wrote most of the arrangements for this project. Even though the record featured a fine guitar ensemble and rhythm section supporting soloists Brookmeyer, alto saxophonist Phil Woods, and trumpeter Carisi, it didn't seem to garner any critical reviews by the jazz press until much later, after quite a few years in obscurity. Here is an excerpt of an excellent review by award-winning blogger and jazz journalist Marc Myers, which I retrieved from the January 13, 2024, issue of the online jazz magazine *AllAbout-Jazz*: "It's certainly fair to call this album one of the finest jazz interpretations of any Broadway musical. This *Showboat* has been in drydock way too long."

A real shame, since there are many lovely moments from track to track, all bolstered by the well-crafted arrangements (one of which was penned by Brookmeyer). While all of the solos are quite attractive, Bob's take on "Old Man River" is another example of his trombone singing the lyrics. His sound on this track is husky and funky, creating an overall effect of a grumpy, tired, yet resigned old man who, toward the end of his lament, yawns expansively through the valve trombone, as if bidding adieu to us as he sinks into a well-deserved slumber.

"Time After Time"

One afternoon at Bob and his wife Janet's New Hampshire home, Bob related the following story to me about the *Samba Para Dos* project; this is about as close as I can get to remembering all of the particulars:

Sometime in early 1963, composer/arranger/pianist Lalo Schifrin invited Bob to be part of a thirteen-member ensemble to record Schifrin's *Samba Para Dos* for Verve Records, featuring Schifrin's new arrangements of tunes that were part of what's often called the Great American Songbook, which included popular favorites like "Just One of Those Things," "What Kind of Fool Am I," and "Time After Time." The creative plan was to feature vocals by a singer who would come to New York from Brazil to sing each song—probably in Portuguese, although that remains a mystery.

In any case, once in the recording studio, the vocalist was unable to sing a note due to a serious case of nerves. As Brookmeyer tells it, Schifrin approached him to replace the singer and to play each tune's melody, followed in most cases by a brief solo. Undoubtedly it was a tough spot for Schifrin, and the best idea possible seemed to be to have Brookmeyer fill in for the singer. The liner note writer, Mort Fega, explains why Schifrin chose Bob to be a co-leader on the session: "[In preparing the liner notes] I found myself singing the lyrics to the standards that Bob Brookmeyer was playing, almost as though it were a vocal album, with the trombone singing the lyrics. . . . Bob Brookmeyer's lyric trombone stylings and Lalo

Schifrin's excellent scoring made me aware that this album, if you would, is a vocal-instrumental album. . . . Bob sings the lyrics with his horn, shading each reading as any sensitive vocalist would."[9]

The 1947 Sammy Kahn-Jule Styne ballad "Time After Time," although only three-plus minutes long, offers us a sterling example of Bob's lyrical sensibilities, especially in contrast to Schifrin's intense pianistics. Within the confines of the brevity of the track, Bob's solo never veers too far from either the song's melody or, equally important, the emotion that the words of the song portray. Squarely in the spirit of the lyrics themselves, he honors their sentiment and crafts his solo statement in a gentle, unpretentious fashion. Schifrin, on the other hand, leaves no notes unplayed, and while his solo statement exhibits great technical skill, it has little to do with the song's emotional meaning. In other words, he misses the point that this is a love song and not a boppish fireworks display. Interesting contrast, to be sure.

"Willow Weep for Me"

While Bob's solo on this wonderful Brookmeyer orchestral arrangement of the old Ann Ronnell song was one of a number of highlights on Thad Jones/Mel Lewis Orchestra's premier recording for Solid State Records, it continued to be in Bob's repertoire throughout his life. He recorded two large ensemble versions with Thad and Mel (1966), one with a Stan Getz sextet (1978), another on a Brookmeyer quintet album (1979), and lastly on Bob's final recording (2011)—this time a return to his original orchestration for Thad and Mel—on an entire album of standards, orchestrated by Bob and featuring vocalist Fay Claassen. I say "orchestrated" rather than "arranged," even though the latter is usually the more common bit of nomenclature, because I feel that Brookmeyer's approach to orchestrating someone else's compositions was—along with Gil Evans' masterpieces—incredibly original. Whereas writing an arrangement of a song in which the melody and harmony are easily recognizable, the process of orchestration often places greater emphasis upon a wider variety of tonal colors and how the layering of those sounds on top of one another serves to redefine the original melody in a new and unique way, without compromising the original melody. Think of it like this: When a painter portrays the silhouette of an elm tree at twilight against a dark-blue background, then juxtaposes a crescent moon in the center of the tree instead of in the sky above it, that moon brings something new and perhaps refreshing into what might ordinarily be a rather banal nighttime scene.

Bob's orchestration of "Willow Weep for Me" not only showcases his and Thad Jones's relaxed and beautifully wrought solos on the Jones-Lewis studio recording but also highlights the orchestration itself, which is sculpted in such a masterful manner that it cushions the accompanying brass and woodwind voicings around and through the solos with great empathy, and supports both Thad and Bob beautifully and without distraction.

There are many other examples of these particular aspects of Bob's solo style and I'm sure that those who are well acquainted with his improvisational mastery could identify their favorite Brookmeyer solos on selected recordings—and perhaps even sing along with some of them! I have no such list. There would be too many favorite solos to compile. And I can already sing too many of them by rote after so many years of listening to them. If that's an affliction, it's a damn good one.

Boom Boom: Brookmeyer and the Drums

> I'm still a frustrated drummer, but I'm getting over it.
> —Bob Brookmeyer, Southern California (late '70s)

One morning in the early '80s, when Bob was in LA to play a gig with our quartet, he spent a couple of nights at our home in Canoga Park. Thinking he was still asleep, I went down to the music room and played one of those Music Minus One jazz recordings. I picked up my miniature Eb alto valve trombone and began playing along with the track. I never heard Bob enter the room. Never heard him sit down behind the drums in his bathrobe. Never heard him pick up the sticks: Splang-Splang-a-lang-splang-a-lang. I stopped playing and turned around and faced my ad hoc

Bob at the drums (late '70s). Photo from author's collection.

drumming accompanist. I was speechless. As the track ended, Bob looked at me, looked at the little horn, looked back at me, and said, "I see you dabble in the occult."

Bob did more than just "dabble" at the drums; he actually sounded good. His time was solid and he knew how to extract a resonant sound from the cymbals. At least he didn't hit me with, "ANYone can play the drums."

To be sure, there are lots of deprecatory jokes about other instruments like the accordion and the banjo; however, history shows us

A ridiculous notion. From author's collection.

that drummers are at the butt end of such jokes more often than not. Ironic in a way, since many kids seem to choose the drums as their first instrument of choice. I don't think that many aspiring young musicians put band instruments like the tuba, the oboe, or the French horn at the top of their wish lists.

Number one at the top of Bob Brookmeyer's wish list was the drums; however, his dream of being a drummer evaporated very quickly, and when it did, he began the journey that brought him to the valve trombone. He describes it this way: "At age thirteen . . . I worked all summer as a day laborer to be a drummer—I had a set of drums picked out and everything and when I got back to my house right before school started, the school band director left and I was the new sixth trombone player at Central Junior High School in Kansas City, Missouri."[10]

In retrospect, that Bob chose the drums as his first choice comes as no surprise. One of his most attractive characteristics as a soloist down through the years was his ability to get inside a groove of any song and play a solo that was rhythmically swinging and melodious at the same time. Bob frequently liked to play on the beat in his solos with a rhythmic feel that drummers really could get into. In short, he was easy to play with and he added to the vitality and spirit of every one of his groups that I had the pleasure of being associated with.

Bob also had a knack for choosing the most simpatico drummers to play with, including Frank Isola, Osie Johnson, Dave Bailey, Mel Lewis, Elvin Jones, Joe LaBarbera, Adam Nussbaum, John Hollenbeck, John Riley, Danny Gottlieb—great players all!

Of all of the drummers mentioned, Mel Lewis had the longest running relationship—both musical and personal—with Brookmeyer. Mel was originally called The Tailor by vibraphonist Terry Gibbs, because according to bassist Bill Crow, Terry said Mel looked and walked just like his tailor; however, Mel became more widely known as a sort of musical tailor, in that he had the ability to weave into and out of the brass and woodwind figures "inside the time"—that is, he didn't play the notated band figures so prominently that they interrupted the incredible rhythmic buoyancy of his drumming or the swinging feeling of the rhythm section. Instead, his time supported the brasses and woodwinds in an organic and uncontrived way. In Chris Smith's remarkable Mel Lewis 2014 biography, *View from the Back of the Band*, dozens of jazz historians, critics, and musicians place Mel Lewis in the upper echelon of big band jazz drummers, although he was also an incomparable small group drummer—always in the moment; like Brookmeyer, always absorbing and adding to the language of what was going on around him.

Bob loved Mel not only for his creativity and musicianship but also for his camaraderie. The two became friends in 1949, notably due to the time they spent together as members of the Tex Beneke Orchestra. In the '50s when Bob would bounce back and forth from the East to the West Coast, he would occasionally stay with Mel and his family at their Southern California home in Sherman Oaks. One of the stories that Bob told me supposedly took place during the time he was staying with the Lewises. One morning after sleeping on the sofa, he was awakened by several neighborhood children standing next to his bedside who had paid a small tariff for the opportunity to witness Bob's stentorian snoring performances.

In my time playing drums with Bob in numerous quartet and quintet configurations over the years, Bob's input and tutelage helped shape the contours of my playing and my improvisatory skills. Thanks to Bob, I was able to transition from being a drummer to being a more open-minded, creative musician. In our many discussions, he would talk about the value of such things as nuance, shading, coloring, meshing, flow, intuition, dynamics, and, of equal importance, the ability to dance around the silence. "Understand the power of one note" is a wonderful comment he made to Dave Rivello in the latter's invaluable book highlighting Bob's extensive conversations with him.[11]

In addition to opening up a whole new musical world for me, Bob taught me by example the importance and inherent value of knowing the structure *and the lyrics* of a song and how to use those elements in both accompanying and soloing. Of course, he was an absolute joy to play with. Every performance was a deep learning experience. Our relationship was special in that regard. Over the years, playing and recording with Bob taught me how to play the drums in a more musical way and, as mentioned above in his conversations with Dave Rivello from Eastman School of Music, how to use silence as a way of giving more meaning to the notes that came before and after the rests. Thanks to Bob I was also able to learn how to play more dynamically. If he were here right now, he'd probably laugh that deep, gruff laugh of his and say, "You know, there *are* such things as soft drum solos."

Bob was as great a mentor as one could hope for, although in my case he probably would have added the word "accidental," since he never intended for me to be his student, nor he my teacher. Here, in Bob's generous words, is how he summed up our almost four-decade relationship: "Michael, you are my younger brother, in music and life."[12]

And this, his beautiful paean, was an absolute gift—one that lit up my website: "Michael is one of the most involved, sensitive, and musical drummers I have known, plus—he swings!! Calling him a drummer isn't really good enough—he inhales the music and gives you a lovely breeze in return."[13]

How on earth one lives up to accolades like that is beyond me.

Chapter 2

Awakenings Along the Way

Traveling isn't always pretty. It isn't always comfortable. Sometimes it hurts. It even breaks your heart. But that's OK. The journey changes you . . . It leaves marks on your memory, on your consciousness, on your heart. . .you take something with you. Hopefully, you leave something good behind.
—Anthony Bourdain, *The Nasty Bits*

When all's said and done, all roads lead to the same end. So it's not so much which road you take, as how you take it.
—Charles de Lint, *Greenmantle*

We learn more from our mistakes than our successes.
—Bob Brookmeyer, *Bob Brookmeyer in Conversation with Dave Rivello*

Florida: Jive Hoot, 1960–64

I first heard valve trombonist Bob Brookmeyer when I was in my midteens. My family and I were in Jacksonville, Florida, visiting some relatives, and while out walking around town one day, I happened into a record shop and bought an album by baritone saxophonist

From what Bob called "our coast-to-coast tour of Arizona" (circa 1980).
Photo courtesy of Theo Saunders.

Gerry Mulligan and the Concert Jazz Band, mostly because I liked the cover art. To make a long story much shorter, I brought the record back to my cousin's house, took it out of its glossy black sleeve, and plopped it onto the phonograph. The first cut I heard was one of those finger-snapping things that sort of chugged along like a big old Hudson Hornet, lumbering from side to side, rooty-tooting down the street. The piano solo was interesting but sort of unmemorable; however, the solo that followed it brought me square into Brookmeyerville. It was a funky, raspy, downright greasy trombone solo that changed how I would hear and play music over the next six decades. It wasn't a slide trombone solo, even though initially I knew it was some sort of trombone. This was a different breed of animal—one that wheezed, bleated, belched, farted, yowled, and groaned. This was down and dirty and really resonated in me! Somehow I knew that, even though I lacked mature listening skills, this was the real deal: a solo that was fiery, blues drenched, and swinging hard all the way! This was my first exposure to the genius of Bob Brookmeyer.

Now, even an uneducated, green-gilled teenager like me back then could figure out that Brookmeyer didn't play slide trombone. He played the valve trombone, which has always been considered the illegitimate stepchild of the more conventional slide instrument. But it wasn't only the valve horn that caught my attention. It was *the way* that Brookmeyer was playing it that completely turned me around; for example, by depressing the valves halfway down rather than all the way, Brookmeyer could bend and twist notes. He could simultaneously "sing" the same note he was playing into the horn and make the note being played sound wet and raspy, like a bull elephant with a cold. Sometimes he would not play a note at all but just move the valves and breathe through the horn, sending a column of air loudly out of its big brass bell. These kinds of techniques made the valve trombone sound incredibly like a living, breathing thing—a gruff, yet fundamentally primordial voice that dug down deep into something I could not identify. It sang and resonated! It mesmerized! It glowed brilliantly like an infinite carpet of stars and planets blanketing the night sky. Something about the way Brookmeyer played it released a kind of psychic adrenaline in me that made me want to hear much more of the Brookmeyer trombone. And so I began buying every record where he was either the leader or one of a group of featured soloists.

Even though I was a young, naïve, and somewhat overzealous jazz drummer, I wanted to be as soulful and hip as Brookmeyer. Not Gene Krupa, Buddy Rich, or any of the other great drummers. It was a valve trombonist, for heaven's sake! Whoever said that imitation is the sincerest form of flattery would've been amused at just how much I embodied that statement. I cut my hair in an Ivy League style like Brookmeyer's. Every chance I got, I dressed in that early sixties New York hip couture like he did. I even tried to affect his mannerisms. It was quite ridiculous, really; it was idol worship at its most pathetic. When no one was home, I would crank up the volume on the stereo in my room and play air trombone to Brookmeyer's solos, bending forward and arching backward, swaying from side to side, like an old Hassidic rabbi singing and praying on the Sabbath. I was pretty far into it after school one day when my father (who came home early that afternoon) opened the door and leaned in to ask me to turn the music down. Catching me in a particularly dramatic pose, as I pointed my air trombone toward the ceiling at the zenith of Bob's solo, my father looked at me with bewilderment before closing the door, leaving me to feel like someone who had just got caught with his hands deep in the cookie jar. What does one say at a time like that? In my house, the exchange probably would've gone something like this:

> Oops. Excuse me, Dad, I was pretending to be Bob Brookmeyer.
>
> Who? Bob who?
>
> Brookmeyer. The famous jazz valve-trombonist. You know, the guy who plays with Mulligan and Getz and—
>
> A jazz musician? A jazz musician? This is your hero? What happened to Mickey Mantle, Sandy Koufax, President Kennedy? A ball player, I understand. A president, I understand. Even Jimmy Hoffa, I understand. But a jazz musician? Is this Brookmeyer Jewish, at least?

Given the circumstances in my house, had this been a real scenario, I probably would've lied and said yes. And somehow, at least for a little while, that would've made it all right. But my father merely closed the door behind him, leaving me to the demons of self-doubt who laughed, pointed at me, and shouted, "You are being ridiculous!" before I chased them away with a swat of my invisible horn.

New York: Big City Blues, Mid-'50s–1968

My first brush with the Big Apple and Brookmeyer was a near miss. Let me explain. By the mid-'60s I was a student at the University of Miami and a member of its big band and a variety of small groups. I also landed an occasional writing assignment for *Tempo*, a magazine published by the School of Music. I remember asking one of the editors if I could write a profile of Bob Brookmeyer since I was making a trip to New York City anyway. He was quick to say, "Bob who?" before saying no, offering some lame excuse about Bob being an "unknown quantity." To be utterly truthful, I was using my request as a vehicle to contact Brookmeyer and see whether or not he would be amenable to a face-to-face interview, even though I knew that *Tempo* wasn't interested in my proposal. I was able subsequently to contact Bob's then-wife, lyricist-singer Margo Guryan, who kindly arranged for me to meet Bob after his gig on a given day outside of the theater that hosted *The Merv Griffin Show* in the theater district of Midtown Manhattan. Once the show ended, the audience came streaming out, followed a few minutes later by the band. The brass players and saxophonists came out first, followed by the guitarist and the bassist. No Brookmeyer. Finally, the drummer exited with his cymbal bag. I introduced myself and asked him if Bob was still inside. He said something like, "Nope. He called in sick."

I was beyond crestfallen, beyond disappointed. When I returned to where I was staying, I called Margo and she said apologetically that Bob had the flu and was sorry he couldn't meet me. We did ultimately have a phone conversation that lasted around ten or fifteen minutes, and the only thing I can remember about it was offering some corny sounding platitudes and mentioning Bob's great pianistic capabilities, a remark that he laughed off. He called himself a "parlor piano player" and said how much he enjoyed Thelonious Monk's pianistics.

So I returned to Miami with only our short and empty phone conversation during which I was too nervous and inexperienced to ask even one perceptive question. I think that Bob could sense my unease, yet even so was gently patient with my ineptitude. When I asked Bob about that incident years later, he had no memory of it at all—thankfully.

New York in the late '50s and throughout much of the '60s continued to be a fertile environment for the growth of the music, as it had been decades before. It lived up to its nickname as the Jazz Corner of the World via the many clubs and recording sessions that were extant at that time. Bob was very successful and had become quite well-known not only in the Big Apple but also nationally and internationally. In the studios he was surrounded by longtime friends and musical compatriots, had opportunities to write arrangements for singers like Ray Charles and Carol Sloane, and, best of all, he was an integral part of the busy New York jazz community. Some of Bob's most notable recorded work, as both a leader (*Gloomy Sunday and Other Bright Moments*) and co-leader (with trumpeter-flugelhornist Clark Terry and saxophonist Stan Getz), and as a sideman (with baritone saxophonist Gerry Mulligan and multireed player Jimmy Giuffre) came out of the aforementioned period, and he began to receive positive recognition in jazz magazines like *Metronome* and *DownBeat*. He was on the cover of the latter numerous times and was the subject of feature articles in both magazines; in 1960 Bob was also a moving force behind Mulligan's Concert Jazz Band (where he was a major soloist, a respected arranger and was the band's "straw boss," i.e., rehearsal coordinator, personnel manager, etc.). And sometime after the Mulligan CJB disbanded in 1965, Bob became a charter member of the Thad Jones–Mel Lewis Jazz Orchestra, where he was once again a vital part of the assemblage, and once again a soloist, but perhaps most importantly a uniquely gifted composer and arranger. His original composition "ABC Blues" remains a classic to this day, and his arrangements of well-known songs like "St. Louis Blues" and "Willow Weep for Me" have been influential for succeeding generations of composers and arrangers as well. In short, Bob's tenure in New York City during those years was enormously fruitful, and as his recordings during that period show that Bob was evolving, not only instrumentally but also as a composer and arranger.

Lost (and Found) Angeles, 1968–78

So why abandon all of his New York successes and move to LA? I would attribute that relocation to Bob's restlessness and his subsequent desire to try something different. So, then, in 1968 Bob traded the Big Apple for sunny Southern California and an environment where he eventually spent a decade sloughing through a state of ennui in the studios, moving farther and farther away from the jazz world, all the while struggling with what seemed to be a losing battle with alcohol addiction—a battle that he eventually won through sheer determination and thanks in part to a few of us who believed in his creative virtuosity and offered our support when possible.

Let me back up a bit to provide some context. Here's how our relationship began. I finally met Bob in the mid-'70s, about a month after moving to Los Angeles from the East Coast. We gradually became friends, first socially, then shortly thereafter, musically. We got together at other musicians' homes and at first began by simply playing familiar songs. I'm sure that Bob wanted to see if there was any potential for further development as a quartet. As luck would have it, he was pleased, and so we continued by putting together a song list for future gigs. Those first sessions were a thrill for me; part of my dream was becoming a reality!

Even so, as great as it was to be playing with Bob, I could feel that something was wrong, something definitely out of kilter for him. That something, I came to discover, was alcohol. In retrospect those years in LA were rough for him. He found the sameness of studio work to be boring and humdrum, not very challenging and only sometimes musical. In short, Bob had what some therapists call the Buzz Aldrin Complex. Like the astronaut, when you've been to the moon, coming back down to earth can be a real bore.[1] So drinking heavily became Bob's escape route.

This is how the next part of our journey played out:

The proverbial straw that broke the camel's back occurred when we were able to secure a gig for our quartet sometime in early 1977 at Donte's Jazz Club, one of the legendary jazz venues that was going full steam ahead since its inception in the mid-'60s. The club was a famous watering hole for the best jazz musicians in the city and for internationally well-known jazz musicians who happened to be passing through town. It was also often a hangout for many movie stars and other well-known media personalities. In other words, Donte's was a destination of choice, and many local and nationally known musicians made it their home away from home.

So with our Donte's date in the offing, we rehearsed, gathered a repertoire, and played weekly for Brookmeyer's first appearance at Donte's after quite a long hiatus from jazz, buried in the LA studios.

The night of the gig, Bob arrived in a taxi in somewhat less-than-sober condition. I seem to remember that pianist Theo Saunders and bassist Fred Atwood were my rhythm section mates, but not the names of the songs we were to play. All I remember was that Bob was in pretty bad shape from the start. The unthinkable happened after the first several songs: Bob had a barstool on the stage so he could sit down while others were soloing. At some point after his solo, when he went to sit down, he missed the stool and took a tumble. Fortunately, he was not hurt, except for maybe his pride and what might've been left of his self-esteem. To see one's musical role model reach a low point like that was heartbreaking, and to witness what I was sure was the end of a stellar career was deeply unsettling. Fortunately, saxophonist Lew Tabackin saved the day and came in to play the next couple of sets. We sent Bob home in a cab.

Several days after the Donte's fiasco, I tried calling Bob at his apartment in North Hollywood. After repeated tries and no success, I decided to go to his apartment to see if he was okay. I knocked on his door and waited. I heard movement inside and knew he was there. Finally, after three or four attempts, I leaned into the door and said, "I know you're in there. I'd like to talk with you. Please." The voice on the other side of the door was less than civil and the words were slurred and running into each other. "Go away! Leave me alone!" It was midmorning and Bob was already drunk. I regret to this day how I responded: "Okay, I'm leaving. You can drink yourself to death if that's what you want to do! I won't try to stop you."

Feeling frustrated, sad, and helpless, I turned and walked down the steps back to my car. I was sure that I would never see Bob Brookmeyer alive again.

That, of course, was not the case. A week or two later, he called me and informed me that he was checking into a hospital rehabilitation program and would be out of touch for some time. His voice did not waver, and his words were not slurred. I remember him saying something to the effect that his choice now was between living and dying and that he was opting for the former.

With the initial help of fellow trombonist and Synanon associate Frank Rehak and the spiritual guidance of two beacons of light, both of whom Bob spoke about often—known to me only as Sister Clare and Father Webber—Bob began the long and challenging journey back to music and life, and his amazing rebirth as both a person and an artist. On the musical side of things, Willis "Bill" Holman and I got him playing again, in both big band and small group settings, respectively. Willis, in particular, convinced Bob to come and rehearse with his big band on a regular basis and was a positive force in helping Bob regain his self-confidence. Around that time, with the aid of the late bassist John Heard, I set up some weekly quartet rehearsals for Bob at John's North Hollywood home with a number of excellent musicians. Eventually, Bob mentioned that his old boss, saxophonist Stan Getz, heard that he was playing again and contacted him to do a three-month tour of Europe, as well as to appear as part of Getz's current group on Johnny Carson's *Tonight Show*. So helping Bob get his chops back together became even more important. Thanks to the love and support of those who played in these foursomes, Bob grew stronger and more self-assured as time passed.

Bob offered these words on one of his comeback recordings in 1978: "Returning to life is long and lonely without the help of friends and I had a surfeit. A brief and incomplete list would include Emil, Mike, and Bob; Willis, Michael, and Redmond; Marilyn, Lou, and Nancy; Stanley, John, and Norman. Who didn't stop caring. Thank you."[2]

In that same year, Bob moved back to New York City and rejoined the vigorous Manhattan jazz scene. Even so, he returned frequently to the West Coast and we played some successful and inspiring club gigs and concerts, which featured some very creative LA musicians, including guitarists Larry Koonse, Ron Eschete, and the late Joe Diorio; pianists Theo Saunders and Alan Broadbent; and bassists Putter Smith, Darek Oles, Tom Warrington, John Gianelli, and the late Eric Von Esssen.

From Here to There: On the Road with Brookmeyer, 1977–87

Here are some highlights of our various excursions:

The White House, Late 1977

No, no—not *that* White House! This one was an upper-crust oceanside club in the charming little California habitat of Laguna Beach, ostensibly a playground for the uber-rich and weekend wannabes. This time Bob brought in a very good quintet with Bill Stapleton, a fine trumpeter/flugelhornist, bassist John Gianelli, Theo Saunders, and me. This was one of the last gigs we played before Bob moved back to New York. As I recall, we played a few things that Bob wrote for the band he co-led with Clark Terry years earlier; however, he also brought in some tunes I'd never heard of and, to my knowledge, were never recorded. These were called "Sensible Rock" and "Facile Waltz"—typically arcane Brookmeyer titles.

In retrospect, this was a very good band. Bob was in excellent form, as was Stapes. The rhythm section gelled right out of the gate, and playing with Theo and John was very inspiring. The most memorable moment, however, came at the end of the night. We packed John's van and headed back to LA. After three energetic sets, we were pretty pooped, and facing the long drive home was not something we were looking forward to at 2:00 a.m. I was sitting up front next to John and noticed about a dozen miles out that he was gradually driving slower than when we started. I didn't pay much attention until John began coasting slower and slower. He was literally asleep at the wheel! That was when a miraculous thing happened: the van veered slowly to the right and, while still asleep, John coasted off onto an exit and rolled to a stop. Thank heavens the traffic on the freeway was light! Needless to say, we were all wide-eyed for the rest of the trip.

Arizona, 1980

During the early '80s, Bob cooked up what he called our coast-to-coast tour of Arizona. We played for a solid six nights at a jazz club in Phoenix, which was fantastic since it allowed the quartet to really dig into both the songs and Bob's mode of presentation. For example, rather than a straight quartet reading of each song in our repertoire, Bob liked to play duos (and sometimes trios) with each of us. He picked the right guys to be in this band. Pianist Theo Saunders, bassist Putter Smith, and I fell right into Bob's concept, and we veered away from the conventional trombone-with-rhythm-section approach common to jazz foursomes and moved into uncharted territory. Many times during that week, the audiences were attentive, probably because Bob taught them to expect the unexpected in each of the sets we played.

However, there were some unforgettably weird stops along the way. We played a concert in Yuma, Arizona (near Gila Bend), and without knowing what we were getting ourselves into, Bob also booked a brief preconcert performance on a local TV show called *The Aunt Gracie Show*, a half-hour community events show hosted by this down-home Sophie Tucker–type woman who, as I remember, introduced us as "Bob and the boys." The only other thing I recall is that after she introduced us initially, Aunt Gracie cut to a commercial for some store in town, after which she said "and that's a great deal, folks. Why, you can't beat it with a stick!" Talk about being woefully out of place.

We also played a concert in the student union at Yavapai Community College in Prescott, which was preceded in the early afternoon by a "clinic" in the activities room at the local middle school. About twenty or twenty-five kids sat on the floor in a semicircle and were either intrigued by the music or distracted by their neighbors, who apparently had the attention span of gnats. Bob seemed to be having fun playing for these kids, and when we concluded the music portion of the program, he asked them if they had any questions. After two or three predictable questions like "Why do you close your eyes when you play?" and "How come the slide doesn't move?" and so on, one rotund, grumpy-faced little kid in the front row raised his hand and asked, "How much money do you make a year?" Bob smiled and, without missing a beat, replied, "Not nearly enough, kid. Not nearly enough."

Amsterdam, Netherlands: The NOS Jazz Festival, 1987

A year or so after recording *Oslo* for Concord Records, Bob was invited to bring a group to Amsterdam to play the NOS Jazz Festival in mid-August of 1987. He decided to bring pianist Theo Saunders (who was slated to do the *Oslo* recording a year earlier but had to cancel due to an injury), the gifted young bassist Eric Von Essen, and me. While I had played in South America, Australia, France, and Canada, I had never visited a Scandinavian country before and was looking forward to being on the festival stage with Bob, Theo, and Eric. The NOS Festival was broadcast on Scandinavian radio that year, and, happily, we were able to secure a recording of our performance. Certainly a step up from recording many of Bob's small band gigs with a cassette recorder!

Our repertoire included five songs from the *Oslo* record and three additional tunes, one each by guitarist John Scofield, Brookmeyer, and Rodgers and Hart. It's a shame that—at least to my knowledge—the recording was never released. Bob was, as usual, in fine form, as was the rhythm section. I remember the communion among us was inspiring from song to song. One of the standouts was Scofield's "Yawn," a very slow and wistful waltz with lovely solo statements from Bob (who tells the audience that this is his favorite song) and Theo, who was at his most lyrical. There was also an oblique, tongue-in-cheek version of "Have You Met Miss Jones" and an absolutely stunning version of "Alone Together," with memorable solos from

Bob, Theo, and Eric. This particular version featured the "splintering" of the quartet, beginning with Bob playing an out-of-tempo chorus, followed by a duo melody statement with Eric, then a trio romp with Theo, Eric, and me, followed by an incomparable bass solo by Eric. The performance ended the way it began—sparsely, as we each dropped out gradually until it was Bob alone. An on-the-spot arrangement at its very best.

Someone mentioned to me that audiences in Amsterdam were quite reserved, and sometimes the best a performer could hope for was polite applause. I thought that it might be an accurate observation, but as I listened recently to the audience's response to our music that night in 1987, I realized that while you could hear a pin drop during our set, the response at the end of the majority of each song was enthusiastic. There was even some scattered vocal approval in addition to energetic clapping. I think that when attentive audiences experience the give-and-take musical conversations of groups like ours, it really resonates for them, as it does for us. And so goes the universal power of music. As Theo Saunders once said to me, "We are vessels through which the music of the Universe passes." And ironically, that was Bob's credo during his later years, where he saw himself as a sort of vessel for music waiting to be composed, both on paper and spontaneously. He might have even said that if we listen closely with our hearts, we become the recipients of those musical gifts. Bob was certainly one who channeled music that always told a story, one that continues to resonate for many, many listeners even now.

Someday, it's my hope that the music from this quartet performance sees the light of day. It was a gift to have the opportunity to preserve it and bring it into a world that, in my estimation, needs every note.

Brook and Smith: Stanford University Jazz Workshop, 2000

This concert was very special to me, since I was sharing the stage with both Bob and pianist Smith Dobson, a musician of great importance to me when I was coming up while living in the Washington,

DC, area in the late '60s through the early '70s. Smith was one of the most genuinely joyous people I'd ever known, and we just seemed to click, both on and off the bandstand. Ultimately, after getting out of the service, Smith relocated to the West Coast and established himself as one of the leading jazz pianists in all of Northern California. We lost track of each other until 1999, when we reunited to play some gigs in San Jose, Santa Cruz, and San Francisco. I have never known anyone who exuded so much positive energy on the concert stage. Smith exemplified the pure joy of making music, and I found his attitude toward music and life to be highly contagious. Unfortunately, we lost him to a senseless automobile accident a year or so after this concert.

Smith and Bob sounded beautiful together, and Bob was in good spirits throughout, joking with the audience and playing beautifully. The program Bob had selected was all standards, particularly those he always seemed to enjoy playing. Smith was a great accompanist for Bob and played intuitively, listening to and complementing Bob's linear twists and turns harmonically. It was exactly how I thought it would be. As usual, bassist Tom Warrington (the bassist on our *Stay Out of the Sun* album) provided a lovely sonic cushion, both as an accompanist and a soloist.

All in all, it was great to play on the stage with two of my inspirations, witnessing how beautifully they connected with each other, with Tom and me, and with the audience.

Looking back on these gigs, varied as they were in terms of venues and audiences, the one constant was always the quality of the music. No matter where we played, Bob's presence, his stature, and the way he always made audiences feel welcome via his comments and humorous asides, kept listeners engaged and, in the end, made them feel happy to have spent time with our quartet.

In the Studio

Two of Bob's California visits were among the most memorable:

Oslo (1986), Concord Records

In the mid-'80s Bob called from New York and said, "I think it's time we made a record together." And so another dream was coming true for me. We recorded *Oslo* for Concord Records in September 1986, which featured pianist Alan Broadbent, bassist Eric Von Essen, and me. Unfortunately, Bob's pianist of choice, Theo Saunders, was unable to play on the *Oslo* record date due to an unfortunate mishap a month earlier that affected one of his hands. Fortunately, we were able to secure Broadbent, who, like Theo, was an intuitive accompanist and brilliant soloist. So having Alan on board was a stroke of luck for us.

Every minute in the studio with Brookmeyer was magical and educational as well. His disciplined and focused approach to recording was inspiring and challenging. We recorded nine songs, four of which were Bob's original compositions, and five of which were standards that Bob liked to play. Bob had a unique way of creating equanimity in small ensembles—in this case, the quartet setting. As mentioned earlier, at any given time during a Brookmeyer quartet performance, you might hear Bob duetting with the bassist, the pianist, or the drummer. Other times, the pianist might play alone, as would the bassist and drummer. Most of the time those decisions were made spontaneously or via hand signals from Bob. And that's exactly what happened when we recorded *Oslo*.

At the beginning of the session, I was a little nervous and was hoping that Bob would be happy with my playing; after all, making a record with one of my all-time heroes was a big deal for me. I think Eric Von Essen felt the same way. As great a musician as he was, he too could feel Bob's quietly immense presence that day in the studio. I think that of the three of us, Alan was the most calm and assured.

All of our anxiety disappeared quickly, however, once we began playing. Bob chose a standard called "With the Wind and the Rain in Your Hair," and he talked us through its structure: Alan, Eric, and I were to play a vamp, and when Bob entered, that would be the first statement of the melody. As he was counting off the downbeat, Bob may've said something like "nice and loose." From there on out, it was all intuition, deep listening, and instantaneous intercommunication. Instead of playing the entire melody of the song, Bob played only parts of the melody, staggering his note choices. I'm sure it was a surprise to each of us, but it also served as inspiration to dance around his fragmented statement, supporting it without distracting from its sparseness. As good as it felt throughout the take, I dreaded listening to the playback, because what I thought was some good playing on my part might have been a total illusion and then it would be downhill in the drum department for the rest of the afternoon. However, the track turned out to be a pleasant surprise. The rhythm section was swinging right out of the gate. Bob merely smiled, and from that point on, we dug in and were squarely in the moment from track to track.

Another highlight was our rendering of "Detour Ahead," which is one of the most beautiful ballads in the jazz standard repertoire. I first heard it on one of the classic Bill Evans Trio records recorded live at the Village Vanguard in New York City, and then later heard the Brookmeyer orchestral version from Bob's brilliant *Gloomy Sunday and Other Bright Moments* album, which I still believe is one of the greatest big band albums to emerge from the second half of the twentieth century.

And then there's the penultimate vocal version by Billie Holiday . . .

Our quartet version for this recording is a Brookmeyer arrangement that, in this case, consisted of Bob's very simple "road map": It would begin with Alan playing a very delicate, sparse rhythmic pattern, supported only by Eric's single metronomic quarter notes, which sound sort of like a low-pitched brass bell being struck gently with a soft yarn mallet. At roughly the fourteen-second mark, I begin playing softly with wire brushes as Bob enters with the lovely melody.

He states it simply and you can almost hear the opening lyrics sung by Lady Day:

> Smooth road . . . clear day . . .
> but why am I the only one . . . travlin' this way?'
> How strange the road to love . . . should be . . . so easy . . .
> Can't you see the detour ahead?[3]

After completing the entire statement of the melody, and with only Eric's bass for support, Bob begins—and ultimately sustains—a two-note rhythmic figure for the bulk of his solo, digressing occasionally here and there with a slight alteration of the repetitive pattern he began his solo with. It's not something he planned to do; rather, it appears to be a spontaneous decision, and he builds upon it, actually enhancing the somber feeling of the piece. It's like he's using these short two-note phrases to create a sense of frustration, telling us that when one travels down that road, the path to love seems smooth at the outset, yet it can become a negative experience—hence, the detour.

Broadbent's piano solo follows, supported by bass and drums, and maintains the mood that Bob has created, until Bob re-enters, sounding anguished for a moment and then settling into what seems like resignation—that life is, indeed, what can happen when one is making other plans.

Years later Alan Broadbent called me and in the course of our conversation said something like, "I listened to *Oslo* recently and damn, it still sounds great." And having withstood the test of time, it still does.

Stay Out of the Sun (2000), Challenge Records

Sometime early in the new millennium, I approached Bob with the idea of another recording project, one that he and I would coproduce. He liked my proposal and off we went, planning instrumentation and repertoire. Bob had been making trips to California in the '90s, and when he did we would always play a number of quartet gigs. One of the quartet configurations around that time included the inimitable and endlessly inventive guitarist Larry Koonse and virtuoso bassist Tom Warrington. Bob had played with both previously and, as stated in Bob's portion of the recording's liner notes, "Larry . . . is a part of me now," and he described Tom as "an immensely gifted and melodic bassist."

Moving this project into the light was a true team effort. Bob wrote four of the nine compositions *in the hotel room* the night before our first and only rehearsal the following evening. He also provided verbal "road maps" for the other five tunes, which ultimately made each sound as though it was an actual written arrangement. Larry brought "Longing," his beautiful tango that featured a delicate turn by Bob on piano, and also a waltz called "Wistful Thinking" by our late friend and colleague, bassist Eric Von Essen, which sounds like it was written expressly for solos by Bob and Larry. Rounding out the repertoire were several tunes I chose that I thought would fit the vibe of the date. I always wanted to hear Bob play "If I Loved You" by Rodgers and Hammerstein and, most particularly, Bill Evans's "Blue in Green," which at my behest was a duo vehicle for valve trombone and guitar. Elsewhere, in chapter 7 of this book, Larry describes what it was like to play the song as a pas de deux with Bob. His humble and beautifully penned description of the spontaneous intimacy they achieved on the track is remarkable in its clarity.

Bob's four new hotel room compositions were examples of an amazing mind at work. I recall him telling me that he frequently wrote while traveling on airplanes and even wrote amidst the hustle and bustle in airport terminals. In fact, when he gave me a copy of *Paris Suite*, which he recorded with his European quartet in 1993, I seem to recall that when I expressed curiosity about one of his compositions called "Airport Song," he mentioned composing that piece while waiting for a flight at de Gaulle Airport. Coincidentally, in his excellent five-part interview with Bob in 2009, *JazzWax.com* blogmaster Marc Myers commented about that very song:

> **Marc:** In 1993, you recorded "Airport Song" on your Paris Suite album. It's so beautiful.

Bob: Thank you. I wrote that while at the Charles de Gaulle Airport in Paris waiting for a plane. I had music paper and my flight didn't leave for an hour.[4]

Jan mentioned much later that Bob always got more work accomplished when under the time constraints imposed by deadlines. How he could produce such beauty in such a short space of time is still a wonder. To say that these four pieces exemplified his genius would be an understatement.

The first piece, "Turtle," is a humoresque—a short, lively piece of music. It humorously describes the waddle of the terrapin in "The Tortoise and the Hare," one of Aesop's most beloved fables. Brookmeyer's turtle just sort of ambles along through the piece, ignoring the taunts and teases of the hare, and miraculously wins the race, coming to a complete and victorious STOP at the finish line.

"Janet Planet" was written for Bob's wife, Jan. Many of us who knew Bob would agree that Jan was the best thing that ever happened to him. She is a woman of exemplary grace, compassion, and wisdom, and Bob adored her. Accordingly, this piece is a musical portrait of Janet Planet, painted in pastels, delivered gently by the quartet. It begins with Bob stating the melody with a lovely harmonic cushion provided by Larry. Bass and drums enter softly, almost imperceptibly, and become more integral during the guitar solo. Finally, Bob enters again, this time duetting with bassist Warrington and joined by guitar and drums to bring the song to a whisper. As I recall, Bob gave very few if any hand signals to indicate who would play and who would tacit throughout the track. It just unfolded the way it did, spontaneously—almost telepathically.

Bob named "Kathleen" after my better half. Katie joined us when we played a concert in Tahoe, and the day after the performance, she rode back to Los Angeles with Tom, Bob, and me in our rented van. Bob and Katie sat in the back seat and had a long and, at times, deep conversation. They became friends immediately and remained so for the duration of Bob's life. I knew that Bob respected Katie for her perceptiveness, her gentle spirit, and for her world view. At one point later, Bob looked at me wryly and said, "You done good, kid."

Some words about the title track: Sometimes it's best to tread carefully when a composer titles his or her compositions in a rather surreal manner. Jazz composers are really adept at doing this. Thelonious Monk was a master of quirky titles, like "Boo Boo's Birthday" and "Trinkle, Tinkle." Charles Mingus wrote "Orange Was the Color of Her Dress, Then Blue Silk" and "All the Things You Could Be if Sigmund Freud's Wife Was Your Mother." The list of unique song titles by jazz composers goes on and on, from the mysterious to the wacky to the just plain weird.

Brookmeyer was no exception. The first Brookmeyer song title I ever saw that was downright funny was "Oh, Jane Snavely," which I think he may have lifted from *MAD* magazine. Other early ditties that followed included "Thump, Thump, Thump," "In a Rotten Mood," "Bad Agnes," and "Dancing on the Grave." Later titles, mostly attached to his large ensembles, included "The Nasty Dance," "Say Ah," "Me, Her, and You," and "Harumph."

So whenever the opportunity came up to ask Bob why he named more than a few of his compositions in a manner that was, shall we say, left of center (and sometimes self-deprecatory), I always passed on it because I thought he might see that as a stupid question. However, when the title track of this Challenge Records release came up in the first decade of the new millennium, I figured, what the hell, I'll ask; but before I could, Bob explained that his doctor suggested that he avoid prolonged exposure to direct sunlight for medical reasons. So he decided to name his final "Hotel Room" composition "Stay Out of the Sun." Simple as that.

And that was the *only* simple thing about it. "Stay Out of the Sun" was the most challenging of the four, at least for me. After our rehearsal the evening before the recording session, I went home and wrote an actual drum part to replace the master score in order to better familiarize myself with the music using my own notation. This piece was like a miniature stylistic version of some of his large ensemble music. There were changes in tempos, constantly shifting rhythmic feels, and weird stop-times to throw some oblique drama into the mix, all with dollops of tongue-in-cheek humor scattered throughout. It was certainly a challenge, but thankfully, I seem to remember that we recorded "Sun" in only one or two takes.

The end product was (and still is) a beautifully realized recording, buttressed by the imagination, on-the-spot creativity, and dedication of all hands. Bob was exceptionally pleased. When he asked me if I'd like to be co-leader on the record, it took me very little time to say "No thanks. Just put my name under yours." I really couldn't see "Bob Brookmeyer–Michael Stephans" as a co-leadership thing. On one hand, I felt that I wasn't enough of a leader in this situation to merit a co-leadership; and on the other hand, I think that Larry and Tom contributed just as much as I did musically, if not more.

One final comment, this one about the track called "Bruise." Even though Bob gave the track its title after the fact, it was completely improvised, start to finish. It is a classic example of how four-way musical interplay, when based upon a foundation of mutual trust among improvisers, can produce completely spontaneous compositions. In retrospect, I feel that we achieved that goal on this track. The fact that "Bruise" ended up being a blues is beside the point since none of us planned for that to happen. The music played us, not the other way around!

Brookmeyer regained his stature as a well-respected jazz soloist, composer, and teacher both here in America and in Europe. And our relationship continued to flourish, even though we didn't play together nearly as much as we used to. But when we did have the opportunity to make music together, it was as though we never stopped. It was always very personal music, filled with joy and humor and even a touch of sadness. I continued to dot Bob's i's and cross his t's, and he would always turn around and smile at me when we moved along through the music on the same wavelength: the teenaged kid from Miami and the suave, world-class hipster from New York-cum-Kansas City. The stuff dreams are made of . . .

Enter Janet Brookmeyer (1986)

In Her Own Words

The first time I met Bob was in 1986. I was married and living in Kansas City and Bob was living in New York but visiting Kansas City to see his aunt Reta and dating my beautiful sister-in-law. I knew nothing about Bob but found him easy to be with, and I loved his sense of humor. Within months after our first meeting, both my marriage and his relationship ended, and I thought I would never see him again.

However, the following February Bob was in Kansas City to accept an award from UMKC and tried to arrange my attendance at the ceremony. It didn't happen and instead he called and we went out on our first date with my ex–in-laws. It wasn't love at first sight, but I loved being with him. When he wasn't in town, he would telephone from wherever he happened to be—New York, Germany, Sweden. Bob loved to talk and I loved listening to all his stories. It was a connection I had never felt before and I loved the attention. After months of a long-distance relationship, I moved to Goshen, New York, on December 31, 1987, to see if we could stand each other on a daily basis. Those first six months of 1988 were the sweetest and silliest months of my life. We biked, grocery shopped, found our favorite restaurant, and listened to a lot of music. When he was in his studio writing through the night, I would be in the kitchen making bagels!

Life together was good, and we decided to marry sometime in early July. Bob was playing with Jim Hall at the Kongsberg Festival in Norway at that time, but with the help of Bob's friend Jan Horn, a Norwegian television producer, we filed our papers and were married in a former water bottle factory by a woman minister in Kongsberg, Norway, on July 1, 1988. As we left the building, we were greeted by other musicians from the festival and walked under an arch of trombones and escorted back to the hotel by a young woman playing a Hardanger fiddle.

Our marriage was a late-in-life find for both of us. Bob was 58 and I was 50. We were married twenty-four years until his death in 2011. One of the secrets of a good marriage is to marry someone very funny, and

Bob was very, very funny. As an example, Michael pointed to the 2009 interview Bob did for Marc Myers's *JazzWax* blog. Marc and Bob were talking about our late-in-life marriage. At one point near the end of that part of the interview, Bob said, "I had been married three times before Jan. We've only had love and happiness since being together. I guess the lesson here is, 'Don't get married until you turn 58 [years old].'"[5]

Our Wedding Song, 2003

> Congratulations to you both!!!!! Well-deserved for two of the best humans gracing our troubled planet.
> —Bob Brookmeyer

In mid-October 2003 Bob and Jan, as a prewedding gift, flew my soon-to-be life partner, Kathleen, and me out from the left coast to New Hampshire. We were married in nearby Woodstock, Vermont, at

Exchanging wedding vows at the altar of a Universalist Church in Woodstock, Vermont, with (*left to right*) Reverend Dr. Clare Bamberg, Bob, me, Kathleen, and Jan (2003). From author's collection.

Bob and Kathleen share a quiet moment before the ceremony (2003). From author's collection.

a small Unitarian church that Jan found for us. Bob and Jan were our best man and woman at our wedding; in fact, they were the only other people in attendance. Even so, having the Brookmeyers bear witness made our wedding even more deeply personal.

It was a magical time. The church was empty, save for the Unitarian minister, Dr. Clare Bamberg, and Bob and Jan. Facing Kathleen up on the altar, I read a beautiful poem by Elizabeth Spires called "Two Shadows," which, in retrospect, mirrored us perfectly.

In fact, now that I think of it, as much as Jan was a beacon of light for Bob, Kathleen continues to be the same for me. The last part of the poem still resonates with me each time I read it:

> When we are shadows watching over shadows,
> We will not speak of it but know, and turn
> again toward each other tenderly,
> shadow to shadow.[6]

What an emotional moment! An internal earthquake! I was shaking inside and rather numb—the way someone might feel in their gut when a life-altering change is about to take place. Kathleen looked absolutely beautiful and had an aura around her that almost made my knees buckle. I remember just before the ceremony began, Bob and Kathleen were having a conversation; he was sitting in the first row and she was standing in the aisle alongside him (see the photos above). I was hoping he wasn't saying something like, "Are you sure you want to marry a drummer?"

After the ceremony we were spirited away to a lovely restaurant for a celebratory dinner. Bob and Jan were the perfect couple. I don't think I've ever known two more loving and compassionate people. We were so honored that they were happy to share those special moments with us.

We spent our first days as a married couple at the Brookmeyer home on Allen's Drive in Grantham, New Hampshire, and continued to visit in subsequent years. Oftentimes, when Jan and Katie were upstairs, Bob and I spent time down in his studio, listening to and talking about music and swapping stories about great musicians, past and present. Bob and Jan became family, and as I look back on it, that was the greatest wedding gift of all.

Chapter 3

For the Record I

Stretching Out: Selected Brookmeyer Small Group Recordings, 1953–2003

Creating a complete annotated discography of Bob Brookmeyer's many small group recordings as a leader or co-leader would be, in this context, like adding an anvil to a life raft. Instead, this chapter and the next two include recordings that, in my opinion, are important hallmarks in Bob's creative growth. Consequently, these chronological entries are by no means definitive and represent only a portion of Bob's recorded output. Couple them with additional recordings, touring, other types of studio work, club and festival appearances, and his activities as a composer and arranger, and you have an artist who was beyond busy.

Please note that Bob's work with baritone saxophonist Gerry Mulligan is not represented in this chapter, since Bob did not co-lead Gerry's quartets and sextets, even though he was an integral member of these groups. More detailed information about the Mulligan-Brookmeyer relationship can be found in the next chapter.

The Oslo Quartet in Sage and Sound recording studio (Los Angeles, 1986). *Left to right*: Bob, me, bassist Eric von Essen, and pianist Alan Broadbent. From author's collection.

1953–54

Bob Brookmeyer, Complete 1953–1954 Quintet Studio Recordings with Stan Getz was reissued in Spain under Bob's name by Fresh Sound Records in 2004 for reasons unknown, especially since it was Stan's quintet. Actually, most if not all the tracks were originally released by various Clef, Norgran, or Verve Records publications under Stan Getz's name. In any case, the quintet was an exceptional unit, due largely to the blending of the Getz-Brookmeyer tenor-trombone sound and the wonderful interplay between them. They would reunite years later with two of the most memorable recordings of each's career.

1954–55

The first Brookmeyer recordings as a leader were released early in 1954 and 1955, mostly in quartet settings, recorded in either New York or Los Angeles. The repertoire often consisted of a mix of standards culled from the Great American Songbook and Brookmeyer originals. The foursomes were usually trombone and piano, bass, and drums, with the addition of tenor saxophonist Al Cohn in 1954, and Zoot Sims or Phil Urso added for quintet recordings in 1956.

Bob Brookmeyer Plays Bob Brookmeyer and Some Others was recorded for Clef Records in Los Angeles the day after Christmas in 1954, and it features the rhythm section of pianist Jimmy Rowles, bassist Buddy Clark, and drummer Mel Lewis. As the title suggests, the program includes a mix of standards and a number of Bob's originals. The rhythm section is a little looser than on earlier recordings, perhaps because of the presence of Rowles, whose rhythmic concept was more oblique and less percussive than his predecessor, John Williams. Also, Mel Lewis's drumming lent a more flowing feel, one that meshed perfectly with Rowles and Clark. This recording was reissued as *The Modernity of Bob Brookmeyer* by Fresh Sounds in Spain and features Bob with both the Rowles quartet and the Williams foursome.

The recording from this period that stands out as completely unique is called *The Dual Role of Bob Brookmeyer*. The original 1954 release on Prestige Records was a ten-inch recording that contained four tracks. Bob played valve trombone on two and piano on the other two, and he was accompanied by guitarist Jimmy Raney and by Teddy Kotick and Mel Lewis on bass and drums, respectively. Bob shines on both instruments, as does Raney, and both are well supported by the rhythm section. They are some delightfully relaxed and swinging performances due to the great chemistry between Brook, Raney, Kotick, and Lewis.

1956

Of the three saxophonists mentioned previously, John Haley "Zoot" Sims and Bob co-led a quintet and recorded three albums as such. The two that stand out were recorded for Storyville Records. *Tonite's Music Today* and *Whooeee!* were rereleased years later by Black Lion Records, with the *Whooeee!* title being changed to *Morning Fun*.

The Zoot and Bob collaborations were high-energy, good-spirited affairs that swung mightily, with the aid of pianist Hank Jones on both recordings and of bassist Bill Crow and legendary Basie drummer Jo Jones on *Morning Fun*, and bassist Wyatt Ruther and another Basie alumnus, Gus Johnson, on drums on *Tonite's Music Today*.

1957

One of Bob's most fully realized and consistently enjoyable small-band recordings is *Traditionalism Revisited*. I don't think it would be hyperbole to add that the music here is timeless and wears well, even now, over a half century later.

Simply put, this recording is NOT merely jazz versions of old-time tunes. It is much more the end result of a twofold process of revisiting the original songs and reimagining them in a way that brings each one back to life without blatantly copying the style in which they were originally conceived. Bob's arrangements and his instrumental virtuosity coupled with Jimmy Giuffre's eloquent clarinet, tenor, and baritone sax voices and Jim Hall's lovely, expressive guitar playing—all bolstered gently by bassists Joe Benjamin or Ralph Peña and Dave Bailey's sensitive swinging drumming—make for a great listening experience. *Traditionalism Revisited* is a recording you may well find yourself returning to time and again.

Another 1957 release that is recommended is *The Al Cohn Quintet Featuring Bobby Brookmeyer*. In addition to the fine, high-spirited playing from track to track, it's interesting to hear a small group recording led by two composer/arrangers. Of the twelve songs, Cohn arranged half and Bob the other half, and each contributed three original compositions. The other interesting thing here is that unlike so many other small group recordings, these arrangements could've easily been converted into big band charts, what with the way the horn lines are written out, both in the melody statements and the variations. This would've been difficult to achieve without the right rhythm section, and this one fills the bill, with pianist Mose Allison, bassist

Teddy Kotick, and especially drummer Nick Stabulas, who admirably supports all of the tricky ins and outs of Cohn's and Brookmeyer's arrangements.

1958

October was a busy month for Bob. In addition to multiple record dates with Manny Albam and his first recording as a member of Jimmy Giuffre's trio, the end of the month found him in Olmstead Studios in New York City, recording his own project, *Kansas City Revisited*, a joyously loose, swinging homage to that city, its jazz joints and dance halls, and its movie theaters that would not only show films but also feature big bands like Count Basie's on matinee days. When one thinks of Kansas City jazz, the conversation often immediately turns to Count Basie, and Basie's stamp is all over this recording. In fact, one of the two tenor saxophonists on this date was Paul Quinichette, who played with both the Basie band and the band of another KC stalwart, Jay McShann. Other members of the septet included tenor saxophonist Al Cohn, pianist Nat Pierce, guitarist Jim Hall, bassist Addison Farmer, and drummer Osie Johnson; and the icing on the cake was "Big" Miller, whose wonderfully soulful vocals graced two tracks. Bob's playing throughout was very vocal: shouts, growls, meows—breathing KC fire through the horn!

1959

One of the high points of all of Bob's small band recordings was his meeting with pianist Bill Evans in March of 1959 when they recorded a two-piano album called *The Ivory Hunters*. I asked Bob how this came to pass, and he recalled that when he walked into the recording studio with his trombone case, he asked the producer Jack Lewis why two pianos were set up in the middle of the room. Lewis, who had produced two Brookmeyer albums for United Artists the previous year, said that he envisioned a two-piano album with Bill Evans, rather than the more conventional horn with rhythm section date. Bob agreed and provided some in-studio sketches for each of the songs, all six of which were recognizable standards. Thanks to the advent of stereophonic recording, a listener can hear Bill Evans on the right channel and Brookmeyer on the left.

Bill and Bob worked together previously, mostly at the Half Note in NYC, usually in a quintet setting with a saxophonist but, to my knowledge, never with a trombone and rhythm section type of quartet. These two guys were (and still are) my heroes, and to hear them together in a foursome—Evans's piano with Brookmeyer's valve trombone—would've been nirvana. But Jack Lewis had other ideas, and so a different kind of jazz history was made that day and, admittedly, the results are quite enjoyable. To say that Bob held his own playing with Bill is an understatement. The piano had always been more than a second instrument to Bob, as he had quite a bit of experience early on as a piano player with both big bands and small groups. On that date the two complemented each other perfectly, and bassist Percy Heath and drummer Connie Kay, both members of the Modern Jazz Quartet, created a subtly propulsive cushion throughout. Forty-two years later Bob would record his first and only piano trio record called *Holiday* for Challenge Records.

1960

Bob recorded what many fellow musicians have said is one of the best—if not THE best—trombone and rhythm section albums of all time! Now that's pretty hefty wordage, and Brook would probably scoff at that notion; but if truth be known, I can think of no better example extant that came before *The Blues Hot and Cold*, nor any that came after. This June 1960 recording is so perfect a vehicle for the new ways that Bob approached his solos. He found a way to merge past and present jazz stylings adroitly, without any pretentiousness whatsoever. More specifically, his solos often became very "vocalized"; that is, he could emit cries, grunts, wheezes, shouts. He could end a solo or a phrase with a single raspy note that would curl upward or end with a "yuh." He could "cluck" repeatedly, sort of like a chicken.

In other words, the valve trombone became Bob's other voice, one that honored the great trombonists of the past: "Tricky Sam" Nanton, Quentin "Butter" Jackson, Miff Mole, and his hero, Bill Harris, whose sound and attack influenced Bob's approach to developing a bigger sound and technique. I also feel that Bob's vocal approach at that time was as far from gimmickry as you could get. If you listen closely to any of these tracks, you can feel Bob's *and our* humanity. It's all there: the joyful exuberance and the sadness, the tongue-in-cheek humor. And the anger. It's who he was . . . and who we are.

These word descriptions don't really do Bob's vocalisms—or his musicality—much justice. Each track on *The Blues Hot and Cold* tells the story. Even though I've described Bob's rendition of "On the Sunny Side of the Street" in an earlier chapter, there is much more to hear on the other five tracks as well. If Bob's opening notes on "Languid Blues" don't typify a sluggish, lethargic feeling, I don't know what does. The final "note" that he plays at the end of "Sunny Side of the Street" is something most anyone can relate to before heading into their medicine cabinet for the Alka Seltzer. His solo on "Smoke Gets in Your Eyes" is both passionate and lyrical, and "I Got Rhythm" is pure joy by all hands from start to finish.

Finally, a few words about the rhythm section. If you listen to *Bob Brookmeyer Plays Bob Brookmeyer and Some Others / The Modernity of Bob Brookmeyer*—the recording mentioned earlier in the 1954–55 segment—and compare it to this recording, it's hard to believe that these are the same three gentlemen who played on Bob's album five years earlier. For that matter, it's even harder to fathom that it's the same Bob Brookmeyer! While the earlier recording was a well-conceived, relaxed, and a somewhat unremarkable affair, this time Bob, Jimmy Rowles, Buddy Clark, and Mel Lewis pulled out all the stops and turned in six utterly soulful, inspired performances. There's much more emotion at play here that, to my ears, makes the earlier recording sound bland by comparison.

The Blues Hot and Cold was originally released on the Verve label in June of 1960 and unfortunately languished in the company's vaults for decades until 2009, when it was rereleased by a small European label called Lone Hill Jazz in tandem with another long-out-of-print Verve album by Brookmeyer called *7 X Wilder*. It is available on the internet and is an excellent addition to any jazz collection.

1961

Late in the '50s and into the '60s is often considered one of the most vibrant periods for jazz, particularly in New York City. On any given night, you could go to Birdland and hear John Coltrane's classic quartet, then head over to the Village Vanguard and immerse yourself in the innovative and resonant music of the Bill Evans Trio. You could then move on to the Village Gate to catch the last set by Sonny Rollins and his adventurous quartet. And the next night, you would plan to do it again, this time starting with the Half Note and the poll-winning Clark Terry–Bob Brookmeyer Quintet.

It was also a great time for recording: Sonny Rollins's *A Night at the Village Vanguard* (1957), Miles Davis's seminal classic *Kind of Blue* (1959), *The Thelonious Monk Orchestra at Town Hall* (1959), John Coltrane's *Giant Steps* (1960), Gerry Mulligan's *Concert Jazz Band at the Village Vanguard* (1960), Bill Evans's *Live at the Village Vanguard* (1961), Art Blakey's Jazz Messengers' *Meet You at the Jazz Corner of the World* (1961), and Stan Getz's *Focus* (1961). And that was just a prelude to what came later in the decade!

Bob Brookmeyer was also a member of this preeminent group yet was known only to a smaller audience and even then often as a prominent sideman with Gerry Mulligan and Stan Getz, rather than as a more well-known member of the pantheon of jazz stars listed previously. Even so, he recorded four albums as a leader or co-leader, as well as the brilliant *Gloomy Sunday and Other Bright Moments: The Bob Brookmeyer Orchestra*, that were critically acclaimed by various jazz magazines and listeners. He even appeared on the cover of *DownBeat* magazine on two different occasions during that time and was the subject of profiles in both.

Sometime in the early 1960s, I bought a Brookmeyer album called *7 X Wilder*. Honestly, I had absolutely no idea what the title meant, but hey, it was Bob's new album and, being a devout teenage fan, I plunked my money down and headed for home and my record player, hoping that it would be some swingin' soulful music like *The Blues Hot and Cold*. To my surprise, this record was completely different. All the songs except one—an impromptu blues—were by composer Alec Wilder, someone I'd never heard of, and the rhythm section consisted of guitar, bass, and drums rather than piano. Guitarist Jim Hall and Bob had recorded together under Bob's leadership in 1957 and 1958, and they also recorded as members of Jimmy Giuffre's trio in the latter year. Bassist Bill Crow was also on Bob's *Street Swingers* album and was a natural choice for the bass chair. And drummer Mel Lewis was, without a doubt, Bob's first choice on this and many other dates to come.

The Hall-Crow-Lewis rhythm section brought a loose, intuitive feel to this session, and its accompaniment suited the songs perfectly. There are three tracks on which Bob plays only piano, and these tracks ("While We're Young," "The Wrong Blues," and "Blues for Alec") are each sensitively rendered in an understated way. The opener, "While We're Young," is magnificent. It has a chamber music feel that speaks softly rather than shouts and is the perfect gateway for the rest of the album. Bob plays Wilder's melody in a stately and somewhat regal manner. Hall's solo meshes perfectly with Bob's accompaniment, and Mel Lewis's drum solo is completely antithetical to the louder/faster school of drumming. Lewis paints pictures with his cymbals and drum punctuations, staying within the feeling of the performance. And here, as elsewhere, Bill Crow's bass playing brings the right kind of depth to the proceedings.

I should also note here that Bob solos on both valve trombone and piano on "I'll Be Around" and "Who Can I Turn To?" and valve trombone only on "That's the Way It Goes" and "It's So Peaceful in the Country." In this day and age of too-often predictable modes of performance, it's refreshing to experience a unique album like *7 X Wilder* to enjoy the diversity of approaches that exist from track to track by this imaginative quartet. It was from here that I began to understand a little more of why Bob was so unique. He simply refused to rest on his laurels and wanted to move forward when he felt it was time to do so. This album was, and still is, an early testament to his credo, and sounds as fresh today as it did then.

Stan Getz–Bob Brookmeyer Recorded Fall 1961 continues to be one of the most revered small group recordings in all of Bob's discography. The music never sounds old or dated, and both Bob and Stan bring a relaxed elegant maturity to the entire date. This is not a recording one buys, listens to once or twice, then shelves. Like *Traditionalism Revisited*, there is a timeless quality about it, a knowingness that never loses its focus, thanks in no small part to Bob's skills as an arranger.

A bit of history: Bob began his musical relationship with saxophonist Stan Getz as a member of Getz's new quintet in December of 1952, when they debuted at the Hi Hat Club in Boston. The quintet was something special in that the contrapuntal interplay between Bob and Stan became one of the main characteristics of their performances. In their hands the simultaneous weaving of the tenor saxophone and the valve trombone created a third voice, a kind of mellifluous timbre that horns in that melodic range could achieve.

Even though the two hadn't played together in some time, the kind of intimate, almost telepathic improvisational quality they began to develop years earlier in Stan's quintet had deepened when they improvised together on this 1961 recording. Each of the six tracks was arranged by Bob and each has its own unique appeal. Take for example the opening track, "Minuet Circa '61," a lilting Brookmeyer waltz. After the solos by Bob, Getz, and pianist Steve Kuhn, the lovely, improvised duet by Bob and Stan offers a classic example of the interplay between them, and how closely they listened to and complemented each other before stating the melody one last time.

Listen to Bob's interesting arrangement of his composition "Who Could Care," the first ballad on the album. After the brief piano introduction by Steve Kuhn, Stan plays the melody, followed by Bob playing the first half of the bridge; Stan plays the second half of the bridge with Bob supplying background, and then plays the final part of the melody with Bob echoing Stan's eloquence with some of his own. The solos function the same way, in that the interactions are partially arranged, giving Stan and Bob ample room to support each other subtly without getting in each other's way. The final bridge finds both playing sixteenth notes softly until moving into a brief, eloquent call-and-response moment between the horns before returning to the final melody statement and Bob's single-note ending.

The rhythm section here, as well as throughout the album, provided empathetic support, especially pianist Steve Kuhn, whose approach to each of the songs often reminds me of Bill Evans. Boston-based bassist John Neves was a great choice, as was the legendary Roy Haynes on drums.

Loren Schoenberg, who wrote the liner notes for the Verve reissue in 2000, interviewed Steve Kuhn, who remarked that "Stan was happy with the date, and didn't belabor things with a lot of retakes. He loved the rhythm section so much that he featured us in clubs. In fact, he eventually said, 'This band has to disband,' because he felt that we were outplaying him night after night."

Schoenberg, elsewhere in the liner notes, posits that "few artists in any genre evolve beyond the conventions of their first maturity. Getz and Brookmeyer managed to keep the melodic imperative of their playing throughout their long careers, no matter how the contexts changed."[1]

1962–63

These years found Bob playing and recording with a variety of musicians, most notably a group he co-founded and co-led with trumpeter/flugelhornist Clark Terry, which in time would become a very popular, poll-winning quintet. Bob also continued his on-again, off-again musical relationship with baritone saxophonist Gerry Mulligan in a variety of quartet and sextet settings, as well as with Mulligan's Concert Jazz Band, which came into existence in 1960 and lasted through the end of 1964.

Even though Bob didn't lead his own small group during those years, he did record an album called *Trombone Jazz Samba* on the heels of the enormously successful *Jazz Samba* album by Stan Getz and guitarist Charlie Byrd. Both of these albums were released in 1962 by Verve, the Getz-Byrd album first in April, followed by the Brookmeyer recording only a few months later. Whereas *Jazz Samba* took off like a rocket, *Trombone Jazz Samba* was left to linger on the launching pad. While Bob and I never really talked about it at any length, I got the feeling that producer Creed Taylor thought that a follow-up recording to *Jazz Samba*—pairing Bob on valve trombone and piano and a mix of familiar jazz musicians such as Jim Hall (solos), Jimmy Raney, guitars, and Gary McFarland, vibes, and a trio of Latin percussionists—might be equally attractive to the listening public. Unfortunately, the wind didn't blow that way, and *Trombone Jazz Samba* came and went with a handful of good reviews and little else.

The following year saw the release of another Creed Taylor Verve project, this one co-led by Bob and Argentine composer/arranger/pianist Lalo Schifrin. As described earlier, *Samba Para Dos* was a semi–happy accident that resulted in Bob stepping in for a Latin American singer who was unable to record as planned. With the exception of the title song by Schifrin, all the rest were his arrangements of standards set to bossa nova and samba rhythms. Not really a substantive addition to the Brookmeyer canon, it is still of interest when considering how Bob saved the session by assuming the solo voice on every song and creating masterful improvisations on each as well.

1964

One of Bob's most important small group recordings, *Bob Brookmeyer and Friends*, was produced by one of the jazz world's most famous producers, Teo Macero, for Columbia Records. Stan Getz and Bob were reunited for this date, their first since the 1961 quintet recording for Verve. The brilliant vibraphonist Gary Burton may have been chosen by Stan and okayed by Bob since he was a member of Stan's group at that time. The stellar rhythm section included pianist Herbie Hancock, bassist Ron Carter—both with Miles Davis's second great quintet—and drummer Elvin Jones, a member of John Coltrane's classic quartet.

One interesting observation is that Herbie Hancock, Ron Carter, and Elvin Jones never once had to sacrifice their stylistic identities to accommodate the music. Track to track, everything they played fit perfectly in the Brookmeyer-Getz universe. An absolutely wonderful musical pairing throughout.

Even with all of the planets in alignment, there were problems between Bob and Teo Macero. Future record sales—particularly jazz records—may have prompted producer Macero to surprise Bob by bringing into the mix singer Tony Bennett, who, in Macero's mind, would assure a boost in sales right out of the gate. Bob was very unhappy about the intrusion, especially since he wrote four of the eight compositions, arranged the remaining four, and rehearsed the group as needed between takes. This was Bob's project, and, as such, I remember him saying that he felt that Macero had no business bringing Tony Bennett into the studio to record impromptu versions of "Danny Boy" and the Billy Strayhorn–Duke Ellington composition "Day Dream" with the sextet. Of course Bob being Bob, the altercation between him and Macero was more than likely less than pleasant.

One of the later CD reissues includes two more of Bob's originals, as well as the track featuring Tony Bennett singing "Day Dream." I am also aware that more than a few of the tracks had multiple takes, and it's my hope that they all see the light of day in the not-too-distant future. *Bob Brookmeyer and Friends* is a recording for the ages, one of Bob's best.

1962–65: Mumbles and Grumbles

Trumpeter/flugelhornist Clark Terry and Bob Brookmeyer were quite a pair, to say the least. The chemistry between them, both on stage and off, was borne out of a deep mutual admiration for each other. Clark earned his nickname Mumbles after recording a swinging wordless mumbling vocal blues on an Oscar Peterson quartet record date. The album, *Oscar Peterson Trio + 1*, became a big hit thanks to the quartet's consummate musicianship and Clark's blues-drenched mumbling. Since it was added on as an additional track, the blues became known as "Mumbles," hence the nickname.

Grumbles was not really a bona fide nickname for Bob, but he could be a card-carrying grumbler about just about anything in the world that ruffled his feathers. Plus, anyone who knew Bob was aware that his low-pitched voice—particularly his laugh—could sound incredibly sinister. So you put these two guys together on or off stage, you have high spirits as well as great musicianship. The brass powered two-horn frontline, particularly the melding of Bob's and Clark's sound, was attractive to listeners, and the repertoire was very pleasingly diverse.

Speaking of high spirits, Bob and Clark were also known as cutups; that is, putting the two of them together often yielded funny results. One story goes that when walking down a street in New York, they would stage a faux argument that would intensify into a shouting match, drawing the attention of passersby who would stand back just far enough to avoid anything that might become physical. Once Clark and Bob had an audience, they would smile and hug each other and continue on their way, arm in arm.

Their home base was usually the Half Note, the popular jazz club and restaurant located on Hudson Street and Spring Street in the Village (now known as SoHo) from 1957 to 1972. In fact in 1961 one of the two owners, Frank Cantarino, invited Bob to form a group to bring into the club on a semi-regular basis. Clark Terry was Bob's choice to co-lead, and the rhythm section included pianist Eddie Costa, bassist Joe Benjamin, and drummer Osie Johnson. The group recorded a live album there in 1962, but the album was shelved, ostensibly because the piano was noticeably out of tune.

Other excellent musicians came and went through the group, including pianist Hank Jones and bassist Bob Cranshaw. The stable personnel ultimately became pianist Roger Kellaway, bassist Bill Crow, and drummer Dave Bailey; both Crow and Bailey had played and recorded with Bob previously and were a good fit in the quintet. Roger Kellaway was a new voice, and he more than proved himself to be a great addition. As usual, Bob wrote some originals (such as "Hum" and "Dancing on the Grave") and arranged many of the standards.

In terms of recordings, there are numerous collections and reissues of this group. Some have been renamed numerous times. Some of the titles include *Tonight*, *The Power of Positive Swinging*, and *Clark Terry & Bob Brookmeyer Quintet: Complete Live Recordings, 1962–65*. Anything you can find would be worth adding to your collection. Great jazz by a poll-winning, masterful group.

1978

There was little to show for Bob's decade in Los Angeles, except the last couple of years when he crawled out from under the dark specter of alcoholism and began reinventing his life for the better. Playing the valve trombone completely sober was new for him, and it was really something to witness the beginning of that transformation. We played in quartet settings whenever we could, and with Bill Holman's encouragement, Bob began playing with Bill's big band. Perhaps those final years in LA helped Bob decide to pull up stakes and return to the East Coast.

Bob recorded two albums as a leader upon his return to New York. The first, recorded in May of 1978 (and released in 1979)—aptly titled *Back Again* for European-based Sonet Records—was a gathering of old friends: Thad Jones (cornet and flugelhorn), Jimmy Rowles (piano), George Mraz (bass), and his old friend drummer Mel Lewis. The repertoire was mostly standards, particularly those that Bob liked to play, like "Skylark," "Sweet and Lovely," and two Brookmeyer originals, "Carib," an up-tempo samba, and a typically titled blues called "In a Rotten Mood."

Two months later, in July of 1978, Bob took a quartet for a two-night stay into Sandy's, a club located just a twenty-seven-mile jaunt outside of Boston. As luck would have it, both nights were recorded, and the album was released as a two-record set on the DCC

Jazz label. Simply titled *The Bob Brookmeyer Small Band*, the quartet featured a terrific lineup. The guitarist Jack Wilkins was the perfect choice for Bob, not only because of his pure sound and great solos but also due to his ability to comp perfectly behind Bob's solos. I've heard bassist Michael Moore in different settings and have always admired how he manages to sound at home in any group I've ever heard him in. And drummer Joe LaBarbera is—as always—swinging, sensitive, and totally in the moment. Their two nights at Sandy's were, like *Back Again*, a welcome return to the East Coast. If Bob's playing is any indication, both recordings are a tribute to his incredible resilience as both a musician and a person.

1980–83

Around this time a significant shift occurred in Bob's approach to both composing and playing. While he was already heading in this direction, notably with the Thad Jones/Mel Lewis Jazz Orchestra over a decade earlier (and later, upon Thad's departure, Mel Lewis and The Jazz Orchestra), the shift away from the more traditional conventions of his early work was much more pronounced, as evidenced by his 1981 sextet recording, *Through a Looking Glass*. For one thing, Bob's compositions were becoming more complex and more orchestral in nature. There was much more movement from tempo to tempo in a number of the pieces, and the entire traditional modus operandi of written melody followed by solos, then a return to the melody went out the window in some instances. Also, this recording was the first time Bob ever multitracked his written parts and some of his solos as well. So while this was a sextet recording, it often sounded like a larger ensemble.

It's also important to note that the sextet was comprised of open-minded younger players like saxophonist Dick Oatts, trumpeter Tom Harrell, pianist Jim McNeely, and bassist Marc Johnson, all of whom took the leap into the music so impressively, with Bob and Mel Lewis at the helm of the ship on each of the seven pieces.

Unfortunately, for one reason or another, *Through a Looking Glass* never reached a broader listening public. Sad, because the overarching importance of this recording is that it provided listeners with an entirely new perspective of Bob as composer and as one who firmly believed that moving forward rather than mining the past was an essential part of his growth as a creative artist.

Several years after *Looking Glass* was released, Bob invited Oatts, McNeely, and Johnson, as well as tenor saxophonist Joe Lovano and drummer Adam Nussbaum, to be members of what I call the 1983 Sextet, which Bob may have envisioned as an assemblage that would be a step well beyond the repertoire of the previous group. The music of this group was not all "through composed" and, if anything, veered much further into the outer realms of free improvisation, which at times brought to mind modern classical composers like Elliott Carter, John Cage, Ligeti, Berio, and Lutoslawski—not only for their music but also for their desire to break free from the bonds of the works of their predecessors. More specifically, in one of his conversations with Dave Rivello, Bob mentions the influence of both Berio and Ligeti: "they became part of my writing because they freed up my dependence on the classic jazz harmony. They showed me a different way to color things, and the melodic structure was so different than what we were used to in jazz."[2]

And Bob also had high praise for the work of the American composer, Elliott Carter: "I love his piece Triple Duo and think it's one of the most welcoming Carter pieces I've ever heard. He invited you right in. You cannot not respect him and like him; he's a giant figure in American music. He is probably one of our greatest composers in history."[3]

The influence of compositions like Carter's *Triple Duo* was very much present in Bob's experimental music as early as 1983, when he formed his new sextet. While there is no commercially available recording of this group, I had the opportunity to hear some of its music. Several years before his passing, Bob gave me a cassette of the group, which included five tracks, including Brookmeyer compositions "Mountain," "Oslo," and "Suits," as well as two untitled works. It's interesting to note that one of the nameless pieces begins with a very abstract, pointillistic group improvisation that ultimately morphs into an intense postmodern version of the standard "What Is This Thing Called Love." Maybe someday this recording will see the light of day. It is an example of Bob exploring and extending certain elements of jazz's conventions in a very interesting and challenging way. It seems clear to me that he was feeling his way through these small group performances, some of which would eventually find their way in one form or another into his work for large ensembles.

Brookmeyer Small Groups and Challenge Records (1999–2003)

Bob's recorded output for the Netherlands-based Challenge Records is an interesting mix of his small group projects. His first release for the label was a remarkable never-before-released 1979 duo concert with Jim Hall at the North Sea Jazz Festival in the Hague. As one might expect, the performance was nonpareil and fortunately was recorded, although why it took twenty years to be released is a mystery. In any case, Challenge stepped up to the plate and released it in 1999, not surprisingly to very favorable reviews.

The second release, in my opinion, provides yet another important shift in Bob's musical thinking. Bob gave me a copy of *Paris Suite* quite a few years ago in the early 2000s; I'm not sure why, but I never really paid much attention to it; however, after listening to it in its entirety the other day, I can't praise it enough. Here's why:

Unlike the earlier 1983 sextet recording, where the "[dis]connect the dots" free improvisational approach seemed to be at Bob's behest on most tracks, this recording is all about the compositions *and* the solos. Bob wrote four of the pieces; his pianist, the brilliant Kris Goessens, wrote three; and Bob's friend Henning Berg wrote one. The group members' empathy for one another runs deeply through each song, and the quartet sounds as if it had been playing together for years. The bassist Riccardo Del Fra and drummer Dre Pallemaerts play sensitively and intuitively throughout, coloring and shading each song as well as their own solo statements.

It is Kris Goessens, however, whose contributions to this recording are enormous at every level—composing, accompanying, and soloing—who illuminates much of *Paris Suite*. And of course Bob shines like the North Star throughout. A perfect balance between beautiful compositions and inspiring solos from every member.

Other Challenge recordings included *together*, a 1998 duo recording (released in 1999) with bassist Mads Vinding. Three of the nine tracks featured Bob playing piano. Bitten by the piano bug, Bob and Mads were joined by drummer Alex Riel, and together they recorded *Holiday: Bob Brookmeyer Plays Piano*, which was released in 2001. Finally, Bob's last small group album for Challenge was cryptically titled *Stay Out of the Sun* (released 2003), which featured guitarist Larry Koonse, bassist Tom Warrington, and yours truly in the drum booth. A description of that LA session can be found in chapter 2 of this book.

Also released in 2003 was *Island*, an intriguing CD/DVD set from Artist House featuring Bob co-leading with trumpeter/flugelhornist Kenny Wheeler, and including drummer John Hollenbeck, pianist Frank Carlberg, and bassist Jeremy Allen. In contrast to the much more extroverted Brookmeyer-Terry outings, this date is more subdued and like *Paris Suite*, more introspective. As you might imagine, Bob and Kenny and the rhythm section navigate their way through the compositions very well. Admittedly, I found myself listening more to fellow drummer John Hollenbeck, who is always consistently imaginative and supportive, whether it's with a large ensemble or small groups.

Full Circle

I am going to take the liberty of saying that the last small band recording to be included in this chapter is called *Full Circle*, which Bob co-led with his old Kansas City friend, tenor saxophonist Ed Dix. It was completed in February 2003. Actually, *Island* was recorded seven months later, making it the *very* last Brookmeyer small group recording. But why quibble over minutiae? As the old and very trite cliché goes, "Close enough for jazz."

A brief explanation is in order. Bob and Ed grew up together in Kansas City, Missouri. The magnetic pull of KC jazz was part of the glue that cemented their lifelong friendship. Their heroes were many of the fine jazz musicians on the KC scene—famous guys like Count Basie, Jay McShann, Ben Webster, Joe Turner, and many others.

As Ed tells us, "This CD with Bob has been a work in progress for over 55 years. It is in celebration of our long and close friendship that started as teenagers growing up together in Kansas City, a magic place and time for young and aspiring musicians. We co-led big and small bands and cut our teeth in the shadows of so many of those greats who, along with Bob, went on to make jazz history."[4]

And Bob adds, "This CD is a testament to my longest, strongest, and most enduring friendship—that's the one with Ed Dix. He and I have been best friends since 1946 and we were inseparable, musically and personally. He was the bandleader and I was the arranger . . . I am proud of him beyond words. He is living proof of that fact that 'once you got, you don't lose it.' He always had it, the swing, the energy, and the musicality, and he still has it."[5]

Full circle indeed—returning to his starting point over a half century later to reunite with his oldest friend and record some music together. The love and mutual respect these two men had for each other was strong and lasting enough for Bob and Ed to "come home" to KC from New Hampshire and Texas, respectively, to honor their friendship. *Full Circle* is a lasting testament to that friendship.

Chapter 4

For the Record II

"Ding Dong Ding": Selected Brookmeyer Large Ensemble Recordings, 1955–82

One of the major challenges faced by many writers when describing a musical performance—especially one that has been recorded—has been finding the most effective way to portray what is happening in each recorded track, from the first note to the last, without losing the reader along the way. That said, I encourage you to seek out the recordings I introduce and discuss, particularly throughout this chapter, and to read the written descriptions of each, either before or after listening. Really, there's a big difference between reading a description of, say, Brookmeyer's arrangement of "Don't Mean a Thing if It Ain't Got That Swing" and hearing it on Bob's Atlantic album, *Portrait of the Artist*. Try to hear the tracks I've described whenever possible. In my opinion, listening to the music brings the descriptive words to life, and the words serve as road maps for each individual listening experience.

Bob conducting the New Art Orchestra at IAJE (New York City, 2004). Photo by Tak Tokiwa, courtesy of the Bob Brookmeyer Special Collection, Sibley Music Library, Eastman School of Music, University of Rochester, NY.

In the Beginning There Was Brookmeyer, the Arranger

Let's begin by setting the stage for this chapter with an excerpt from part 1 of an excellent five-part interview that *JazzWax* blogger Marc Myers conducted with Bob over a five-day period in June 2009.

> JW: How old were you when you started earning money as a musician?
> BB: I was 14. That's when I became a commercial arranger and copyist.
> JW: How did you pick it up so fast?
> BB: I was already playing with dance bands, and I sort of knew how harmony went. So at age 14, I was writing for a professional dance band. The first chart I brought in was "Do You Ever Think of Me?" and it worked out OK. From that point on I had a contact in Omaha who would order the arrangements.
> JW: How busy were you?

BB: I'd write a chart a week, copy it and send it off and get paid $15 bucks. I don't know how I pulled that off. I was arranging for three tenors, three trumpets and a rhythm section. The band was too poor for a violin [laughs], which was popular then. That was my steady gig for a while. Eventually the volume they needed got so large that it required someone else to copy the parts from my charts.[1]

So there you have it: Bob Brookmeyer, 14-year-old arranger for hire, beginning in 1943. Almost ten years later, as a member of Stan Getz's quintet, Bob would write many of the arrangements for much of the quintet's repertoire. And shortly thereafter he began writing quartet arrangements during the times he was a member of Gerry Mulligan's foursome and his Concert Jazz Band. Bob also wrote original compositions and arrangements for his own three big band recordings. Finally, in the mid-'60s Bob wrote many of the arrangements and some of the originals for the popular quintet he co-led with trumpeter Clark Terry.

Bob's Day Gig, Circa Late 1950s

Sometime toward the end of the decade, Bob could be found "ghost writing" arrangements for a variety of recording projects. If you don't know what "ghosting" is, Bob explains it briefly (and concisely) in part 3 of his *JazzWax* interview with Marc Myers: "When you're hired to ghost for someone, you want to write in their style. No one is supposed to hear that the arranger was anyone but the person who's credited."[2]

Bob ghosted for top-shelf arrangers like Ralph Burns and Bill Finnegan, the latter being one of Bob's biggest influences. Among the most memorable Brookmeyer ghosting gigs were the two Ray Charles sessions *The Genius of Ray Charles* and *The Genius Hits the Road*. I remember hearing Ray Charles's recording of "Come Rain or Come Shine" from the former album on the radio one day sometime in the '60s, and it began with a soulful four-bar intro by Bob with strings in the background, after which Ray began singing the melody. Well, of course

I had to go out to our local record shop in Miami and buy the album as soon as possible, because the mere idea of Brookmeyer playing with Ray Charles was huge, especially since I loved most things that Ray Charles did. Bob plays brief obbligatos behind Ray throughout the track that beautifully complement the feeling portrayed in Ray's vocal, although you have to listen carefully for them because they're a little far back in the mix. Moments of pure beauty on both their parts. I only wish that Bob had been given more room to play on several of the other tracks.

The Genius Hits the Road found Al Cohn and Bob ghosting for Ralph Burns, who arranged only one song on the album while Al and Bob wrote all of the other arrangements. Looking back, it seems odd to me that Burns was credited for arranging the entire album when in fact he arranged only a single track, while Bob arranged seven others and Al arranged the rest, including "Georgia on My Mind," which became one of Ray's signature pieces and one of the most popular renditions of that song—maybe even *the* interpretation that stands alone among all the other versions of it.

At the mercy of some really corny and dated songs like "Alabamy Bound" and "Mississippi Mud," Bob's arrangements were appropriately suitable for the gig and for Ray's vocals, which at times seemed a little bit tentative, probably due to the nature of the material. However, Ray Charles could elevate most anything he sang, and Bob's arrangements offered ample support, even when some of the songs he had to deal with were no match for Ray's gifts as a musical storyteller.

The process of ghosting in the music industry may have always been a business-as-usual phenomenon and may still be a flourishing endeavor today whenever musical arrangements are necessary, and a first-call arranger needs help meeting a deadline. In any case, ghosting was a gig and put food on the table.

1953–64: Mulligan Stew

Due to the unique and long-standing relationship that existed between Bob and baritone saxophonist Gerry Mulligan, I'm offering a brief introduction to the birth of the legendary Gerry Mulligan

Concert Jazz Band and Bob's importance to the development of the band's organization, repertoire, and, to a great extent, its longevity. However, first things first:

Bob's musical and personal relationship with Mulligan began a short while after trumpeter Chet Baker left the original Mulligan Quartet sometime in 1953. Bob had begun his career earlier that year as a member of Stan Getz's quintet. When Getz brought the quintet to play at several venues in Los Angeles, including the Tiffany Club, Mulligan's quartet was playing nearby at the Haig, and Bob and other members of the quintet often spent their intermissions at that club, listening to Gerry, Chet, and Mulligan's piano-less quartet. Their repeated late returns for the next set at the Tiffany cost them the gig. The owner of the Tiffany fired the Getz group, and Bob returned to his hometown. One of the eventual plans, which unfortunately fizzled out, was the idea of a sextet with Stan, Gerry, Bob, and Chet, plus bass and drums. However, Gerry wanted to be the leader and so did Stan; hence the group never materialized. It was around Christmas in 1953 that Gerry asked Bob to take Chet's place, because Chet wanted to pursue a solo career.[3]

The change from trumpet to valve trombone created a new sound for the group, largely because the combination of trombone and baritone saxophone—especially the way both men complemented each other musically and when they soloed simultaneously—gave the group a buttery warmth that many listeners found attractive at that time. While Bob was integral to the group's success as both a player and composer/arranger, he was never invited to be a co-leader, which I think was a shame.

Bob ping-ponged in and out of the quartet and Gerry's sextet for several years. In 1957 Bob stayed with Mulligan only briefly this time, leaving after a few months at the end of that year. This time the hiatus from Mulligan was longer—over two years. During his leave of absence, Bob established himself as a New York studio musician and also became the third voice in the iconoclastic Jimmy Giuffre 3 with Giuffre and guitarist Jim Hall, both of whom played on Bob's 1957 recording, *Traditionalism Revisited* (World Pacific).

In addition to *Traditionalism Revisited* the previous year, Bob did quite a bit of recording as a leader from 1958 through 1960—six albums to be exact: *The Street Swingers* (World Pacific, 1958), *Kansas City Revisited* (United Artists, 1958), *The Two-Piano Ivory Hunters*, co-led with Bill Evans (United Artists, 1959), *Jazz Is a Kick* (Mercury, 1960), *Portrait of the Artist* (Atlantic, 1960), and *The Blues Hot and Cold* (Verve, 1960).

Bob's more lasting reunion with Mulligan came about due to his early involvement with Mulligan's newly formed Concert Jazz Band. Bob describes that reunion as follows: "Gerry came by early that year [1960] and had a week at Basin Street East and wanted to know if I'd write an arrangement for him. We hadn't played together for a couple of years, and I think that he was depressed that I quit—I quit in '57. So we got to be a little tighter, and the one week at Basin Street turned into a band. I saw the opportunity to be part of a band that I'd wanted since I'd been a kid."[4]

In January 1960 everything changed with the birth of Mulligan's Concert Jazz Band. Gerry asked Bob if he'd write more arrangements for the band's weeklong stint at Basin Street East in New York City. Bob did so, and after the selection of personnel and a few rehearsals, the Concert Jazz Band made its debut. Bob became the chief arranger and contributed a whopping twenty-one arrangements to the band's repertoire. While not exactly a small band, nor a "big band" (by traditional definition) the CJB consisted of three trumpets, three trombones, four saxes, and bass and drums, plus the leader on baritone saxophone—a dozen plus one. The scaled-down size of the CJB, as well as a number of the compositions and arrangements by Gerry and Bob, tended to capture the intimacy of the Mulligan quartet, both in solos and contrapuntal duets (most notably with Bob) within the larger band framework. Note that the rhythm section consisted of only bass (Bill Crow or Buddy Clark) and drums (Mel Lewis), maintaining the piano-less airiness of both the quartet and Gerry's sextet. Mulligan's biographer, Jerome Klinkowitz, likens this type of compositional approach to the concerto grosso technique of scoring, "indicating a style in which a small group is framed by the larger orchestra with the listener's attention being passed back and forth."[5]

So what does describing the early days of Bob's introduction to and participation in Mulligan's small bands have to do with the importance of Bob's presence in Gerry's Concert Jazz Band? For me the answer is as simple as it is somewhat paradoxical. The attempt to capture the intimacy of Mulligan's small groups within the context of a "twelve-tet" has the CJB straddling the fence. Either way, the music is timeless and was successful in its efforts to defy convention without distracting from the small-band-within-a-larger-band framework.

About two of Bob's CJB arrangements:

Several compilations from a number of the band's recordings are available as part of Verve's Jazz Masters series. Among the numerous songs arranged by Bob, there are two in my opinion that really stand out. Each displays a different resonance inherent in Bob's writing. His arrangement of legendary guitarist Django Reinhardt's "Manoir Des Mes Rêves" (also known as "Django's Castle") is the first. When you listen to it initially, you may notice that the brass and the woodwinds softly play warm, burnished long tones that just seem to float in the air, creating a hymnlike soundscape that brings a rather ethereal quality to Reinhardt's original melody, which the guitarist recorded in 1943 with two clarinets and a second guitarist, among others. Unlike that original recording, Bob's version is slower, and the rhythmic "chunk-chunk" provided by the second guitarist in the original was eliminated, which suggests that the Brookmeyer arrangement may have been conducted—perhaps by Bob—or that bassist Buddy Clark anchored the tempo by playing "walking" bass very softly through most of the piece. While I don't doubt that Mel Lewis might have been playing brushes very softly, it's really hard to tell, since he is mostly inaudible.

The other Brookmeyer arrangement, "You Took Advantage of Me," is anything but "hymnlike." It swings joyously from the first note to the last, opening with Mulligan playing the first eight bars alone and the band joining in on the ninth bar and completing the first section.

Bob's solo begins on the bridge, and I don't think it's an exaggeration to say that from there on out, he *owns* the tune! His solo is lusty and swings hard all the way. Saxophonist/author Bill Kirchner notes, in his perceptive essay that accompanies Mosaic's Gerry Mulligan box set, tell the story: "There's plenty of charm and vitality here, and Brookmeyer's solo in particular is one of his best with the CJB; check out the bluesy minor third he 'lays' on in the second eight bars of it and the vocalizations he uses. Marvelous!"[6]

The arrangement is joyous without being ponderous and was one of Bob's best. Great solo, great chart.

Besides being a great orchestrator/arranger and a phenomenal soloist, Bob was as important to the success of this band as its leader was. He was, in his own words, the "Straw Boss" (i.e., he had the authority to hire and fire musicians who were incompatible with the creative vision that he and Gerry had for the band). If anything, he should have been the co-leader, given his leadership abilities and the substantive contributions he had already made from the start. As he said to writer Gordon Jack, "I wanted that band to succeed, because I felt it was partly my band."[7]

The Concert Jazz Band lasted until December 1964. It played its final gig at Birdland, which, ironically, was closing its doors at the end of the CJB's run. While there have been various opinions as to the cause of the band's demise, I don't believe that any of those matter. What does matter is that it was and still is a vital part of jazz history . . . and Bob was an integral key to its success.

Intermezzo 1: A Little Primer About Big Jazz Bands

First of all, there have been many famous big bands throughout jazz history: Fletcher Henderson, Jimmy Lunceford, Duke Ellington, Count Basie, Benny Goodman, Artie Shaw, Chick Webb, Woody Herman, Stan Kenton, and many others. In Bob Brookmeyer's formative years in Kansas City, one of the most influential of these was Count Basie's band. Another was the expansive music of the Duke

Ellington Orchestra. While all of the big bands mentioned above were excellent and quite popular in their day, I think it was both Basie and Ellington that had the biggest impact on Bob. Basie's band personified swing through and through, and Duke's imaginative and evocative compositions took large ensemble music to another place—one filled with different sonorities and colors, in addition to swinging, danceable grooves. Both bands were also blessed with legendary soloists.

Modern-day big jazz bands are borne into existence for a variety of reasons. Some, which are often called rehearsal bands, may exist mostly for the benefit of composers and/or arrangers who bring their music to a rehearsal—usually in order to hear the fruits of their labor and to make modifications to their work if necessary. Others are often called kicks bands, whose main purpose might be to get together at a certain time of the week and play all manner of big band "charts" in order to just sharpen their music reading and improvisational skills. In these settings, participating musicians frequently come and go, and the personnel may change regularly.

In specific cases, big jazz bands in the mid-twentieth century were formed because a singular figure (e.g., Woody Herman, 1944, and Gerry Mulligan, 1960) or several musicians (Toshiko Akiyoshi–Lew Tabackin Big Band, 1973, and Thad Jones & Mel Lewis Jazz Orchestra, 1965) wanted to create working units that would not only utilize the talents of various writers but also feature excellent soloists in the modern jazz idiom, both those who were well-known and those who deserved wider recognition from the jazz community; the goals of these types of groups (especially from the '40s to the present) would be to perform in clubs and concert venues at home and abroad and to record their music and release it to wider audiences across the country and around the world, via all available media.

While Bob Brookmeyer's first three big band albums featured many excellent players and great compositions and arrangements, his musicians were hired each time to make a record and were probably not thinking about staying together to promote it, or about making a commitment to being part of a working band. Perhaps it just didn't seem feasible economically, and the demands of making a living and supporting oneself or a family were too great to risk compromising whatever stability existed for many musicians at that time. However, Gerry Mulligan and Thad and Mel envisioned the creation and development of their own big bands, and due to their tenacity and commitment, they were successful in creating two of the greatest big bands in the history of modern jazz. And Brookmeyer was instrumental in each one's success.

1956, 1958, 1961: A Brookmeyer Triptych

So far we've looked briefly at Bob's involvement with Gerry Mulligan's Concert Jazz Band as soloist and arranger (1960–64). He also appeared as a soloist on a number of other big band recordings, including those by Manny Albam (*The Jazz Greats of Our Time*, 1957), Chubby Jackson (*Chubby Takes Over*, 1958*),* George Russell (*New York, New York*, 1959), Bill Potts (*The Jazz Soul of Porgy and Bess*, 1959), and Cannonball Adderly (*African Waltz*, 1961).

This seems to be a good time to look at the three big band sessions that Bob recorded under his own name. It's really interesting to follow the progression from album to album as a listener and to try to note the stylistic and structural changes extant between each. Now if I were a Brookmeyer scholar and was offering a hypothesis or two, I'd be able to dig into some of the pedagogical stuff regarding composition and arranging; but I'm not, so I humbly defer to my colleagues who are much better suited to cross that terrain than I.

1956–57: A Maiden Voyage

Bob's first solo outing as a composer and arranger for a big band, *Brookmeyer*, was recorded in 1956 and released the following year on the VIK label, a subsidiary of RCA Victor Records. Unfortunately, due to the fact that the company's choices of artists in its stable were pretty obscure and often completely unrelated to jazz, VIK closed its doors in late 1958. In scrolling through their catalog, I think I'd heard of fewer than 10 percent of their artists, from any genre, let alone jazz. I never had the chance to speak with Bob about the sad fact that *Brookmeyer* wound up being relegated to obscurity a mere year after it was released. Fortunately, a company called Collectable Records was able to rerelease the complete recording in 1999.

The music is excellently performed, and the choice of material is quite diverse. Bob wrote and arranged five of the tunes ("Oh, Jane Snavely," "Open Country," "Gone Latin," "Confusion Blues," and "Big City Life") and arranged the old standard ("Just You, Just Me"). Saxophonist Al Cohn arranged the remaining three.

There are several things that make *Brookmeyer* unique. First, there are three different instrumental combinations, rather than one big band playing on all tracks: The first configuration consists of four trumpets, one valve trombone, four saxes, and three rhythm (piano, bass, drums) and can be heard on "Oh, Jane Snavely," "Open Country," and "Just You, Just Me." The second grouping is an octet, which includes three saxes, one trumpet, one valve trombone, and three rhythm, playing "Confusion Blues," "Gone Latin," and "Zing Went the Strings of my Heart," which was arranged by Al Cohn. The final grouping is the most unusual in terms of its instrumentation, which consists of Bob playing valve trombone and piano (on "Nature Boy"; piano only on "Big City Life" and valve trombone only on "I'm Old Fashioned"), and two trumpets, French horn, tuba, and two reeds, doubling clarinet and English horn, respectively. Al Cohn arranged "Nature Boy" and "I'm Old Fashioned."

Another thing that makes this recording unique is that each of the three groups are a bit unorthodox in contrast to the standard big band instrumentation that existed at that time—generally four trumpets, three trombones, five saxes, and piano, bass, and drums (with the addition of perhaps rhythm guitar a la Freddie Green).

Altering the number of players in the woodwind or brass sections could often change the sound of the band. After not really listening to this album for many years, I realized that one of the things this time around that held my interest was the color changes that existed between each of the three groups. Al and Bob's arrangements reflected those differences, in some cases very subtly. For example, when one track features four trumpet players and another has only one or two, a skilled arranger may write for the latter in a manner different than they would for the full section. And if we close our eyes and place ourselves *in the music* without intellectualizing about why it sounds different than the other tracks on the recording, and see how the difference makes us *feel*, then we're on the way to immersing ourselves in a total musical experience.

Intermezzo 2: Deep Listening, a Theory

I'm of the opinion that when we really listen to any music, we move through three levels of experience: I call it Ears > Mind > Heart. The first level is physiological (i.e., we merely hear some music). The second level may be where we use our cognitive ability to tell us exactly what we're hearing (e.g., "That's pianist Bill Evans and his trio playing a ballad called 'Spring Is Here'"). We may or may not get to the third level, depending upon whether or not we can relate what we're hearing to some personal experience we may have had that had a subtle or even a profound effect upon us at some point in our lives. So if I'm driving down the street after a gig at 2:00 a.m. and I hear the Bill Evans Trio playing "Spring Is Here," I may recall some singular instant that occurred in my past that brought great sadness (level two). That's where level three comes in. We often land there, replete with some feeling that takes us back to a certain time and place—or perhaps instead, doesn't remind us of anything, but enters our being for no particular reason other than to resonate in some way that draws us closer to our inner selves. Music has that capability, if only we open ourselves up to it.

If Bob were here, he would have you think about how to experience his music. You might be, in Bob's words, hearing the music but not really listening to it. He has said numerous times that hearing music is a passive act, but that truly listening to it entails something deeper and more personal. It's about emptying all the mental clutter and approaching the act of listening completely and without an agenda. It's what happens when you lose yourself by tossing your daily monkey-mind baggage out the window and quieting your mind in order to let the music in. As an author I have used the word "experiencing" in place of "listening" because for me listening is the first crucial step—the gateway—to experiencing a musical offering fully. It simply takes us away and plops us down into uncharted territory.

Take for example the ballad, "Big City Life," the seventh track on *Brookmeyer*. It begins with Bob introducing the theme on piano, joined first by English horn, then by the ensemble, which provides a lovely cushion of sound throughout Bob's improvisation. For me this track really rings some bells. It's New York City at 4:00 a.m. and it takes me to a lonely place that I've never been to before, for no particular reason. And I think about that, even though I am not, by nature, a lonely person. "Big City Life" puts me in touch with a feeling that brings me back to myself—which is what experiencing music is all about. Straight to the heart.

Other tunes on *Brookmeyer* are more conventional and swing as one might expect from the likes of Bob and Al Cohn, who certainly tip their hats to Count Basie and Duke Ellington. And yet there are tracks like "Big City Life" and one other piece that really sets this album apart from many of the other big band albums coming out of the mid-'50s. It's the beautifully impressionistic Al Cohn arrangement of the popular Eden Ahbez song "Nature Boy," which was popularized by Nat "King" Cole in the late '40s. Here, the piece begins in slow waltz time with the winds playing long, almost reverential tones for eight measures, followed by a four-bar setup, then the French horn begins stating the melody, which is continued softly by the winds, until Bob enters in the second half on trombone, followed by the low brass, completing the first part of the song. Bob then enters playing a very meditative piano improvisation, after which there are solo turns, presumably by trumpeter Nick Travis and a rare appearance by Al Cohn on clarinet. Bob returns on trombone one last time, supported by the winds, who return once again to the introduction of the piece, and this time with a final chord supplemented by a lovely trombone coda by Brookmeyer.

1959–60: Homage to the Blues

"Big City Life" and "Nature Boy" give us an idea of where Bob was going in his quest to present big band jazz in a somewhat unconventional setting, one which he would continue to explore in his next solo recording, *Portrait of the Artist*, which consists of eight tracks: an original multipart suite, three standards, and a Brookmeyer original.

According to Nat Hentoff's liner notes, the album was recorded in 1959 and released in 1960 by Atlantic Records.[8] Hentoff informs us that "Blues Suite" was Bob's first extended composition for big band. The key word here is "extended," in that the "Blues Suite" is divided into four distinct movements, totaling almost twenty-one-and-a-half minutes, whereas "Big City Life" from the VIK recording was a standalone composition that clocked in at just over four minutes.

I'm not going to devise a critical analysis of each movement, because I fear that we—you and I—would get lost in a jumble of intimidating techno-speak. I will say that "Blues Suite" needs to be heard to be appreciated, not just because it's Bob's initial effort to compose a multipart composition but also because the music is, by turns, atmospheric and swinging and deserves to be heard on a one-to-one level.

I therefore encourage you to cast whatever preconceptions you may have aside and *experience* the music. As Bob says in his liner notes to *Kansas City Revisited*, "You just grab a nice glass of Dewar's Finest, one big old and easy chair, turn the volume up and listen."

Here, however, are a few notes and impressions:

"Introduction and First Movement" begins with a variety of introductory statements from both the band and Bob, who is heard exclusively on piano throughout all four movements. This first movement feels very much like a bow and tip of the hat to the Kansas City of the

'20s and '30s; the mood is slow and bluesy for a while, then makes several tempo changes before settling back into the original theme. The entire feeling is relaxed and, for me at least, somewhat wistful. This movement—and, for that matter, each of the others—paints an affectionate and at times subtly humorous portrait of a bygone era.

The second movement is quite brief and begins with a medium tempo, repetitive tick-tock pattern played in fourths in the lower register of the piano. Once again there are numerous tempo changes and what seem to be mini chordal interludes (sort of like little oases in the middle of a metronomic desert) before the original tick-tock pattern resumes. Hentoff writes that this structure feels somewhat ominous, and I couldn't agree with him more.

I can hear echoes of Count Basie and Duke Ellington in the third movement. In the liner notes, Bob calls this section his "Jump tune" because it practically swings right "from the get-go."[9] The brass and woodwind sections support Al Cohn's tenor solo with riffs that leap out of the Basie vocabulary, and Bob's solo feels very Duke-ish and more than a little playful.

The final movement of "Blues Suite" sounds and feels very much like the first, very reverential, very . . . after-hours Kansas City. However, it incorporates themes and tempo changes from the previous movements before bringing us back home, just before the sun comes up.

The other tracks are nothing short of amazing in their originality and respective energies. "It Don't Mean a Thing (If It Ain't Got That Swing)" bubbles over with great solos (particularly from Bob on valve trombone) and ensemble passages that, even today, are incredibly exciting.

In the previous chapter and elsewhere, I've alluded to Bob's oblique sense of humor. It's in full bloom here on "It Don't Mean a Thing (If It Ain't Got That Swing)." Bob's arrangement of the Ellington-Mills favorite begins like this: Four short military-style drumbeats followed by a very dissonant chord from the horns, which in turn, is answered by one raspy, greasy note from Bob; then another ominous chord from the horns, followed again by more short commentary from Bob.

That conversation between Bob and the band happens a number of times more and seems to become less intense each time it's repeated. Once that pas de deux ends, the band comes in with a brief series of chords, at which time there is a brief silence, after which Bob plays four descending quarter notes that lead directly into the melody of the song. Bob weaves in and out of the band as it plays his arrangement and then takes the first solo, which offers a fine example of the improvisational style that Bob had developed during that period: it was puckish, playful, and completely organic—all without compromising the lyricism he was known for.

After several other fine solos by trumpeters Nick Travis and Ernie Royal, and altoist Gene Quill, the band picks up steam and brings it back home, at which time Bob (now on piano) brings the ship to a soft landing and the song ends.

Compared to the VIK recording, *Portrait of the Artist* feels more centered. While he arranged five of the nine songs on *Brookmeyer*, he was the sole arranger on *Portrait*. His arrangements of the three standards breathed new and exciting life into each one. To my way of thinking, Bob's stamp on this album was significantly greater than his first release, perhaps due to the fact that he'd matured as both a writer and as an instrumentalist.

1961: The Diamond in the Tiara

When I was in my late teens and on the way to becoming a real jazz head, I remember catching the Eighth Street bus to go downtown with my friend Steve and roam around in and out of the department stores, five-and-dime stores, and specialty shops. While navigating our way through Burdine's, the biggest department store in all of downtown Miami, I found a small area that sold records. I was already a Brookmeyer fan (albeit a recent devotee). There wasn't much there except for a couple of bins and a vertical display of newly released records. I think it was a Verve Records display. That was where I found the latest Bob Brookmeyer record. It was a handsome twofold album with a beautiful oil painting by Olga Albizu

Gloomy Sunday and Other Bright Moments (Verve Records, 1961). "The Diamond in the Tiara." Bob called this recording his pride and joy.

set against a black background. The album title, *Gloomy Sunday and Other Bright Moments*, was one that went right over my head, because I had yet to know anything about Bob or his reputation as a darkly funny guy, or about the origin of the song and what it represented. All I knew was that it was a new record by Brookmeyer. Truth be known, I owned only a few of Bob's records, and those were mostly small group recordings with other leaders, and of course I had the record that started it all: *Gerry Mulligan and the Concert Jazz Band at the Village Vanguard.* At that point I didn't know about Bob's two previous big band albums on VIK and Atlantic, so this big band thing of his was a total surprise.

Later that day I plopped the new record on my stereo and sat down for a first listen. When the needle met the groove, what I heard knocked me back a few feet! It was the opening fanfare at the beginning of "Caravan." From that moment on, I knew somehow that this was a recording that would expand my perception of big band jazz well beyond Count Basie, Duke Ellington, Benny Goodman, and Artie Shaw. Okay, I now humbly admit to everyone who reads this book, I am extremely biased about this particular album. Not because it reminds me of any one person or thing in particular. My bias comes from listening to the music itself and the sheer commitment of the musicians to make the best music possible. Their effort is so evident throughout, and Brookmeyer himself gives 110 percent each time he solos. If he were still with us, Bob might've said that this was not *his* record; he would say that *Gloomy Sunday* was *their* record. What an orchestra!

And because of the collective effort by all hands, *Gloomy Sunday* still sounds fresh and new. Every track resonates deeply, and I always manage to hear something new every time I listen. It is indeed an absolute gem. I remember telling Bob years later how much I loved the album and that it continues to be my favorite big band recording. He smiled and said something like "Mine too." More specifically, in Marc Myer's Brookmeyer interview for *JazzWax*, when asked about *Gloomy Sunday*, Bob opined, "I consider it my pride and joy. I took many creative risks here, most based on the heels of working with Bill [Finnegan]. I used woodwinds, double reeds, and other configurations I hadn't used before. My attitude toward the orchestration was really a big step forward in my development."[10]

Gloomy Sunday and Other Bright Moments was a tremendous undertaking for everyone involved. First of all, the sound of the orchestra is clear and vibrant, thanks to the combination of a great recording engineer and the location of the sessions, which was, in all probability, Webster Hall in New York City. Secondly, the arrangements by top-shelf people like Ralph Burns ("Caravan"), Eddie Sauter ("Gloomy Sunday"), Al Cohn ("Some of My Best Friends"), and Gary McFarland ("Why Are You Blue?") are incomparable. Each was commissioned to write one arrangement (although Cohn and McFarland composed and arranged their songs). Of the remaining four songs, two were composed and arranged by Bob ("Ho Hum" and "Days Gone By, Oh My!"), and the other two ("Detour Ahead" and "Where, Oh Where") were his arrangements—all exquisite as well.

Just as there are elements of uniqueness to *Brookmeyer* and *Portrait of the Artist* that set those two albums apart from the more traditional repertoires of many other big bands that existed during those years, there is another element that illustrates Bob's growing mastery as both arranger and composer of a new kind of big band music, and that was his desire to further expand his use of tonal colors to create a new kind of aural landscape. To do so for *Gloomy Sunday and Other Bright Moments*, Bob utilized instruments not often heard in big jazz bands in 1961. If you listen closely to the recording, you'll hear timpani (or low tom-toms), chimes, xylophone, flute, piccolo, bass clarinet, oboe, English horn, bassoon, flugelhorn, and miscellaneous percussions. Their presence greatly expands the palette of colors one can hear throughout the recording, notably in the Burns, Sauter, and especially Brookmeyer arrangements. Couple these with the other tracks and the powerful virtuosity of all of the soloists, and you'll be rewarded time and again with a beautifully realized listening experience. In short, *Gloomy Sunday* is timeless. My hope is that, upon experiencing it, you will enjoy its many riches. To paraphrase Nietzsche, "Without music, life would be a mistake."

Here are some descriptions of four of the tracks:

"Detour Ahead": I remember hearing this lovely ballad a long time ago on a Bill Evans trio record (*Waltz for Debby*) and after that years later on a remarkable performance by Billie Holiday, originally recorded in 1951. Both recordings do the song justice. Brookmeyer's pensive arrangement of it here on *Gloomy Sunday* is a worthy addition to those memorable recordings. This is a song that suggests that while the road to love may be smooth at the outset, it can become bumpy down the way, and perhaps disastrous, especially if you don't see the bumps coming. In a way, the song is a warning to turn back and retreat to safety before she or he breaks your heart. Both Lady Day and Bill Evans capture the poignancy of those lyrics in their respective interpretations, especially Lady, who always sang every song as though she were living the lyrics—often subtle, but always convincing.

When you listen to Brookmeyer's orchestral version, it speaks with the same degree of feeling yet maintains its own kind of subtlety. Let me take you through what I hear when I listen. Keep in mind that my interpretations are just that—and nothing more. I'm more of a tour guide than a critic.

"Detour Ahead" begins with the bassoon playing a slow and repetitive three-note figure, which is soon joined by the winds, also playing the same solemn three-note figure, over and over. I'll stop here for a minute to admit that, to me, this trudges along, sort of like when we are tired and there seems to be little energy in our gait (this almost feels intentional on Bob's part). We're going somewhere, but the farther along we go, the more energy we expend, and perhaps we become disheartened. Then the flute enters and plays the first part of the melody, soon to be joined by the valve trombone. All the while the three-note dirge continues quietly in the background under Bob's solo, until the orchestra takes up the melody of the bridge of the song. The sonic textures here are lovely and reminiscent of an andante movement of a piece by Brahms that a chamber music ensemble might play. Once again, Bob is front and center and weaves in and out of the orchestra until they begin a crescendo to introduce the last section of the arrangement, which returns us to the beginning, when the bassoon reprises the lonely three-note figure and Bob re-enters, playing what becomes a last plaintive note. After that note, just close your eyes, sit quietly for a few moments, and give "Detour Ahead" the chance to sink in.

We move now from detours to waltz time. It's no secret that Cole Porter was incredibly prolific and that he composed dozens of hits, such as "Begin the Beguine," "Night and Day," "I Get a Kick Out of You," and "Anything Goes." Many of these more well-known songs have lent themselves nicely to jazz musicians' repertoires over the decades; however, considering the sheer volume of Porter's work, it's always nice to discover one of his songs that you've never heard before. "Where, Oh Where?" is such a song. If you've ever seen the movie *Lili*, starring Leslie Caron and Mel Ferrer, you would probably remember the song "Hi-Lili, Hi-lo" in which Ms. Caron sings a duet with a marionette. That song was written by Bronislaw Kaper, who also wrote "Green Dolphin Street" and "Invitation," two songs that have been jazz standards for many years.

The reason I mention "Hi-Lili, Hi-lo" is that it is an infectiously happy waltz, and although you may find that this next observation is a real stretch, if you place "Where, Oh Where?" alongside "Lili," it has the same kind of saccharine-free sweetness that pervades Kaper's tune, only in a much more colorful way.

After a gentle eight-bar introduction in waltz time, which ritards into a held note, Bob sets the tempo into the melody, which he plays with orchestral background, until the tempo slows once more, this time led by the English horn and the bassoon, which decelerates and holds the last note briefly until the waltz tempo is introduced once again, this time by the vibraphonist as the leading voice, playing another eight-bar intro with the brass and the rhythm section into Bob's restatement of the first part of the melody; from that point on, there is significant interaction between Bob and the orchestra until we hear the chimes, which introduce a longer and exceptionally lyrical valve trombone solo, one that would be easy to sing. Bob's trombone voice has never been more singsong-like than it is on this tune. After more interplay with the brass and woodwinds, the brass section plays a variation based on the chord changes from the bridge, followed by a musical conversation between trombone and the orchestra, which leads into a reprise of the woodwind introduction from the beginning of the song, which ends quietly.

"And now for something completely different" is a trite and hyperbolic phrase that has been overused since tent shows and vaudeville. However, it is a completely accurate term to introduce this next track. "Some of My Best Friends" was penned and arranged by Al Cohn and is a joyous romp that allows the orchestra to stretch out and turn the heat up; indeed, it is a fiery performance from the beginning to the fade-out ending.

It begins with a brief, raucous two-trumpet duel above low brass figures and resolves just before Bob enters with three notes into the melody, supported by the brass and woodwind sections. The two trumpets return to play the bridge, after which Bob surfaces briefly. Then it's solo time. Trumpeter Joe Newman takes the reins and pulls out all the stops with an explosive turn, followed by flugelhornist Clark Terry, whose solo is a bit cooler, though no less intense. Bob jumps in with a wonderfully melodic solo that ends with a raspy wail, punctuated by eight nearly identical notes ("wap-bap! bap-bap! bap-bap! bap-bap!") sounding very much like something a drummer might play to drive the rhythm forward. No surprise there.

Speaking of drummers—and rhythm sections—special mention should be made of drummer Mel Lewis, who is one of a pantheon of the greatest big band (and small band) drummers of all time. The bassist George Duvivier was a versatile conservatory-trained musician and a much in-demand bassist on the New York scene. Pianist Hank Jones, along with brothers Thad (trumpet) and Elvin (drums), was part of one of the most famous of jazz families in the history of the music. Collectively, Lewis, Duvivier, and Jones drove the bus on each track of *Gloomy Sunday*.

Of all of the tracks on *Gloomy Sunday and Other Bright Moments*, "Gloomy Sunday" stands out as the one that is closest to being a classical composition, largely because it is almost entirely through composed. The song itself was written and first published in 1933 by two Hungarian musicians and was also called "The Hungarian Suicide Song." Urban myths claimed that many people both here in America and in Europe committed suicide after hearing it. Like many such legends, that claim has never been supported by fact.

When you listen to Eddie Sauter's arrangement of the song, you'll notice that even though Bob and alto saxophonist Phil Woods play short solos with the ensemble supporting them, it's the entire orchestra that breathes as one entity throughout. The level of interpretation and execution here is very impressive. While "Gloomy Sunday" is considered a sad song—and begins that way here—this version takes it to a place that is energetic and almost boisterous before it returns to the rather ominous quality we heard at the beginning.

These kinds of descriptions may seem useless unless you use them as a road map before listening to each of the selected tracks. For example, read the description of "Where, Oh Where!" then play the track; finally, reread the description, then distance yourself before listening again. I've used that approach with my students and found it to be successful. They seem to enjoy the music more once they've eliminated all distractions and cozied up to it.

If you think that, once again, I'm trying to convince you to actually listen to *Gloomy Sunday and Other Bright Moments*, you'd be absolutely correct. The attempt here is to illustrate, by example, the brilliance of this recording—the compositions, the arrangements, the soloists—and the mind that brought all of these songs and musicians together. If Bob were still around, he might express his hope that you would find a comfortable space, slip on some headphones, and sit back and spend some quality time getting into this exciting music

Until recently Verve offered *Gloomy Sunday and Other Bright Moments* on Amazon as part of a twofer, coupled with Gary McFarland's *How to Succeed in Business Without Really Trying*, featuring almost the same ensemble, recorded just days after *Gloomy Sunday*. Fortunately, at this writing, there is an MP3 of the recording available on Amazon.com. There are also digital versions of this recording available at Amazon.co.uk (United Kingdom) and Amazon.co.jp (Japan), provided that you create an account at either country's Amazon site. If you are looking for a vinyl copy, check Amazon.com, eBay, Apple Music, and online or brick and mortar record stores like New York City's venerable Jazz Record Center. My hope is that the entire album will appear eventually on YouTube.

1965–67: The Thad Jones/Mel Lewis Jazz Orchestra

When cornetist/flugelhornist Thad Jones and drummer Mel Lewis were beginning to put together their new big band, Bob was one of the first to be invited to join, along with three other in-demand players: lead trumpeter Snooky Young, bass virtuoso Richard Davis, and legendary baritone saxophonist Pepper Adams. While a charter member of the band, and one of its notable soloists, Bob contributed what has long been considered a number of masterworks: His arrangements of Fats Waller's "Willow Tree," W. C. Handy's immortal "St. Louis Blues," and, particularly, Bob's incredibly beautiful rendering of Ann Ronell's "Willow Weep for Me." Among his original compositions, "ABC Blues" is still considered an all-time classic of modern big band literature.

Actually, Bob arranged "Willow Weep for Me" originally for the Mulligan Concert Jazz Band, but Gerry didn't like the arrangement so it was shelved. However, in Marc Myers's *JazzWax* interview, Bob remembers that Gerry "came down to the Vanguard and heard Thad's band play it. He said 'Wow, that's a nice arrangement.' I told him it was the same one he rejected."[11]

Bob's time with Thad and Mel afforded another opportunity to move forward and continue to seek new sonic avenues. As Chris Smith has pointed out so accurately in his book *The View from the Back of the Band*, "It cannot be stressed enough how important Brookmeyer's compositions were to the evolving style of the Thad Jones/Mel Lewis Orchestra. His concepts of harmony, form, and texture both contrasted and complemented Thad's compositional style."[12]

The first inkling I had as a listener about the beginnings of another Brookmeyer transition was hearing Bob's first contributions to the Jones-Lewis big band on their initial 1966 recording for Solid State Records, *Presenting Thad Jones/Mel Lewis & The Jazz Orchestra*. The band was overflowing with top-shelf musicians, including those identified above, as well as saxophonists Jerome Richardson, Joe Farrell, and Eddie Daniels; trombonist Tom Macintosh; trumpeter Bill Berry; and, once again, pianist Hank Jones.

The first of Bob's charts was his arrangement of the aforementioned "Willow Weep for Me," a beautifully oblique interpretation that begins with a series of mysteriously somber chords by the winds. Richard Davis sets the tempo before Thad Jones enters, staggering bits and pieces of the melody before embarking on a deeply personal solo, all the while accompanied sparsely by the band, culminating in a slow series of ascending marcato notes, followed by Thad's final statement. At that point the band reprises the opening chords, which introduce Brookmeyer's trombone solo. As you might expect by now, it shows once again what a superlative ballad player he was. At the conclusion of his solo, Bob leads the band into a final bridge, only this time we hear a bit of group improvisation led by Thad and Bob before moving ultimately into another return to the opening of the song. This is a perfectly symmetrical arrangement that really illustrates the path Bob was following at that time.

In retrospect, I think that Bob's "ABC Blues" is one of his most memorable compositions, one that certainly helped to exemplify his desire to move ever forward into uncharted compositional territory in the world of big band music. And I also believe that it differed enough from Thad Jones's compositions and arrangements and did not distract from them.

"ABC" begins ominously, with a brief free-form improvisational conversation between bass and drums, followed by a pyramid of cascading notes into a layer of sustained and somewhat dissonant long tones from the band. It then moves back into a short rubato statement from bassist Davis before he sets a medium tempo with a walking bassline that moves into the first part of the dark sounding theme, before dissolving quizzically into a mini-interlude by pianist Hank Jones, who introduces the medium tempo again. His brief solo sets the stage for the band to restate the theme, and we now find ourselves sitting squarely in blues-ville, with Mel Lewis's deep groove providing a funky momentum throughout. The first solo is by Thad Jones, followed by tenor saxophonist Joe Farrell and altoist Jerome Richardson, and finally, Brookmeyer enters with a bit of down-home commentary.

By the way, the band interlude that sets up each soloist in the first eight measures, then moves into a strong four-beat approach for four measures, reminds me of Bob's Kansas City roots, and Count Basie in particular.

After a brief group improvisation from the four soloists, bass and drums return to the dialogue they began at the beginning of the track, followed by a return to the top of the tune and a partial restatement of the theme. Finally, after brief rubato solo statements from Davis and Lewis, the band comes in with a rhythmic two-note vamp that fades into the end of the track.

While the band recorded many other fine albums, *Presenting Thad Jones/Mel Lewis & The Jazz Orchestra* continues to be a favorite among many musicians and listeners. The level of writing and playing, in my opinion, set the bar very high in the mid-60s. And Bob was integral to the band's appeal and success.

. . . However

In 1968 Bob left New York for a variety of reasons and had the opportunity to move to Los Angeles, where he was welcomed into the LA studio music community. As discussed in chapter 2, even with the opportunities that came his way doing abundant studio work, Bob pretty much hit rock bottom. As some folk singer wrote, You can't run, you can't hide when it comes from inside. As we know, Bob finally realized that only he could alter the disastrous course he was on and change his life. Alcoholism was a dead end—almost literally for Bob. I think that the one good thing that came out of that period was that Bob exorcized his demons, thanks to his newfound determination, a hell of a lot of willpower, and those of us who helped him as much as we could to get back into playing and living again.

1978: Back to the Apple and Mel Lewis

And so the pendulum swung in reverse and Bob moved back to New York in 1978. The Big Apple was a different place in the late

'70s, and many of the faces in the jazz community were new to Bob. Perhaps one of the biggest changes was Thad Jones's abrupt departure from the Jones-Lewis big band in early January 1979 in order to accept a position with the Danish Radio Orchestra. Soon after the dust settled a bit, Mel asked Bob Brookmeyer to be Thad's successor, a position that Bob turned down due to his commitment to Stan Getz and a lengthy European tour. So rather than select someone else to co-lead, Mel made the decision to go it alone. Ultimately, Bob agreed to step in as the band's musical director in 1980, which initiated some significant additions to its repertoire. Bob's compositions and arrangements were very different from Thad's and were not received enthusiastically by some band members. When interviewer Paul Rubin asked Bob what kind of reception he received from a younger generation of musicians, he said,

> they didn't care what I'd done. They wanted to know what I could do.... They were all new to me. And I came down, and I was the old geezer who'd written some of the fifteen-year-old arrangements that they were playing. They could look at me and say, "Well, he did that," but that was no wedge for me in the door. I had to spend the next year and a half in New York, getting to know them, and saying, "Well look, here's what I do. What do you think of that?" So it was really reestablishing credentials.[13]

This real challenge upon his return to New York was grounded in the fact that Bob was spending quite a bit of time immersed in studying the works of contemporary classical composers, possibly with the idea of pushing the envelope and some boundaries, thereby enriching his own approach to composing and arranging music for large jazz ensembles. In his interview with Gordon Jack, he says, "I hadn't learned anything new in a long time, and my approach was now old fashioned. I wanted to do some writing and I started studying scores and going to a lot of classical concerts. My favorite writers are people like Berio, Boulez,

Morton Feldman, Ligeti, Lutoslawski, Shostakovich, and my good friend, Earle Brown."[14]

Even though Bob agreed to be the orchestra's musical director, he knew that the generation gap between him and some of its younger players might make the road to acceptance a bit bumpy. As trombonist and band member John Mosca remembers it, "It was a natural mistake to assume he [Bob] would bring in charts that resembled the ones we knew. The new things were for the most part through composed, meaning much less rest for the brass and [less room] for soloists. As a result, the band was slow to accept the new music."[15]

The best thing about Bob's tenure as musical director of Mel's orchestra was that he didn't just talk the talk, he also walked the walk, especially when it came to composing music that spoke volumes about his level of creativity, his imagination, and his ability to draw from a wide variety of sources and genres, past and present. That's how he won the support and admiration of the skeptics in the orchestra.

Come to think of it, that type of honesty was engrained in Bob's personality. As you might guess by now, Bob did not suffer fools lightly, and he could spot bullshit a mile away, and if you tried to put one over on him, he would eviscerate you completely if he felt that you deserved it. I suppose that's why he inadvertently may have intimidated some people. As you continue reading, you will learn a lot more about Bob through the voices of some of his protégés, fellow musicians, family members, and friends—all to complete the picture of who he was as an uncompromising artist and, at the same time, as a much beloved human being.

It was no coincidence that in the early '80s Bob and Mel would work together again in such a closely knit way after so many years. While no one could replace Thad Jones, Bob stepped in and—with the support of key band members like saxophonist Dick Oatts, trombonist John Mosca, pianist Jim McNeely, and, of course, Mel—he produced some of the most vibrant, audaciously original, and swinging big band music ever written and performed.

The Inimitable Mel Lewis, world-renowned drummer and bandleader and one of Bob's oldest friends and collaborators. Copyright Raymond Ross, courtesy of Archives/CTSIMAGES.

Intermezzo 3: Mel, the Tailor

Time out for a few accolades for Mel Lewis. Mel met Bob in Chicago in the late '40s and the two were close friends for over four decades until Mel's passing in 1990. In Chris Smith's excellent biography *The View from the Back of the Band*, here's how Mel described their first meeting:

> Bob and I met at a jam session [in 1949] at a little club called the High Note in Chicago. Also that night we met up with Al Cohn, Tiny Kahn, Frank Rosolino, they were all working in Chicago at the time. And we were with two commercial dance bands at the time. . . . We are the same age, in fact I am older than Bobby, six or seven months. So we were both around nineteen years old then and met at that session. It was one of those things where we liked each other, liked the way each other played and we became fast friends.[16]

I met Mel Lewis only once and had a brief but friendly conversation with him. He knew about me through my relationship with Bob, and he made a joke about that, saying something like, "Ahhh, so YOU'RE the west coast Mel Lewis," to which I responded with something like, "Not. Even. On. My. Best. Day."

However, when it came to the music Mel played, I knew him very well. The first time was on the Mulligan CJB at the Vanguard recording. From that point on, I listened to and was influenced by quite a few of the big and small band records he played drums on. Mel had the magic in any scenario. He was extremely consistent and achieved a level of excellence that, in my opinion, few could match.

Mel was often called the Tailor by many of his fellow musicians. The original moniker came from vibraphonist Terry Gibbs, who provided this explanation to Chris Smith: "There was this little Jewish tailor in my Brooklyn neighborhood who had bunions on his feet, and never lifted his feet when he walked. Well Mel shuffled his feet when he walked too. So I nicknamed him 'the tailor' and it stuck with him."[17]

While that was the original reason for Terry Gibbs's nickname for Mel, it garnered another explanation altogether, one that was no less accurate. Mel played the way a good tailor sews, knitting the written parts of a reed or a brass section together by playing underneath and inside whatever they are playing on the page and accentuating it within the time rather than on top of it. Now that may seem like complicated verbiage, but it really becomes much clearer when you hear what Mel does on a tune like "Lady Chatterley's Mother" from the Mulligan CJB Vanguard record, or "Days Gone By, Oh My!" on *Gloomy Sunday and Other Bright Moments*. He incorporates whatever figures the band is playing within his own time feel and without breaking his stride; plus, his openness to new forms of music and great ability as a musician were elements that effectively facilitated Bob's rebirth as a composer, arranger, and player.

1980, 1982: Mel Lewis and the Jazz Orchestra: Metamorphosis

So far in this chapter, we've had a look at Bob's orchestral work, beginning in the mid-'50s, through the early to mid-'60s. During those years we've witnessed his artistic growth as both composer and orchestrator. His nascency was obvious throughout the aforementioned trio of recordings as he continued his exploration of the expansion of melodic motifs, harmonics, and rhythmic displacement. As Chris Smith suggested, "Brookmeyer treated the big band like a classical chamber ensemble. Each composition was focused on harmonic and melodic developments, textures, and moods, rather than preexisting song forms, or well-known chord progressions."[18]

Bob also began to believe that the ensemble was as important—if not more so—than the soloist. So in Bob's opinion, the background that a band plays behind a soloist can become as important as the solo itself. Actually, you can hear versions of this concept here and there in some of Bob's early arrangements; for example, listen to "You Took Advantage of Me" from the first Concert Jazz Band recording for Verve Records. You'll hear it again on the introduction and first movement of Bob's "Blues Suite" on his *Portrait of the Artist* album. In both cases, Bob wrote the ensemble accompaniment in such a way that he could dance around each of the band's written passages, much like a prima ballerina could weave in and out of the corps de ballet, thereby integrating soloist and background. That technique can also be heard later—albeit a bit more subtly—in Bob's contributions on *Gloomy Sunday* and *Presenting Thad Jones/Mel Lewis & The Jazz Orchestra*.

That being said, Bob's creative modus operandi definitely places the ensemble on equal footing with the soloist, with a variety of whatever backgrounds it is playing at the time. Maybe a simpler way of putting it would be that, rather than the band playing a short passage to introduce a solo (the traditional way), its backgrounds would move to the foreground to actually interact with the soloist who, in turn, would comment musically with whatever the band is playing at that moment.

Pretty heady stuff, I'll admit, but when you listen to Bob's compositions and arrangements, if you start to sense the equal importance of the ensemble throughout the solo, then that's a good start to understanding what Bob means when he says "the soloist is a compositional continuance" of whatever the band is playing. Such an approach would be revisited in his composing and arranging for Mel's orchestra and in later works written for his New Art Orchestra as well.

Mel showcased Bob's compositions and arrangements exclusively on two recordings (both accessible on various internet outlets): *Bob Brookmeyer, Composer, Arranger: Mel Lewis and The Jazz Orchestra* (Live at the Village Vanguard, February 1980, Red Baron Records), *Mel Lewis and The Jazz Orchestra: Featuring the Music of Bob Brookmeyer* (a.k.a. *Make Me Smile*, Live at the Village Vanguard, January 1982, Finesse Records). Both recordings provide a clear picture of how, in just a couple of years, Bob made some significant revisions and additions to his creative skills as a composer and orchestrator. Keep in mind that the word "revision" means "to see again" or, more specifically, to "revisit" something, often with the objective of moving beyond the thing being revised into a new setting or process.

In this context, first we'll compare Bob's approach to orchestrating two well-known ballads: "Skylark" in 1980 and his unique 1982 soundscape of "My Funny Valentine." Perhaps doing so will give you an idea of the influence contemporary classical composers had on Bob's aesthetic transformation.

"Skylark" (1980)

Hoagy Carmichael's and Johnny Mercer's "Skylark" was the first piece Bob arranged as the new musical director for the orchestra. In his foreword to Dave Rivello's *Bob Brookmeyer in Conversation with Dave Rivello*, pianist Jim McNeely recalls the day Bob brought his arrangement to the band's rehearsal: "I remember the rehearsal where we first played 'Skylark,' which he arranged as a feature for [alto saxophonist] Dick Oatts. Bob brought in the parts, copied in pencil in his own hand.

Before we played it he told me, 'If this doesn't work, I'm not going to bother anymore.' Well, it worked. My god, did it ever!"[19]

The song opens with a slow and simple (but slightly altered) piano statement of the melody by Jim McNeely, interspersed by a lush, atmospheric carpet of long tones from the horns. At about at the 1:40 mark, alto saxophonist Dick Oatts enters and begins his solo. All through Oatts's solo, the band weaves in and out, from the background to the foreground and back again. A brief moment or two finds the altoist playing with only the rhythm section, followed shortly thereafter by the bridge, where we hear the band playing soft, very short quarter notes that get progressively louder as Oatts reaches the end of that section. Then everything drops away, leaving the altoist alone with sparse bass accompaniment to complete the melody by holding the last note . . . then silence . . . until pianist McNeely returns to the original melody, once again with the horns responding, then Jim takes us home, providing a final ethereal note that hangs in midair . . .

"Faint as a will o' the wisp, crazy as a loon / sad as a gypsy serenading the moon."[20]

"My Funny Valentine" (1982)

> Brookmeyer was a visionary. He was such a broad musician and took elements of contemporary classical composition and merged them with jazz elements in such an unusual way. He was so fearless and adventurous in some of the things he wrote. He was always going for it.
> —Bob Mintzer, *50 Years at the Village Vanguard*

The 1982 recording of "My Funny Valentine" is not without its challenges, for both performer and listener. Unlike "Skylark," where Bob altered notes and voicings here and there in the original melody without compromising it to the point that it was virtually unrecognizable, "My Funny Valentine" is a horse of a different color. There really is no easy way to describe a series of sequences that move the arrangement forward. Portions of the melody are like buoys in a roiling sea, surfacing here and there for only a moment before disappearing into an undercurrent of sounds.

Actually, Bob called the piece "Valentine"—perhaps a more appropriate title, given that there are only snippets of the original melody present throughout. It was—and still is—a masterpiece of deconstruction.

Even now this piece makes me think of kaleidoscopes, and what a kaleidoscope of tones, harmonies, and rhythms would sound like. For example, just as we look in a kaleidoscope and witness the ever-changing geometric shapes that appear and disappear before our eyes, the shapes of sounds we hear in Bob's orchestration are themselves kaleidoscopic; that is, the orchestra plays one segment, then breaks apart here and there into smaller configurations, only to coalesce into the complete ensemble, which once again breaks apart. And so it goes. This feels to me like musical shape shifting. Rather than have a not-so-subtle, grandiose ending, the piece concludes the way it began—not with a bang but with a percussive whisper.

So how then to approach listening to the orchestra's live 1982 performance of "My Funny Valentine"? Here are two different ways:

For those who've never heard the song, listen to a recognizable recording—that is, one that offers a clear, well-structured statement of the melody, either a vocal or instrumental version. Most renditions that I've heard or played followed the structure of the song with slight differences here and there.

If, on the other hand, you are familiar with the song, another and perhaps a more challenging way to listen might be to abandon any preconceptions you may have about how the song should be performed and to merely immerse yourself in the Brookmeyer version on its own harmonic and structural terms. Actually, try to think of it as a stand-alone concert piece. In fact, Bob handed out parts to the orchestra that were entitled only "Valentine," which may have been his way of suggesting that while there are snippets of the standard here and there, listeners would do well to cast all notions aside of what "beautiful" is and just listen. One of the problems that many people have occurs when they bring personal conceptions of what a song is "supposed to sound like" to the table rather than approaching the listening experience with an open mind. "Valentine" is, in a sense, *not* "My Funny Valentine" at all but Bob's deconstruction of the original Rodgers and Hart song, in that it is almost completely unrecognizable.

You might ask, "Why deconstruct such a beautiful song?" Bob's friend, trombonist John Mosca (who was in Mel's orchestra at that time) mentioned to me that rather than refer to the composition by its proper name, Bob opted for shortening the title to just "Valentine." At the end of the day and repeated listening to the deconstructed version, I can't help thinking that there was a certain amount of bitterness undergirding Bob's elimination of the words "My" and "Funny"— especially knowing him and some of his personal history. Perhaps to him there was nothing funny about some of the events that haunted his past; and maybe this dark and cacophonous "Valentine" reflects the frustration and disappointment of those years.

Addendum: Years ago, in 1981 to be exact, a major TV network filmed a half-hour documentary called *The Making of a Song*, which focused on Bob's arrangement of "Valentine" for the Mel Lewis Jazz Orchestra. To my knowledge it was aired only once and never again. The film features Bob talking about his unique interpretation of the song, and we also get to see him rehearsing "Valentine" with the orchestra on site at the Village Vanguard, where we would see them performing it live on one of their Monday night sets. Fortunately, it has now resurfaced, thanks to Mel Lewis's daughter, Lori, and the Archives Division of the University of Missouri at Kansas City. *The Making of a Song* is now available for viewing, under both Bob's and Mel's names, on YouTube.[21] Enjoy!

Just as the emotional contrast between Bob's two ballad orchestrations was easy to discern, so was his approach to the kind of energy inherent in the up-tempo pieces I've chosen to illustrate the distinction between the hard swinging 1980 performance of Bob's "Hello and Goodbye" and 1982's "Goodbye World," which he wrote as a dynamic duet for Mel and himself, bobbing (no pun intended) and weaving around and through the orchestra, which is the third collective voice throughout. It's been my experience that most "Goodbye" songs are, by nature, depressing (*e.g.,* "Gloomy Sunday," Charles Mingus's "Goodbye Pork Pie Hat," Cole Porter's "Every Time We Say Goodbye," and Gordon Jenkins's "Goodbye," to name a few); however, the Brookmeyer compositions here are anything but sadness set to music. Quite the contrary, they are joyous affairs featuring great ensemble work and inspired solos by several band members, as well as by Mel and Bob, whose lovely singsong valve trombone voice is a rare treat, especially since Bob solos only three times on these two recordings.

"Hello and Goodbye" (1980)

This composition seems initially to be couched in the tradition of the swinging big band repertoire; I say "seems" because there are some untraditional left turns here and there that give this Brookmeyer original the tongue in-cheek uniqueness so typical of Bob's compositional style. It opens with only the rhythm section playing a loose, rather sparse vamp of undetermined length until Brookmeyer cues the first ensemble entrance—not a lot of notes flying around and not very loud, but gradually adding volume and heft to the next part of the melody—followed by the entire "unison shout," bolstered by Mel's rhythmically perfect punctuations. At this point, rather than an exciting ensemble section, the band melts away and is replaced by a light, old-timey four-beat interlude featuring the rhythm section and Oatts's soprano saxophone playing a sprightly little ditty, interrupted by a rather nasty sounding glissando by the trombones. The punctuated quarter-notes continue, this time with members of the ensemble joining the rhythm section. All of this leads to the re-emergence of the orchestra and the return to the traditional swing feel; only this time, what follows is the kind of exciting small group improvisation that was common in Dixieland bands in the early days of jazz. Mel sits on a solid backbeat behind the collective blowing, as the rest of the ensemble provides a layer of long tones (doo-doo-dahh's) that eventually signals the reprise of the unison shout, which sets up an intense solo by tenor saxophonist Rich Perry, who weaves in and out of commentary by the ensemble. After Perry's solo there is another thematic passage that introduces a Gary Pribeck baritone saxophone solo, replete with handclaps on two and four and a constant trill by pianist Jim McNeely, which segues into an exciting shout chorus supported by some beautiful fire from Mel, then a brief return to simultaneous blowing and a Dixieland-style ending. You need only hear the audience response to know how much they enjoyed the ride.

"Goodbye World" (1982)

Once again, the changes in Bob's compositional style are very much in evidence here. The brief opening melody has a lively, pastoral quality that has the kind of energy reminiscent of a folk dance; however, that spirit is interrupted by Bob as he plays a long, low downward smear followed by a momentary silence; then, as the orchestra continues its silence, he moves beyond the upper register, squawking, whinnying, and creating a ruckus. Mel Lewis responds with jagged, percussive, out-of-tempo explosions. All in all, trombone and drums dance around each other until Mel sets a medium tempo, and on cue the orchestra enters into a short back-and-forth with the drums until Bob enters with the melody of the song. All through Bob's solo, he and the ensemble become one entity: the ensemble's written parts support and punctuate Bob's improvisations, which in turn glide around and through the ensemble's written figures. It's quite exhilarating to hear this kind of interaction, mostly because much (but not all) of the big band music at that time was locked into a kind of theme-and-variations approach to big band writing.

At the end of Bob's solo, the ensemble holds on to a chord and lingers for a moment until Mel picks up on a rhythmic figure (which the band repeated throughout Bob's solo) and creates a brief solo interlude of his own, which leads the ensemble into the next transition, one that finds Bob playing alone for a moment before slowing down to a stop. Just when we think that "Goodbye World" is bidding us adieu, what sounds like a cowbell sets a fast but metronomically steady tempo over which Mel begins an extended solo—one that moves away from the strict pulse established by the cowbell into a heated, free-form exchange wherein Mel plays a phrase to which the band responds with out-of-tempo cacophony. Then it's off to the races at a frantic (but controlled) pace, with Mel filling up the space between repeated brass jabs and intense rhythmic passages from the entire ensemble. Very exciting stuff! But wait . . . there's more trombone from Bob, who leads the orchestra quietly back to the beginning melody and a final chord.

Please understand that Bob's unique kind of composing and arranging didn't materialize overnight. If you listen to the previous Brookmeyer big band records, especially the tracks described earlier in this chapter, you'll begin to see a pattern forming—a process, if you will. Bob was changing the face of large ensemble jazz bit by bit. Just as his approach to soloing took on fresh new characteristics, so too did his abilities as a composer and arranger. His legion of influences became very diverse over the years as he moved through these phases. From Al Cohn, Manny Albam, Bill Holman, and most notably Bill Finnegan, to contemporary classical composers like Stravinsky, Schoenberg, Lutoslawski, Carter, Ligeti, Feldman, and many others.

Admittedly, what follows is mostly conjecture on my part, although I think that what Bob was implying is that we as artists are all too often tethered to conventions that were established long ago, and that searching for new ways of expanding and expressing ourselves through our work was (and is) essential.

Maybe that's why the allure of postmodern music, art, and literature appealed so strongly to him. Writers like his friend Donald Barthelme, artists like Joan Miró, and composers like those mentioned above may well have been of like mind.

Postscript: I want to say a few words about one more track on the 1982 Vanguard album. Probably one of the most dynamic and challenging Brookmeyer compositions on either recording, it's called "The Nasty Dance" and features the brilliant tenor saxophonist Joe Lovano as the only soloist. It's a ten-plus-minute tour de force for Lovano, who meets the challenge head on with an absolutely incredible solo. This track has too many disparate sections to write about, and the furious zigzagging between them is stunningly executed by the ensemble.

Experiencing "The Nasty Dance" is like riding on the world's fastest roller coaster without a seatbelt! Listen to the performance while spending some time looking at Pablo Picasso's *Guernica* or Hieronymus Bosch's *Garden of Earthly Delights* and I think you might see the connection between musical and visual art. I firmly believe that in this instance the connection is irrefutable—all in all, a major achievement for Bob, Mel, Joe, and the orchestra.

Goodbye, Mel

Mel Lewis's passing in February 1990, after a lengthy battle with cancer, was a crushing loss to musicians and fans alike. It hit Bob especially hard. Here's a portion of his comments as excerpted from Burt Korall's excellent book, *Drummin' Men: The Heartbeat of Jazz*: "When Mel died, it was one of the biggest losses the music ever had. People all over the world suffered. There will never be another him. Mel was one of the greatest drummers of all. I'd stake my life on that."[22]

And this from Jan Brookmeyer: "While Mel lay dying in the hospital, Bob came to visit him for the last time. Shortly thereafter, upon hearing that Mel had passed, Bob became very quiet for a number of days, grieving for the loss of his old and dear friend."[23]

As I sit here at the computer listening to "Goodbye, World," it feels more like "Hello, World." What became even clearer to me throughout the track is exactly how much Bob and Mel loved and respected each other deeply as both musicians and human beings. Listen to the track all the way through and keep in mind that playing jazz at its best and most personal is all about camaraderie, mutual respect, and a shared love of the music—not only among players but also among listeners as well.

Chapter 5

For the Record III

Europe, the Path to the New Art Orchestra: Selected Large Ensemble Recordings, 1988–2011

Prelude: Moving On

As you may remember from previous chapters, Bob was no stranger to European audiences. As an instrumentalist he performed in France, England, Germany, Spain, the Netherlands, and other countries with Mulligan, Getz, Jim Hall, Clark Terry, Mel Lewis, and his own small groups. Europe always welcomed Bob, as it did with many American jazz artists over the years. It was not a surprise to those who knew Bob that, given his artistic trajectory, he would be the recipient of multiple composition commissions, directorships, and teaching opportunities, most notably in Germany, Sweden, and the Netherlands. It also became inevitable that he would be able to record some of his finest, and perhaps most intriguing, orchestral compositions while in residence in these countries.

That being said, this chapter focuses upon the final transitional turning point in Bob's life—this time in Europe. Just as he evolved stylistically from his first big band album on VIK Records in the

Bob and his dream band, the New Art Orchestra, taken just a short time before Bob's passing (2011). Photo courtesy of Lena Semmelhoggen.

mid-'50s to his second and third large ensemble recordings (in 1959 and 1961, respectively), his growth as both composer and arranger was significant. As we have begun to find out, there was something markedly different about Bob's compositions and arrangements. His early influences included the big bands of Count Basie, Duke Ellington, Woody Herman, and others; and the works of composers and arrangers like Bill Finnegan, Willis (Bill) Holman, Manny Albam, and Gil Evans played an important part in Bob's evolution, which moved ever forward as Bob became a charter member of the Thad Jones/Mel Lewis Jazz Orchestra in the mid-'60s, and subsequently as musical director of the Mel Lewis Jazz Orchestra in 1979. As we know from his two live Village Vanguard recordings with the Mel Lewis Orchestra, Bob's compositional aesthetic flowered remarkably from the 1980 recording to the second one two years later.

It was around that period of time that Bob's growing desire to further explore and expand his creative abilities as a composer, by fusing elements of ultracontemporary classical music with his jazz sensibilities, led him to disengage from Mel's ensemble. In part 5 of his interview with Marc Myers for *JazzWax*, Bob explains, "I told Mel, 'I think I've written myself out of the band. I think I have to go to work for classical people.' So I left the band and went to Europe to the radio stations in Cologne [Germany] and Stockholm [Sweden] and worked with their orchestras and producers. I even began writing electronic things and a double concerto."[1]

After leaving Mel's band as musical director, Bob intensified his study of modern orchestral music. He bought classical music scores and managed to go to a number of concerts in New York City as often as possible; as mentioned in the previous chapter, he immersed himself in the music of composers whose work began to resonate deeply for him.

Intermezzo 1: What Makes a Piece of Music "Beautiful"?

So how does one go about identifying "beauty" in Bob's orchestral work? As you move with him from his early large ensemble compositions and arrangements in the mid-'50s and early '60s through the next stylistic transition in his writing a few years later with Thad Jones and Mel Lewis, and then through his musical directorship of Mel's Jazz Orchestra in the early '80s, you'll notice a new "wrinkle" in his writing. While the swinging and wistful feelings are ever present, there is a playfulness and a rather oblique métier at work as well. In addition to some very comfortable melodiousness, there is also some dissonance, which brings a certain strident edginess to some of Bob's compositions. This is music that, to me, oftentimes seems ephemeral— almost as though Bob might be saying, "Stay with us now; after a while, we'll get back on the train and begin moving down the road, further into the unknown. But *at this very moment*, share *this* adventure with us. Our music is like life itself: it has its ups and downs and can run the emotional gamut. And why shouldn't it? Music should always tell the truth, no matter what that truth turns out to be." While Bob didn't actually say these things to me in any of our conversations, he intimated them many times in our moments together, both on and off stage. It was who Bob was, both truth seeker and truth teller.

I think that Bob would agree with the following brief meditations about beauty as exemplified in musical composition, performance, and improvisation.

Why is it that we consider some music to be "beautiful" and other music to be extremely hard to listen to? This question can be very difficult to answer! Defining the concept of beauty itself produces more questions than answers; and your answer may wind up being very different than mine, hers, or his; truth be told, the idea of responding with "I know beauty in music when I hear it" is basically another way of saying, "I don't have any idea."

Here are two disparate perceptions that may shed a bit more light on the concept: The contemporary philosopher and writer Roger Scruton, whose little book *Beauty* (2009) brings us squarely into the twenty-first century, suggests that "beauty in music is not just a matter of form. It involves an emotional content."[2] He demystifies that declaration by adding, "The connection between music and emotion is established in the experience of playing and hearing. We understand expressive music by fitting it to other elements in our experience, drawing connections with human life, 'matching' the music with other things that have meaning for us."[3]

And, at the end of the day, he concludes that "real beauty can be found, even in what is seedy, painful, and decayed."[4]

Willis Conover—an American jazz producer and broadcaster known most notably for his tenure as the host of *The Voice of America* radio program, which brought jazz to Eastern Europe for over four decades—amplified Scruton's observations in this quote from Leonard Feather's *Book of Jazz*: "Jazz is a language. It is people living in sound. Jazz is people talking, laughing, crying, building, painting, mathematicising [sic], abstracting, extracting, giving to, taking from, making of. In other words, living."[5]

While Conover's comments precede Scruton's by over thirty years and refer only to jazz, they accurately exemplify the former's suggestion that there is a significant correlation between music, emotion, and everyday life, and that beauty in music can often show itself in the many aspects of living that Conover describes, and not just those that bring us to our "happy places," replete with rainbows, starry nights, and other idyllic settings. While those attributes are certainly valid, the nature of beauty in music—or any art for that matter—can encompass much more than that. Being open to *all* types of music expands our world, particularly as we follow Brookmeyer, on his way to the sky.

In the previous chapter, we charted Bob's metamorphosis as a composer and arranger by having a look at the large ensemble recordings he led (or was a prominent member of), beginning in the mid-'50s through his charter membership in the Thad Jones/Mel Lewis Jazz Orchestra in the mid-'60s, and his position as musical director for the Mel Lewis Jazz Orchestra in the early '80s. This chapter continues exploring Bob's trajectory in much the same fashion, only this time, due to his interest in and study of postmodern electronic music, Bob began including electronic instruments in his compositions for his next three recordings (*Dreams*, *On the Way to the Sky*, and *Electricity*). These three transitional recordings may well have been the stepping stones that led him to the final leg of his journey.

1988–91: *Dreams, On the Way to the Sky, Electricity*

Dreams (1986, 1988)

Thinking about Bob's music in 1982 with Mel's orchestra, I went back and listened again to "The Nasty Dance" and "My Funny Valentine" from the second *Live at the Village Vanguard* album before moving into *Dreams*, which was the first album Bob made after leaving Mel. It was also the first recording to include a synthesizer as part of the ensemble. Recorded in the summers of 1986 and 1988 with the

Stockholm Jazz Orchestra, the differences between the 1982 Vanguard recording and the Stockholm recording six years later seem palpable. There is a well-focused energy throughout *Dreams* that contrasts with the power and intensity of performances that flow through the Vanguard album. To be fair, the New York performances were recorded "live" at the Village Vanguard, whereas the Stockholm Jazz Orchestra recorded Bob's music in the controlled environment of a recording studio, where the level of communication with an audience was largely absent. No matter. Both are outstanding representations of the further metamorphosis of Brookmeyer as composer. Here are two descriptive examples of the music on the *Dreams* recording:

"Lies" (1986)

> Jazz is a personal expression. A Jazzman should be saying what he feels. He's one human being talking to others, telling his story—and that means humor and sadness, joy, all the things that humans have. . . . You tell it freely and honestly, and sometimes you don't make it . . . like telling a joke no one laughs at. But you tell it, whatever it is, and it's yours. That's you, that's human, that's jazz.
> —Bob Brookmeyer, *DownBeat*, 1961

To my way of thinking, Bob's comment back in 1961 could apply with equal acuity to Brookmeyer as composer as well as player.

I listened to Bob's album *Dreams* a number of times before including it in this book. Out of all of the tracks, "Lies" reminded me most of Bob's words about jazz—like "telling his story"—because they are central to one of the most important reasons we take to heart our calling as musicians who not only play jazz but also live it. Which means to me that the stories we tell through our instruments or on score paper are borne out of our many life experiences—both good and bad. As writer Nat Hentoff suggested, "Of all sophisticated forms of music, jazz is the most self-revealing, the music where there is the least room for the performer to hide who he or she is."[6]

Listening to "Lies" is an example. Composed in 1986 and recorded two years later, Bob hides nothing from the listener. This composition unexpectedly elicited a quietly emotional response from me each time I listened to it, much like "Detour Ahead" did on Bob's *Gloomy Sunday* album. I'm not quite sure why, except to say that the emotions that bubbled up reminded me of a panoply of personal feelings that were "wins" as well as those that were bumps in the road: losses, bouts of grief, things that I should've done and didn't do, and so on. So you may ask whether or not "Lies" is a sad song and, further, was it Bob's intention to compose a piece of music that would reflect upon some sadness he may have been feeling at the time?

In conversation with Dave Rivello, Bob had this to say about intentionally setting out to compose a sad piece of music:

> How can I write a sad piece? I really don't know. Some pieces of mine, they say, are sad and some are not. Maybe they're intended to be, but it could also be the way I feel. I might be having a really lousy month or a depressed month or a happy month, but those go by the wayside. I don't sit down to write a happy piece or a sad piece. I sit down to write a piece and try to make it the best piece that I can, and if it turns out sad or happy, I can't control that.[7]

One chilly winter evening, I asked my wife Kathleen to sit with me and listen to "Lies" and to respond to the music with a scenario once it was over. Her response was similar to mine, although I must take the blame for the lapses into cliché.

What follows are our visceral reactions to the music. Please remember that this is merely our interpretation of the story that "Lies" is telling us. Yours may be very different but no less valid. Rather than setting out to manipulate our feelings as listeners, Bob leaves it to us to examine our own reactions and their underlying feelings to the piece. This is what we came up with:

"Lies" begins with Bob alone playing a plaintive melody with very minimal and barely audible synthesizer support—lonely, a soliloquy perhaps. Kathleen, ever the creative imagist, sees a man sitting on a jetty on a late afternoon overlooking the bay, skittering pebbles across the incoming tide. We don't know why he's there or what he's feeling, beyond his apparent loneliness.

The mood changes when Bob plays four loud descending notes introducing the orchestra, which provides a substantial background for Bob's restatement of the melody, this time intertwining with the ensemble, allowing his solo voice to become part of the orchestra for a short time before resurfacing; the man seated on the jetty feels his pent-up emotions rise to the surface and become pure anguish, and he asks the setting sun, "Why was I so cruel and heartless? Why?" It is here that the valve trombone plays a single note, expressing the feeling behind that question repeatedly, with the orchestra filling the space briefly after each one-word question. The man likens his confused and anguished state to being trapped in a house of mirrors, seeing only multiple angry images of himself, trying desperately to find his way out. Then, maybe he finds the exit and answers his own question. Bob caresses each of these moments with his beautifully lyrical trombone commentary. It almost seems at times that he is not playing the horn; the horn is playing him.

The final moments of "Lies" seem to Kathleen and me to be filled with some manner of resolve, even though a slight feeling of loss lingers. The bass drum marks time slowly and strictly, and the brass undergird this segment and build gradually only to ultimately release the tension, and we are once again left with only the trombone and synthesizer, fading as the sun melts away into the Bay. C'est la vie.

Now admittedly you may think our visual interpretation of "Lies" coupled with the music itself sounds like a soap-opera melodrama or a cheesy movie of the week, but we believe that Bob may be unintentionally sharing a personal story here—through his extraordinary trombone voice and his orchestration. And maybe he would ask only that we listen and perhaps discover our own stories along the way. Whether or not he wrote the piece intentionally is not the question, but "Lies" offers us the opportunity for self-reflection and maybe even an epiphany or two. Such is the power of music.

"Missing Monk" (1988)

Brookmeyer's association with Thelonious Monk is somewhat of a mystery. I remember Bob saying that they knew each other (maybe from the loft days?); however, on those rare occasions when I brought up Monk, Bob expressed his admiration for him, especially as a composer. That admiration is in evidence on "Missing Monk," a tour-de-force Brookmeyer opus performed by the Stockholm Jazz Orchestra. Here's an abridged description of the track:

"Monk" opens with keyboardist Anders Widmark's solo synthesizer introducing the theme and adding some of his own bluesy commentary. Once he sets the tempo, Widmark is soon joined by the rhythm section and the theme is then expanded by the synth to sound like a trumpet section. (You have to listen closely here in order to realize that what you're hearing is not really something that multiple trumpets could articulate easily, if at all.) At around three minutes, you can hear the low brass playing half notes as the real trumpeters enter and play a separate melody simultaneously with the synth trumpeters. Then the entire orchestra enters at a little beyond the four-minute mark, plays for eight measures, and melts away, leaving it to Bob, who begins his solo with those same kinds of clipped two-note figures that the synth trumpeters played. Bob expands the two-note figure and embellishes it with additional notes as the orchestra supplements Bob's solo with a syncopated passage consisting largely of a single repeated note. The release comes when they drop out once again, into the background. This kind of interplay continues until Bob passes the torch to two trumpeters (Fredrik Norén and Gustavo Bergalli) whose exciting solos intertwine, underpinned by long tones from the ensemble and a strong backbeat by drummer Johan Dielemans. After some exciting big band shout choruses, the two trumpeters trade four-bar phrases, after which the entire group joins the fray and there is an explosion of simultaneous improvisations. All hands on deck! Then it's back to what begins as one more classic shout chorus, only this time it morphs into a cacophonous wall of sound, bolstered by a heavy backbeat and another brief group improvisation, now supported by a riff from the horns. Drummer Dielemans is the real hero here. He holds all of these sections together with some very authoritative playing.

In the final moments of the piece, the ensemble evaporates, leaving only keyboardist Anders Widmark reprising the feeling he introduced at the beginning, only this time with a sparse and quiet conclusion.

In retrospect, while this is not a tribute to Monk, I can hear rhythmic figures that are not dissimilar to the rhythmic jabs that make up the melodies of Monk tunes like "Evidence," "Criss Cross," and "Teo." What I'm hearing on *Dreams* exemplifies Bob's further development as a composer. He said repeatedly to me and others that he was committed to moving forward into unknown realms in his compositions and arrangements. I think that each of these later recordings, as well as the two live recordings with Mel's Vanguard Jazz Orchestra, and even the compositions and arrangements on each of the Brookmeyer-led big band albums from the late '50s and early to mid-'60s, reveal his insatiable desire to explore new avenues of expression.

On the Way to the Sky (1989)

> I am slowly entering the world of electronic music—the sounds of synthesizers are becoming part of my language.
> —Bob Brookmeyer, 1989

> This work was one that Bob was quite proud of, and for many years was only really known by his students that he shared it with. It was always a dream of his to someday have the recording released for the world to hear, which thankfully came true . . . when the WDR released this wonderful work on CD and digital platforms.
> —Ryan Truesdell, 2006

Commissioned by Wolfgang Hirschmann, producer at the WDR Big Band in Cologne, Germany, *On the Way to the Sky* was performed and recorded for broadcast on German Public Radio in August 1989; however, it was not released in the United States until twenty-seven years later, in 2016. Even though reasons for its delayed release remain unclear, it is now readily available and is an important addition to Bob's discography.

This, from Bob to Dave Rivello regarding *On the Way to the Sky*: "That's one of my favorites, I think. It was really far away from everything I was doing then. It works well as a concert piece. I've done it in concert three or four times."[8]

On the Way to the Sky is a work comprised of six movements: "Awakening," "Earth," "Fire," "Water," "Ascension," and "The Sky." I suspect that Bob intended for listeners to consider experiencing the six movements contiguously, since this is a suite of music, with what appear to be interrelated thematic segments. You will be hearing guitarist Jim Hall, drummer Mel Lewis, and Bob's valve trombone, with the WDR Big Band—one of Europe's finest large jazz ensembles—which on this occasion, consists of five trumpets, four trombones, five woodwinds, guitarist, bassist, percussionist, and two keyboardists.

Unlike the big band albums discussed earlier in this chapter, it's a real challenge for me to describe a movement's structure in a manner that's accessible without becoming overly technical. That said, I can only offer some observations based upon what I'm hearing. Hopefully, what I write here about the two movements will be useful as you experience each movement of *On the Way to the Sky*.

"Fire"

As you listen to this movement, you will be hearing two pianists playing a variety of keyboards, including synthesizers. The liner notes offer no track-by-track description of which keyboards were being utilized, and frankly, I don't believe that such information is relevant to first-time listeners, especially those unacquainted with electronic music. The exciting moments throughout come when the WDR Big Band, with Mel Lewis leading the charge, enters and joins the synths, often creating a herky-jerky electro-acoustic momentum that ignites each movement. Listen to the beginning of "Fire" for a good example. You'll hear a release from the opening intensity when all drops away, leaving the keyboardists to create a warm patina of sounds that move from long placid tones to bursts of improvised multi-note phrases. Once the WDR musicians reenter, the textures begin to change again, this time with Lewis's machine gun–like bursts, which often introduce a repetitive, rhythmic five-note figure superimposed over four beats. Halfway through the movement, there is a short but exciting interlude featuring a fleet-fingered, blues-tinged solo from guitarist Jim Hall. Then the dragon reawakens and synthesized notes spiral up into the air and tumble down to earth, creating an exhilarating effect. The band reenters one final time, and the last few embers of the fire become sparks and then disappear into the void, only to be filled by . . .

"Water"

The beginning belongs to guitarist Jim Hall alone. His beautiful guitar sound complements and sanctifies the silences that surround the notes he plays. Pure magic. And who better to respond to Jim's guitar voice here than Bob, his longtime friend and musical partner. Together they bring their magical lyricism to this movement. If you can picture how water flows through a small stream, such as it does behind our house here in the woods—smoothly, effortlessly, elegantly, and gracefully—then you'll have an idea about the expansive fluidity these two men are capable of. In fact the Brookmeyer-Hall duo can be heard on their live recording at the North Sea Jazz Festival. Challenge Records captures those synchronous moments at their best.

The electronics in "Water" play a supporting role here, remaining in the background. At times Bob scored the synth backgrounds much as he might've done for a concert string section, as if the low drones were being played with bows by an orchestra's bassists, while the short, repetitive notes on each dirgelike beat would come from perhaps the strings and, eventually, the wind sections. Given that this was recorded in 1989 and there was not much of this kind of melding going on between electronics and jazz—particularly in ballads—I think that Bob created something here in this movement that was quite unique and, to my ears, very moving.

In sum, *On the Way to the Sky* is an orchestral piece that Bob felt was representative of a new phase in his life; a more positive outlook began flowing through his music, maybe because at last the harmonious, loving relationship that had eluded him for so many years finally became a reality. To be able to hear that personal metamorphosis reflected in his music at that time was very inspiring to me, both musically and personally.

Even so, it's true that Bob seemed frustrated by the fact that *On the Way to the Sky* hadn't been released commercially. It's truly a remarkable work, one that succeeds in creating a sort of organic bridge between electronic and acoustic music in a very unpretentious way. I think he would be gratified knowing that it is available globally now for all to hear.

Electricity (1991)

> [*Electricity*] is the child of *On the Way to the Sky*.
> —Bob Brookmeyer, 1994

In 1994 Douglas Payne, a reviewer for the venerable online jazz weekly *AllAboutJazz*, reviewed Bob's third electro-acoustic recording, this one moving further into a three-way synthesis of rock, jazz, and electronic music. Payne believed that Bob's compositions and arrangements were intricate and that they, as I put it, "require more than a single listen."[9] While that notion by itself might be enough to turn some listeners off (one friend told me she didn't want to have to work that hard), repeated listening doesn't mean listening to a track and immediately afterward listening to it again; for example, when I first heard "Ugly Music," track two on *Electricity*, there were so many interesting things going on—often simultaneously—that I wanted to wait a bit and come back to the track after a while and listen to it all again. If there's one thing that Bob's music isn't, it is boring. In fact, each time I listen to most tracks on this recording, I always hear something I did not hear when I listened at an earlier time. Listening, then, can be a powerful experience, if you are open to sonic and rhythmic exploration and not locked into one or two kinds of music. Payne does say that "there's much to appreciate in [this] music's richness and depth."[10]

Also, as Payne has said in his *AllAboutJazz* review, *Electricity* "is by no means a look backwards."[11] It is an audacious recording, by turns elegiac, funky, psychedelic, and ambient— actually, a hybrid of all of these wrapped up in an electronic gumbo. Unlike other similar attempts, there's nothing pretentious about *Electricity*. While Bob seemed to be inspired here and there by these genres, he was most interested in the works of modern and postmodern classical composers such as those mentioned previously. There are some interesting dialogues between Bob and Eastman School of Music's Dave Rivello about these and other modern and postmodern composers in Dave's excellent book *Bob Brookmeyer in Conversation with Dave Rivello*.

While writing this book, I spent some time reacquainting myself with Lutoslawski, because sometime in the '80s Bob began giving me cassettes of the Polish composer's music, which I was nowhere near ready to receive with open arms. Those cassettes stayed on the shelf for quite some time before I jumped into the fire. But when I did I was astounded, especially by Lutoslawski's compositions, beginning with his string quartets and eventually his large-scale works. On some nascent level, I could hear how his influence permeated Bob's writing, especially in terms of rhythm and of the use of silences throughout much of Bob's work, especially on the three electro-acoustic recordings presented in this section, *Electricity* being the most rhythmically rigorous.

Some advice if you're thinking about comparing *Electricity* with its predecessor, *On the Way to the Sky:* Don't! It would be like trying to compare a tasty cantaloupe with an equally flavorful honeydew melon. Both recordings are masterworks for different reasons. While the movements on *Sky* are thematically connected, the pieces on *Electricity* are not directly related to one another, except in several instances, like the shocking, seamless transition from the end of the pensive "No Song" into the fiery, high-voltage duet between guitarist John Abercrombie and drummer Danny Gottlieb that acts as a prelude to the final track, "The Crystal Palace."

In a way this recording showcases not only Bob's continued evolution as a composer but also the guitar virtuosity of John Abercrombie. In the same review, *AAJ* writer Douglas Payne is spot-on in his description of Abercrombie's artistry as a multidimensional artist, as follows: "Abercrombie is simply amazing throughout. He can mine the wealth of innovations from Hendrix and Montgomery to Farlow and Frisell and yet never lose his own multiply-talented identities. Brookmeyer's choice of a main soloist with multiple talents (in this case, Abercrombie) is perfect."[12]

And he concludes: "*Electricity* is highly recommended to the those who appreciate the lost art of orchestral jazz in a contemporary setting, and most especially to fans of John Abercrombie—who is nothing short of brilliant in his varied roles here."[13]

Intermezzo 2: A "Moving" Experience

I was listening for the second or third time to *Electricity* the other day while on Route 80, driving out to New Jersey from our home in Northeast Pennsylvania. A huge mistake! One of my favorite tracks, "Ugly Music," had just begun, and about four minutes into the track, Rainer Brüninghaus's intense, multinoted electric keyboard solo was punctuated by sparse offbeat jabs by the WDR brass section as well as Danny Gottlieb's propulsive drumming. And as if that wasn't enough, Brüninghaus's solo segued seamlessly into John Abercrombie's entrance, with the band rocking full-throttle in and out behind him. It was at that point that I noticed that I was traveling at almost 85 miles an hour! Fortunately, the police were elsewhere when I returned to earth and dropped down to a respectable 70 mph. Talk about being mesmerized by this music!

There are times in each of these three electro-acoustic Brookmeyer recordings when it's difficult to tell whether you're hearing the horn sections of a big band or a synthesizer. A question looms in the final analysis: As listeners, should our ability to identify those differences be important? Personally, I think the essential thing is to take the music in viscerally without approaching it in an intellectual fashion—for example, sonic theory and the technological differences between acoustic instruments and synthesizers—ouch! More specifically, I think that if he were here, Bob would hope that you would take the time to sit and listen and maybe just feel the music on an evocative and personal level, rather than on an analytical one. After all, talking about music is not the same as experiencing it—just like thinking about a painting and the technical skill it took to paint it rather than how it evokes certain feelings in you as you spend some time with it for a while.

So, then, does it really matter whether the sounds you're hearing are produced by a brass section or by a synthesizer? My guess is that as a listener, you may not really care. It's the overall effect of the music you are experiencing that may either draw you in or turn you off. The choice is yours.

Second Chances: Gifts From the Universe

Lately, I've been thinking about Bob Brookmeyer's journey and all of the transitions he made, both artistically and personally. We've been looking at Bob two different ways: through the lens of his recordings, both as instrumentalist and composer/arranger, and through the struggles of his decades-long journey from bitterness and anger to a calmer and more positive existence. I think that Bob began feeling that a higher power of some magnitude was at work. In Eric Nemeyer's incisive 2009 *Jazz Inside* interview, Bob alludes to composer Igor Stravinsky, who says that when a composer discovers the nucleus or the central essence of what he is writing, he then finds the "core" of the music, which he calls "Inspiration." In Bob's words, "All of a sudden, or slowly, he [Stravinsky] said that a light shines invisibly on you and that's when you've found the center of the piece. Well, if there's a center to the piece . . . then we're dealing—not quite in spiritual terms, although we should be—because there is a music God who gives you a chance to write music well."[14]

So when Nemeyer asked whether Bob believed that there was a connection between music and spirituality, he responded by saying he believed that there was. Knowing Bob as I did, I really do think that he was given a variety of second chances throughout the last half of his life which would enable him to explore new forms of creative musical expression and for the first time, to find real love and peace in his personal life.

A Dream Ensemble: The New Art Orchestra (1997–2011)

I wonder if in his final years, Bob knew just how beloved he was to so many people. If the New Art Orchestra was any indication, it's clear to me that Bob knew that he had found at last what he had been seeking for so long. In his words: "The players in the NAO are wonderful to work with and have a fresh attitude toward making music. The feeling is unlike anything I've experienced in my life. We were together for three summers at the festival and decided that it was too good to let it go. The good will and beautiful playing of the musicians cannot be described in words . . . just music. They have my eternal gratitude for making my life and music shine."[15]

Beginnings

> After rehearsing and playing as the Schleswig-Holstein Musik Festival's Big Band in Lübeck, Germany, which we did annually for a number of years, Bob would always joke that it's time to tear the "Schleswig-Holstein Big Band" sign off the bus and change it to "New Art Orchestra" as we headed south for more gigs. The young band grew quickly during those weeks of six to eight-hour rehearsal days because we were all in. It was not just a gig, it was more than that, and we all really wanted to be there. We did our best to do everything Bob asked, like when he urged the brass to "make it sound like French horns" or when he told us "there are no short notes, only long notes and long short notes."
> —John Hollenbeck

The New Art Orchestra came into existence during a dinner conversation between Bob and a producer of Germany's yearly classical music festival which John Hollenbeck references above. The result of that conversation was the development of a plan to assemble a big band to premiere Bob's compositions at the festival.

Bob held international auditions, which required interested applicants to submit cassette tapes showcasing their musicianship. After hours of listening to all of the audition tapes, Bob finally made decisions as to who would populate each section. The Schleswig-Holstein Big Band was born!

A pair of Brookmeyer compositions were written, one each for two of Bob's closest collaborators, Gerry Mulligan (*Celebration Suite*) and trumpeter/flugelhornist Clark Terry ("Silver Lining," "Gwen," "Glide," and "Blue Devils," the *Clark Terry Birthday Suite*). These compositions were premiered at the festival in 1994 and 1995, respectively. The third year the band reprised the *Celebration Suite*, this time featuring the tenor saxophonist Michael Brecker due to Mulligan's passing early in 1996.

Even though the festival ostensibly abandoned jazz later that third year, the band wanted to continue playing together. According to Bob, "The band wanted to stay together. They gave themselves a name, The New Art Orchestra. For better or ill, that was our name so we started. The first thing I thought we'd do was make a record. We went to Bauer Studio in Germany and recorded Celebration Suite and some other music and we had our first record."[16]

New Works Celebration (1997)

It's not hyperbole to say that this recording documents the beginning of Bob Brookmeyer's love affair with the New Art Orchestra. Released in 1999 after being recorded several years earlier, *New Works* was the debut recording of Bob's New Art Orchestra that, in addition to Bob's writing, features the brilliant Scott Robinson playing baritone saxophone solos on each of the four movements of *Celebration Suite*:

"Celebration Jig," "Celebration Slow Dance," "Celebration Remembering," and "Celebration Two And." It's important to note that the work was originally written to feature Bob's old friend and musical colleague Gerry Mulligan, baritone saxophonist, who performed it in 1994 with the NAO at the Schleswig-Holstein Musik Festival. However, a major change was about to happen. Drummer John Hollenbeck sets the stage for us: "One of the first compositions Bob wrote for us was 'Celebration Suite' and our first guest [was] Gerry Mulligan. We premiered it at the Schleswig-Holstein Festival in 1994, and after Gerry passed in 1996, we recorded it for the album *New Works Celebration* with one of Bob's favorite players (and mine!) [baritone saxophonist] Scott Robinson. The sound of the New Art Orchestra, which had been evolving, coalesced on this album into a sound that was unique and distinctly ours."[17]

I'd like to offer brief descriptions of each of the four movements of the *Suite*, which I hope will pique your interest enough so that you will consider listening to the entire recording and using these little diving-board narratives as jumping off points into the music itself. You won't be disappointed.

Celebration: "Jig"

Although the exact origin of the word "jig" is unknown, it has come to be thought of as a happy, energetic folk dance, most notably popular in both Ireland and England throughout the histories of both countries.

This first movement of the Brookmeyer *Celebration Suite* was indeed a cause for elation, since Bob finally found and nurtured an ensemble that was truly his own, one that approached every one of Bob's compositions with both humility and youthful zeal. All of that is evident in this first movement with its glorious opening fanfare and introduction to featured soloist Scott Robinson, who, accompanied mostly by drummer John Hollenbeck, sets the stage for the ensemble's punches and colorful bagpipe-like colorations that become part of the saxophone/drums dialogue. The build to furioso keeps us on the edge of our seats, and all too soon the jig is over. The first time I heard "Jig," at the end, I found myself wanting more. Maybe you will too.

Celebration: "Slow Dance"

"Slow Dance" doesn't really fall into the ballad category, in that once it gets going, it is in reality a medium tempo, finger popping, big band swinger, and has a very easy feel to it, largely due to the fact that it was written as a showcase for Gerry; hence the medium swing groove tempo was a good choice, since it gave everyone in both the audience and the orchestra a chance to take a breath, including Gerry in performance and, later, Scott Robinson, whose approach to stepping in for Mulligan after the latter's passing was the best thing that could've happened. Scott doesn't as much try to emulate Gerry's approach to soloing, and he captures the feel of "Slow Dance" in his relaxed, lyrical performance of both the written music and his improvisations.

Celebration: "Remembering"

To say that this evocative ballad is a lament, a tone poem, an elegy, or an eclogue is like jumping into the deep end of a swimming pool filled with folks who always seem anxious to hang labels on this style or that, particularly when it comes to the fine and performing arts. In the case of music—most notably this movement of the suite—maybe any of the labels above could be used when really listening to "Remembering." The feeling that flows through the piece seems to be one that has a kind of quiet melancholy; Scott's first entrance with Kris Goessens's piano tells a story—yours and mine. With the exception of Gerry Mulligan or Harry Carney, seldom have I heard such tenderness come out of a baritone saxophone as I have in Scott's performance. No note left uncaressed.

Celebration: "Two And"

No, that is not a typo in the title of this final movement; it's Bob's famously oblique sense of humor at play once again. Regrettably,

I never had the chance to ask him about the origin of "Two And," and even if I would've had the opportunity to do so, Bob probably would have changed the subject!

"Two And" is built around a two-note figure that is repeated through much of the movement, first briefly by the electric keyboard and the drums, then by the full ensemble. After a minute the baritone saxophone enters to answer the short two-note bursts by the ensemble (typical Brookmeyer). The original motif returns, stated by what sounds like trombone and baritone saxophone. Shortly thereafter, the ensemble reenters with a short, hard-swinging interlude, leading to a more extended solo flight by Scott, who never drops the ball or turns the heat down. The ensemble soon reenters with the same interlude it began with before Scott's solo; then Bob jumps in and treats us to an example of why he has been praised consistently as one of jazz's great solo voices. He builds his solo with economy, spacing his notes between band accents and Hollenbeck's simpatico drumming. And, as always, his sound and articulation is nonpareil, always his own.

And then, a surprise, especially to those of us who are familiar with Bob's work as a key member of Mulligan's quartet, sextet, and Concert Jazz Band. In all three of those configurations, one of the highlights was always when Bob and Gerry would solo individually first, then contrapuntally; that is, they would often solo simultaneously, weaving their melodic lines together to create a third voice. Gerry first experimented with the contrapuntal concept with trumpeter Chet Baker in a piano-less quartet; however, when Chet left, Bob replaced him. In my opinion it was a better match because the baritone and the trombone were in the same register, so playing in unison and simultaneously gave the quartet a distinctly warmer sound.

That warmth is in evidence here: Bob and Scott trade four-bar solo phrases, then one-bar phrases, then begin improvising freely together until Bob plays a phrase that seems like an invitation for Scott to join him. They linger on that phrase, and once the ensemble and the drums drop out, the two deconstruct the phrase to the point at which they sound like a trombone and baritone sax laughing slowly at a not-so-funny joke before ending together on five very languid sounding notes. All of this drama comes to a close as drums roll and the trumpets play two long notes, followed by dirgelike drumbeats that very slowly ritard into a single final chord. The celebration has finally ended.

"Cameo": A Lovely Postscript

Even though it's not part of the *Suite*, I felt compelled to include this track for sentimental reasons, which will become clear in a moment.

When I heard "Cameo" for the first time, I was a bit taken aback. It wasn't just the atmospheric beauty of the introduction played by the winds in the first eight measures; sure, that was part of the magic, and Bob's solo entrance was beautifully fashioned, spontaneously creating a "song" on the spot. It was in those first eight measures of his solo that I realized that, without stating the standard's melody, he was playing what I knew to be one of his favorite ballads, one that we played a lot before he left Los Angeles and even the times when he returned and kept it in our set list.

So hearing Bob playing over the chord changes of the 1936 Vernon Duke–Ira Gershwin classic, "I Can't Get Started"—this time with the New Art Orchestra—was the icing on the cake. If you were to listen to the track, you might notice how Bob is really duetting with the orchestra. Sort of having a conversation, where he plays a few notes and the orchestra responds each time. He weaves in and out of the horns in such a way that their accompaniment becomes an integral part of his solo. We know from chapter 4 that Bob used this kind of technique before on previous recordings, but nowhere that I can think of was it more elegant than it is here on "Cameo." Closing my eyes, all I could envision was a solo ballet dancer moving around and through a troupe of supporting dancers, a la Tchaikovsky's *Nutcracker Suite*, for example. The grace and ease with which the orchestra plays around and through Bob is exemplary—a musical symbiosis, to be sure. *New Works Celebration* is very thematically diverse recording from track to track and its riches are plentiful, and always Bob's iconoclastic genius permeates every note in each movement. One thing can be said for sure: It's very clear that this recording and the successive Brookmeyer–New Art Orchestra collaborations mark the final—and to my ears most notable—evolution in Bob's composing and arranging aesthetic. Here as in the next three recordings, Bob has created music that gifts the New Art Orchestra with a unique sonic and rhythmic persona, one that becomes almost immediately recognizable after a single listening. I have a feeling that these recordings will be elevated to their proper place in the pantheon of distinctive large jazz ensemble music far into the future.

Watering the NAO Garden

While I offered my abridged descriptions of each movement of *Celebration Suite* as well as the stand-alone piece "Cameo" from the New Art Orchestra's debut recording, I'd like to explain my modus operandi for introducing each of the next three NAO recordings.

If you look back in chapter 4, you'll notice that Bob's first three big band albums as a leader for VIK, Atlantic, and Verve Records, respectively, were all recorded with different personnel, each assembled specifically for the purpose of highlighting Bob's creative talents as a composer, arranger, and soloist. I found it almost effortless to write about all three records individually and offer you some highlights of select tracks, largely because I grew up with each recording in the early '60s. Looking back at them now, as well as Bob's two albums as musical director and occasional soloist with the Mel Lewis Jazz Orchestra in the early '80s, I think that the changes in Bob's music—both on score paper and as a soloist—became much more evident to me as the years passed.

However, one of the greatest challenges for me was to immerse myself in Bob's creative development of the New Art Orchestra and its music. Unlike the first three big band albums, the personnel of the New Art Orchestra was largely stable, except for a few personnel changes from disc to disc. So rather than focusing only upon the NAO's soloists, I'd like to offer my reactions to two songs each from *Waltzing with Zoe, Get Well Soon,* and *Spirit Music.*

Waltzing with Zoe (2002)

This second recording is comprised largely of pieces that Bob composed and dedicated to a variety of people, among them the (then) 10-year-old Zoe, daughter of the virtuoso trombonist Hal Crook; protégé Maria Schneider, a brilliant award-winning composer and orchestra leader; and of course, Janet Brookmeyer, the most important woman in Bob's life. In the liner notes to *Waltzing with Zoe,* Bob describes the album thus: "It arrived as 'character pieces,' with a will of their own and I sometimes felt like a transcriber, following orders."[18]

The two compositions I chose couldn't be more different from each other. The first is "Sweetie," which, as mentioned earlier, is a portrait of Bob's wife Jan. From the first measure to the last, "Sweetie" sounds like who Jan is: the mist on the Seine River in early morning; the soft infusion of pastels floating in and out of the mist, offering tranquility and peace. Knowing Jan all these years, I can attest that she is all of that and more. You can hear that in Bob's solo. Listen to it a few times, and maybe it will remind you of someone special enough to be your own "sweetie."

The track begins with a brief (half-minute) single-note melody played slowly by pianist Kris Goessens, with what sounds like a synth providing a very soft cushion of long tones. The orchestra enters at that point, playing three-note fragments of the theme spaced in such a way that we really don't realize that what Bob has done is sliced the theme up here and there, like pieces in a jigsaw puzzle.

The "ah-HA!" moment happens when Bob enters with the first complete statement of the melody, which was only hinted at previously in small, sparse fragments by the orchestra. His trombone voice sings the song and shows us once again why he was one of the most lyrical soloists in jazz history. Not a musical cliché to be found. I can envision Bob playing this solo, holding his horn straight out, parallel with the floor, then moving it slowly in an upward arc and bringing it back down just as slowly as he plays another phrase.

"KP '94" stands for "King Porter," which is short for Jelly Roll Morton's "King Porter Stomp," and the "94" is short for the year 1994, when Bob deconstructed it. If you'll remember from the preceding chapter, when Bob was the musical director of the Mel Lewis Jazz Orchestra, he took apart the song "My Funny Valentine," dissected it to the point where it became almost unrecognizable. I say "almost" because there were snippets of the original melody placed sporadically here and there that you might be able to identify if you were well acquainted with the song. If, on the other hand, you were not, then you were out of luck.

Sadly, if you're looking for *any* trace of Morton's 1923 jazz classic in "KP '94"—musician or not—you will come up empty-handed. Believe me, I tried to find a musical connection between the two. I even listened a few times each to a variety of other renditions, including both the original Fletcher Henderson arrangement as played by his band and the one by Benny Goodman and his orchestra, recorded live in 1938 at his memorable Carnegie Hall Concert.

The final conventional version of "King Porter Stomp," a 1959 Brookmeyer arrangement on *Stretching Out*, features an octet album he co-led with saxophonist Zoot Sims for United Artists. Unfortunately, I hit a brick wall each time I searched for a familiar musical phrase that might be paired with something in one of the earlier versions. I know that Bob loved the swing era versions of the song; so why did he turn it inside out and upside down to essentially create an entirely new composition? I went immediately to Dave Rivello's book of conversations with Bob to seek and hopefully find something from Bob in the way of an explanation that would shed some light on how exactly "King Porter Stomp" could be recognized somewhere in "KP '94." Here is a portion of what Bob said when Dave mentioned the composition: "Oh that was crazy! I love 'King Porter Stomp.' I'd already made two or three records of it, and this time I took it completely apart. There were seven major elements that I extracted and used to create a new piece. I don't like it so much . . . but the band likes it and everywhere we go, it is well received. It has some good things in it and I think it works okay and maybe it gives a hint of the song. I don't know."[19]

And much later in 2013, NAO's drummer John Hollenbeck added this: "Waltzing with Zoe is my favorite in terms of repertoire, which is so varied; and it includes 'KP '94,' which we had to push Bob to record because audiences (who were most likely expecting to hear something closer to Benny Goodman that night) were perplexed by it, making Bob unsure of it. But we knew it was a masterpiece!"[20]

A masterpiece. Indeed it is! I wish only that, after all was said and done, Bob would've given "KP '94" a different title.

Overview: A Few Words About the Music

"KP '94" is the only Brookmeyer composition in his oeuvre that I know of that does not feature any solos. In fact, I see the New Art Orchestra itself as the soloist here, in that it is a showcase for the orchestra as a whole. The brass and woodwind sections are in perpetual motion, often reacting to each other in a kind of call-and-response mode as well as creating separate thematic statements that ultimately weave around and through each other, creating two independent melodic lines—kind of like the way Brookmeyer and Mulligan or Brookmeyer and Getz would improvise together at the same time (contrapuntally), creating sort of a third voice. There is no improvisation here, except from drummer Hollenbeck, who, along with sparse support from his rhythm section teammates, provides a rhythmic commentary that connects the sections together throughout the piece.

A Needle Drop Road Map for "KP '94"

Please note that I have added what we used to call "needle drops" or "time stamps" in parentheses here and there in the narrative which follows. As a rule, I don't often include time stamps because you as reader don't need to know when a saxophone solo begins; you can hear it. So there's really no need to indicate it with a phrase like "when the sax solo begins (@3:27)." However, as mentioned initially, there are no solos in this piece; so if you are listening to "KP '94," read the road map below, either before or—if you are the adventurous type—while listening to the track. I only include what follows as an option.

The piece opens with an ascending rhythmic figure from the trumpet section that gets progressively louder and reaches a rather jarring peak before ultimately becoming more distant sounding, moving us with a similar figure, supported by the trombones and possibly the saxophones, into the next section and a repetitive vamp-like rhythmic figure from the rhythm section that sets the stage for a saxophone section soli (@2:00). The brass soon reenters, this time in the background, and ultimately dances contrapuntally with the saxes until the point where they merge and play an introduction to the next part of the piece, another saxophone soli—this one longer than the first, supported by the drums and pedal tones from the low brass and drums; and suddenly (@2:21) we're transported to some traditional hard-swinging big band shouting for a moment or two, then more movement between the brass and the saxes; then it's back to the rhythm-section figure (@3:18) and a return to the melody first heard near the beginning of the piece, replete with the ascending brass figure culminating in a very shrill, make-your-teeth-hurt explosion from the trumpet section (@4:22)—followed (@4:27) by a fugue-like section with all hands on deck, moving in and out of each other's phrases with staggered entrances and call-and-response moments.

"KP '94" begins to wind down slowly at that point, perhaps a welcome release from the roller coaster we've been riding on for the past five or so minutes. The winds enter once more, winding down, after which we are left with the original keyboard vamp figure, with drums adding commentary between phrases (@5:37). Trumpets and saxophones reenter (@5:57), which leads into a restatement of the original theme (@6:17), followed by a final statement alone from the keyboard and a very tongue-in-cheek, almost corny rubato six-note ending, led by the trumpet section. This left me with a question, rather than the kind of resolution I was hoping for. Why, after so much intensity and excitement, did Bob leave us with an ending that was the complete antithesis of all that came before? All I could think of was that, in the final analysis, Bob has gifted us with an incredible groundbreaking piece of music that concludes with a typically oblique Brookmeyer ending. Maybe the joke's on us.

Get Well Soon (2002)

This third New Art Orchestra album was recorded during the summer of 2002 in Germany and features guest soloist and popular virtuoso German trumpeter/flugelhornist Till Brönner. Bob met Brönner in 1999, where the latter was a guest soloist with the NAO. Here's how Bob describes their first musical meeting: "I had heard a little of him on CD but was completely unprepared when we began 'Tah- DUM' at the rehearsal. The jaw hitting the floor was mine. An amazing player . . . AND—he swung!!"[21]

Instead of beginning with my own accolades with respect to this recording, I'd like to pass the torch to a writer whose work I've come to admire. Jack Bowers has been reviewing jazz records for the award-winning blog *AllAboutJazz* for quite a few years. I find his in-depth reviews to be very perceptive and accessible. Here is his brief but succinct overview of both the NAO and *Get Well Soon*, published in AAJ on August 11, 2004:

> Get Well Soon is the third recording by the New Art Orchestra, an eighteen-piece ensemble formed nearly two decades ago in Lubeck, Germany, as a jazz component of the Schleswig-Holstein Musik Festival and overseen since its inception by the renowned American trombonist and composer, Bob Brookmeyer. Brookmeyer loves the NAO ("It has been my good fortune to become associated with an incredible group of people," he says. "They love what they do, they thrive on their friendships, and they give everything they have to me and my music")—and the NAO loves him back, the proof of which is readily apparent to anyone who peruses the results of their collaborative efforts.

To Brookmeyer, love doesn't mean spoon-feeding his colleagues easily digestible fodder, and the charts he sets before them are as strenuous and sophisticated as one could envision. But the NAO seems unfazed, mastering the tricky metric shifts and harmonic variations with the sort of ease one associates with a leisurely stroll in the park. As a writer, Brookmeyer calls to mind Bill Holman and Gil Evans, among others, singular artists who use the entire orchestra as a canvas on which to paint their elaborate and expressive musical portraits. This is nowhere more apparent than on the exuberant opener, "Tah-DUM!," on which the NAO offers guest trumpeter Till Brönner a lively welcome with pianist Kris Goessens and drummer John Hollenbeck setting the compass while Brönner dances nimbly through and around the changes.

Brönner is also showcased on "Monster Rally," "Over Here" and the entrancing ballad "For You" (on flugelhorn); Goessens on "Song, Sing, Sung" and "Elegy"; tenor saxophonist Paul Heller on "Get Well Soon," the last written for Brookmeyer's Norwegian friend Jan Horne, who is recovering from a recent battle with cancer (and credits Brookmeyer's composition with hastening the healing process). As for Brookmeyer, who now considers himself "a composer who also plays [valve] trombone," he has the two brief "Interludes" largely to himself, and, as always, solos marvelously.

The mournful "Elegy" was penned for another of Brookmeyer's friends, composer Earle Brown, who was near death when it was written. The orchestra doesn't let him down, nor does Goessens, whose eloquent and responsive solo heightens its emotional impact. From "Elegy," the NAO launches into the powerful "Get Well Soon" goaded by Hollenbeck's assertive drumming and animated by Heller's loquacious solo—an altogether suitable conclusion to an impressive panorama by two bright and indomitable forces, Bob Brookmeyer and the New Art Orchestra.[22]

The three soloists on this recording—trumpeter/flugelhornist Till Brönner, pianist Kris Goessens, and saxophonist Paul Heller—are worthy of all possible praise, and are certainly deserving of much more recognition here in the United States. Each can stand side-by-side with the best, most creative jazz musicians playing anywhere today.

Till Brönner is an absolute wonder. He plays with great facility and imagination. And like most virtuosos, he makes it all seem so effortless. His speed-of-light execution at medium and fast tempos is nothing short of phenomenal. However, rather than focus upon Till's brilliance on the faster songs, I'd like to spend a few minutes to highlight his performance on the ballad called "For You." One of the things my mentors impressed upon me when I was coming up was that the true test of a jazz player was how well he or she played on a ballad. A ballad solo should reflect and honor the emotional vibe of the melody and the lyrics (if the song has words), and the soloist should be able to caress and embody the overall feeling of whatever the composer of the song has created. Till offers us a beautiful example of that approach. He takes the time to develop a gentle series of well-connected phrases that celebrate both Bob's melody and the orchestra's accompaniment. It is, in a sense, the perfect marriage of flugelhorn and ensemble, with Till floating above the sonic landscapes that Bob has created.

One day in his basement studio in New Hampshire, Bob introduced me to the music of pianist Kris Goessens, first by talking about Kris's importance as a pianist and composer, and then—if memory serves me correctly—by playing some of Kris's performances in a duo setting with Bob. In Bob's words from the liner notes, "Kris Goessens is one of the world's best kept secrets. . . . He has the depth of feeling and touch that I find unequaled by anyone I have heard. He also has a quiet daring, use of space and register that break accepted barriers, AND patience to allow an idea to unfold and fully speak. His language is his and he feels almost painfully the act of creation."[23]

I've already introduced you to Kris's talents in chapter 3, when discussing Bob's European quartet and what an important contribution Kris's playing and composing made throughout the *Paris Suite* sessions. Kris exhibits the very same qualities that Bob describes in his words about Kris's playing on "Elegy," the composition Bob dedicated to his mentor, the late Earle Brown. I can think of only a few other pianists who play as delicately yet with such emotional power as Kris Goessens.

I am probably biased since for quite a few years I have been listening to a lot of classical pianists, and the one I keep coming back to time and again is Mitsuko Uchida, the Grammy-winning Japanese-British pianist and conductor. Ms. Uchida is my favorite classical pianist, primarily because of her exquisite touch and her phrasing, especially noticeable when she chooses to play Mozart, Schubert, and Debussy. The silence between her notes and phrases is, for me, exhilarating without seeming pretentious.

While the same characteristics Ms. Uchida exhibits in her approach to performance can also be found in Kris's playing, it has also been the hallmark for many of the most gifted jazz musicians who preceded him. For example, the great pianist Ahmad Jamal understood the value and importance of economy and spacing in his solos, as did pianist Bill Evans, guitarist Jim Hall, bassist Ron Carter, saxophonists Sonny Rollins and Wayne Shorter, and, of course, trumpeter Miles Davis, to name only a few. Bob Brookmeyer valued those attributes as well, as evidenced by his unique artistry as both a player and as a composer and arranger. I think that is one of the many reasons Bob loved playing with Kris. "Elegy" exemplifies the quiet emotional level so necessary to the composition, and Kris' playing throughout displays what Bob called his superb "depth of feeling and touch," from beginning to end. For example, in Kris's thirty-second solo introduction at the beginning of "Elegy," it's almost as though he caresses each phrase lightly with an uncanny sense of how best to complement the Orchestra's initial entrance; and throughout the piece, he meshes perfectly with them, especially with whomever is carrying the weight of the melody so beautifully on English horn.

And toward the end, there is a very quiet, magical moment just after minute 7:00 when the orchestra pauses, and in that silence all you can hear is the barely audible chiming of four single midrange piano notes, after which Kris reenters atop the continued chiming with a sparse solo meditation before the orchestra responds and plays the final statement with Kris's gentle obbligatos, bringing "Elegy" to an end.

Kris was a truly important young pianist who passed away unexpectedly in 2013. As with so many other great musicians, he left us much too soon. While I never knew Kris, I feel that this lovely composition could also be thought of as an elegy to him as well.

The third soloist I'd like to focus on in this section is tenor saxophonist Paul Heller. Truthfully, I'd never heard of him until the NAO's appearance in New York City at the final concert of the International Association of Jazz Educators' Conference in 2004. Bob had some very positive things to say about Paul in his liner notes to *Get Well Soon*. Here's an excerpt: "With the flood of tenor saxophonists surrounding us [in the NAO auditions], finding Paul in 1994 was a new beginning for me and the instrument. He looks like an angel and plays like the devil AND—he gets excited!! When the band begins to roar he cannot help feeling the excitement and joins in. This is NOT a normal response for most musicians playing any instrument these days—people have become careful and organized. Not Paul—he screams with delight! A stunning performance [on the title track]."[24]

Some jazz critics, when describing a particular instrumentalist's style, will liken him or her to a past master. In the case of the tenor saxophone, a critic might say that so-and-so "has been influenced by both Coleman Hawkins and Sonny Rollins, with a bit of Chu Berry thrown into the mix." I suppose that kind of description would be helpful for some readers. But I also find that sometimes, those kinds of comparisons tend to compartmentalize a player stylistically, in a way that places him or her in a box—one that tells only a part of that person's story.

You'll notice that in his liner notes excerpted previously, Bob uses metaphors to describe Paul Heller's approach to improvisation (e.g., "he screams with delight!").[25] He has done that before in other liner note writings as well, describing one other saxophonist thus: "My, my, that gentleman can speak such nice language through the horn."[26]

These kinds of descriptions are far more inviting and may well pique a reader's interest, more so that telling us who they sound like.

With that in mind, I read Bob's comments about 31-year-old Paul Heller before listening to his solo, which is the centerpiece of the final track, "Get Well Soon." This composition feels like a fitting finale to the entire recording. It bursts out of the gate with exchanges between the orchestra and Hollenbeck's spot-on fills. After a short orchestral interlude, we get a taste of what's to come, with Heller's muscular sixteen-bar solo at the forefront, after which the orchestra returns, setting up a more lengthy solo statement by Heller, one that builds here and there into an intense foray in the upper register of the tenor horn, as well as some dazzling multinoted phrasing that moves from the bottom of the tenor to the top.

Brookmeyer exemplifies his own close listening skills in his preceding quote, describing Heller's "screams of delight." Coming from Brookmeyer, a metaphor like that is pure gold.

If someone were to ask me who Paul Heller sounds like, I'd be quick to say, "He sounds like Paul Heller!" When the orchestra pulls out all the stops, Heller reaches a fever pitch and indeed, shouts with what sounds to me like great joy borne out of the happiness that comes with being a part of the New Art Orchestra and the ongoing Brookmeyer oeuvre. Bob calls Paul Heller's performance "stunning," and I couldn't agree with him more.

It's wholly appropriate that *Get Well Soon* ends on an upbeat note. With this third recording, the New Art Orchestra continues to maintain its standard of excellence. Once again, every track is a jewel. And once again, if we close our eyes and open our ears, we become an essential part of the experience.

Spirit Music (2006)

First, a few words about jazz critics and writers. It was purportedly composer Jean Sibelius who said something like "Pay no attention to what the critics say. A statue has never been erected in honor of a critic."[27] While there have been so-called jazz critics who truly deserve that brickbat, there are many that I know of who have written about the music and musicians incisively, in such a way that their reviews of performances and recordings (and their jazz writing in general) are accessible and enlightening. As mentioned earlier, I have found that books and/or reviews by writers like Nat Hentoff, Whitney Balliett, Doug Ramsey, Bill Crow, A. B. Spellman, and Amiri Baraka have been most influential to me as a writer. Among the best of the current authors are Ben Ratliff, Scott Yanow, Dave Liebman, Robin D. G. Kelley, and Ashley Kahn, each of whom have been very inspiring and have been invaluable resources for helping us to develop a solid grounding in all aspects of the music—past, present and future; these and others are the writers who have helped to keep the music alive and have contributed significantly to its continued growth and development.

Two wordsmiths whose work I have enjoyed while writing this book are the aforementioned Jack Bowers and David Franklin, both of whom have written reviews for *AllAboutJazz*; you've already read Bowers's review of *Get Well Soon.* Here is Franklin's review of *Spirit Music*, which also appeared in *AllAboutJazz:*

> Bob Brookmeyer doesn't write conventional big band "charts." Instead, he composes sophisticated, creative works for jazz orchestra that fuse traditional big-band techniques with elements from the broader musical landscape. Yet as advanced as Brookmeyer's approach is, it doesn't require either a composer's ear or a theorist's knowledge to relate to it. *Spirit Music*, his latest offering with his superb Germany-based New Art orchestra is suffused with beautiful melodies and gorgeous harmonies—and its pulse is always present, even if it's at times flexible. "The Door" opens the album in simple fashion with an extended pedal point [being a note that is held often by the bass or lower register wind instruments underneath changing harmonies], and in keeping with the composer's aim for an integrated program, a similar pedal closes "The End," the final track. The music in between, much of it projecting a folk like and

pensive—sometimes melancholy—mood, is consistently interesting and emotionally satisfying.

Brookmeyer solos on the most straight-ahead track, "Silver Lining" (a cousin to "Blue Skies"), and on the ruminative "Alone." His valve trombone brings an earthy Kansas City sensibility to both.

The ensemble is as good as they come—precise and cohesive, perfectly in tune and ideally balanced. As Brookmeyer would have it, the fine soloists strive to integrate their improvisations with the compositions.[28]

"Don't Just Do Something, Sit There!" —Sylvia Boorstein[29]

As I've opined elsewhere, sometimes when we overly intellectualize about music—or for that matter, any art form—we take the wind out of its sails. Sometimes unwittingly, we try in vain to explain the unexplainable in music, when all we have to do as listeners is to sit back and let the sonorities carry us into our inner selves. So all I can give you here is how *Spirit Music* made me *feel*:

Joyful	"Happy Song" and "Dance for Life"
Intrigued	"The Door"
Wistful	"New Love"
Sad	"Alone"
Tearful	"The End"
Inspired	"Silver Lining"

I added "Tearful" to the list above, although for the life of me, I don't know exactly why; but at the end of the day, I can admit to you that it's probably because of the title itself. *Spirit Music* felt to me like a swan song, even though I don't believe that Bob intended it to be one; however, in his liner notes, he admits that "2004 and 2005 were rough emotional years at times, and I had trouble bouncing back to my motivated and busy self."[30]

As alluded to earlier, when asked one time if he felt that there was a connection between music and spirituality, Bob responded by surmising that there had to be. I regret that he and I never got around to talking about that. I would have wanted to ask him how that manifested itself whenever we played together, most notably in the midst of a tune, when I opened my eyes and he would be sending a smile my way.

There is sort of an emotional undercurrent at work here, at least for me—a feeling I got through each of the multiple times I listened to this last NAO recording. A gentle mellowness, if you will, even on the up-tempo swingers. This is an ensemble that seems comfortable in its own skin. They appear to be so wired into Bob's music that it feels here and there like a single organism creating each piece spontaneously. There is a palpable motion throughout that invites us to be part of the experience. I know, as do many others who were his students, bandmates, and fans, that being moved by the music is what Bob hoped would be a takeaway for all.

Intermezzo 3: The New Art Orchestra Performance at the International Association of Jazz Education Conference (2004)

It was the final night of one of the last conferences held by the International Association for Jazz Education (IAJE). The auditorium was packed and there was standing room only in the back and on the sides of the room. Attendees were there to hear Bob's New Art Orchestra, made up of mostly Dutch musicians, as well as several from neighboring countries, and American drummer John Hollenbeck.

If memory serves me correctly, after the musicians were in place, once he was announced, Bob entered the stage to vigorous applause.

After all, here was a living legend, the guy whose forty-plus year metamorphosis enabled him to become an esteemed composer, arranger, beloved teacher, and instrumentalist—all of which led to not one but two honorary doctorates: one from the New England Conservatory of Music and the other from the University of Missouri, Kansas

City. Bob was also awarded Jazz Master Status from the National Endowment for the Arts in 2006.

While I don't recall the Brookmeyer compositions that they played, I do remember being astounded by the sheer immensity of the music, its twists and turns and accentuations, and the brilliant playing by all hands, from soloists to section players. With Bob at the helm, playing and conducting beautifully, John Hollenbeck's fiercely supportive and authoritative drumming, and the stunning soloists and ensemble performances, it was as though the NAO was a living, breathing entity—the incredible sum of its parts. I'm reasonably sure the audience felt it too, because at the end of the concert, the entire house stood and cheered! A huge triumph for Bob and the New Art Orchestra.

After so many years of being "the best man," Bob was finally the groom!

The Final Recording: *Brookmeyer/Standards*

Regrettably, *Spirit Music* would be the last recording project to feature Bob's compositions; however, the final NAO recording as an ensemble came five years later in 2011, and was simply called *Brookmeyer/Standards*, featuring the remarkable vocalist Fay Claassen, the equally remarkable New Art Orchestra, and, of course, Bob's arrangements—this time of well-known songs culled from the Great American Songbook.

I remember asking Bob a sometime in the early '80s about the possibility of arranging and recording some more standards; after all, he arranged classics like the Johnny Mercer–Hoagy Carmichael ballad "Skylark," Ann Ronell's "Willow Weep for Me," Herb Ellis, Johnny Frigo, and Lou Carter's "Detour Ahead," and W. C. Handy's "St. Louis Blues"—just a few beautifully realized examples of his growing mastery. Why not continue along that path? In retrospect I think it was a ridiculous question, one that, if I remember correctly, he rightfully shrugged off.

Bob and I also spent time during our various New Hampshire visits in his home studio listening to quite a bit of jazz, including early masters like Basie, Woody Herman, Sauter-Finnegan, Lester Young, and many others from all eras of the music. One thing I remember distinctly during those visits was the enthusiasm Bob had for a singer named Mary Ann McCall, someone I had never heard of. Mary Ann sang with a number of high-profile big bands led by Woody Herman, Artie Shaw, and Tommy Dorsey, and others, and over a period of three decades was in and out of view in the jazz world. Bob played some examples of her work with Woody's big band, but even though she sounded very good and could swing with the best of them, I didn't really share Bob's enthusiasm, since Billie Holiday was my all-time favorite. All told, that was the only time we ever listened to any other vocalists.

I

For a while vocalists in big bands seemed to be on the periphery of big band culture—sort of extra added attractions, if you will. When I was a kid, I looked at photos of jazz musicians in both big bands and small groups, mostly from the 1930s and '40s. At that time I noticed that in many of the big bands' publicity photos, singers would actually be sitting in front but slightly off to the side of, say, the woodwind section, the men in tuxedos or coats and ties and the women in dresses and heels. Each would sit through the band numbers until the leader would announce that so-and-so would be singing a specially arranged version of a hit tune, something like "Up a Lazy River" or "It Had to Be You." In the arrangements for either individual vocalists or vocal trios or quartets, the bands stayed pretty much in the background, maybe because many big bands, Duke Ellington excluded, were providing music for dancing and not for concertizing, hence the name "dance bands." In those instances the band was there to support the singers, who, after their turn at the microphone, would sit back down and wait for their next vocal feature.

This was not always the case, since the more jazz-oriented big bands and combos featured many phenomenal singers like Billie Holiday (notably with pianist Teddy Wilson), Ella Fitzgerald (early on with drummer Chick Webb), Ivie Anderson and Herb Jeffries (both with Duke Ellington), and Joe Williams and Sarah Vaughn (both notably with Count Basie), to name a few. Whether with a big band or a small group, each of the above stepped up the plate and delivered memorable performances.

II

As we have learned earlier, Bob wrote music that allowed the Mel Lewis Jazz Orchestra and then the New Art Orchestra to have equal footing with a soloist, rather than merely supporting him or her underneath the solo with some type of musical phrase here and there and staying in the background until the solo has ended. What Bob had done was to make the orchestra a participant in the solo by moving the ensemble into the forefront at times, even though the soloist continues to improvise. Specifically, it plays the written passages while integrating itself into the solo, if only for a short time.

Take for example, Joe Lovano's brilliant tenor saxophone solo on Brookmeyer's "The Nasty Dance" on the second Mel Lewis Jazz Orchestra / Village Vanguard album. There are moments during Lovano's blistering commentary when he is deliberately overtaken by the entire ensemble, and yet—even though he is thrust into the background as they move excitingly into the foreground—Joe continues to blow underneath the orchestra until the horns drop down to their previous volume level, at which time Joe resurfaces to finish his improvisation. In effect, the soloist and the ensemble trade places: it became the soloist, even though Joe never broke his stride once during that dramatic role change.

Now we come to Bob's final recording. Even though I was certain it would be a masterpiece (given how each of the NAO/Brookmeyer projects was a sonic universe unto itself), I wondered how he would write arrangements for a singer—whose body of work I was unfamiliar with—given his unique compositional oeuvre.

Honestly, while I've heard (and played with) lots of big bands over the years, I've never experienced anything that comes even remotely close to *Brookmeyer/Standards* in terms of singer Fay Claasen's ability to swing so confidently through Bob's challenging writing. She is not simply someone singing with a big band. Not in the least! Fay is an integral part of the NAO. She quite literally gives voice to the ensemble. She makes the lyrics her own, is solidly in the moment, and creates complementary phrases that mesh well with Bob's imaginative tonal and rhythmic settings. And Fay is truly a singer of songs. No fancy pyrotechnics or scat singing excursions to be found here. Her mastery of pitch and her phrasing are impeccable. Not only is she delivering the songs in their purest form, but she does so unpretentiously and with great feeling. Like Billie Holiday, she tells us a story in each song she sings.

The repertoire for this recording includes Irving Berlin's "How Deep Is the Ocean"; three by Cole Porter: "Get Out of Town," "Love For Sale," and "I Get a Kick Out of You"; Duke Ellington's "I'm Beginning to See the Light," followed by "Come Rain or Come Shine," penned by Harold Arlen and Johnny Mercer; "Detour Ahead" by Herb Ellis, Johnny Frigo, and Lou Carter; and the album's only instrumental, "Willow Weep for Me," a return to Bob's classic arrangement for the Thad Jones/Mel Lewis Orchestra. Each of these songs, incidentally, have been an integral part of the jazz repertory for decades.

After listening to this recording a few times, I think that my favorite piece is the third track, "Love for Sale." I always liked this tune because it more often than not seems to work well in the jazz repertoire as either a medium tempo or up-tempo outing. So upon first listening here—and knowing to expect the unexpected where Bob is concerned—I slapped on my headphones and was ready to take the trip. And as I anticipated, from note one it was unlike any other version of "Love for Sale" I'd ever heard; and speaking of "note one," the track begins with John Hollenbeck setting the slow tempo, playing four sets of triplets on the drums (in 12/8 time), after which the low brass plays a thunderous first note, with the other horns hitting the second and fourth note of each measure. After that explosive setup, Bob throws us a curve ball by . . . you'll have to read what follows here, then listen to "Love for Sale" for yourselves.

It turns out that Maria Schneider, someone whom I hold in very high esteem (as do many of the finest musicians in the world) also feels that Bob's treatment of "Love for Sale" is bound to become a classic big band arrangement (and, in my opinion, an important part of the canon of large jazz ensemble masterworks). Maria's vivid description of the performance in her liner notes is proof that words can help us appreciate it even more. In addition to being a great composer, arranger, and bandleader, Maria is also an excellent wordsmith, which she demonstrates in chapter 6 of this book, and with her wonderful liner notes for *Brookmeyer/Standards*. Here is an excerpt of her comments about "Love for Sale":

> I'd say that "Love for Sale" will now be considered one of Bob's all-time great arrangements. Listen to that massive ensemble opening, and how it suddenly comes down to just piano: gutsy, smart. He [Bob] leaves the accompaniment of Fay's verse to Kris Goessens alone. Then that big intro starts all over for the second part of the verse, again giving way to piano and voice. The ensemble transition to the song has such poignant, warm, lush and at times, astringent chords.
>
> Fay is provided with a perfect little pregnant silence before she sings, "Love . . . for sale." And how perfectly he tailored his ensemble transition to weave behind Fay as she sings the melody.[31]

Listening to this recording nonstop from the first track to the eighth is like opening a treasure chest and finding eight jewels, each refracting a brilliant ray of light as you move it around in the palm of your hand, each stone a fount of an incredible array of colors. While "Love for Sale" is a sensational tour de force, the other seven tracks have so much to offer as well. Each is incomparable, due in large part to the symbiosis that existed between Fay's interpretive power and Bob's nonpareil arrangements—and, of course, the masterful musicians who breathed life into every one of the eight songs.

Brookmeyer/Standards was released by ArtistShare shortly before Bob's passing in late 2011. Fortunately, there is a treasure trove of Brookmeyer recordings—both audio and video—from many decades of his contributions to the jazz art. I don't think I've ever known someone who was as beloved by so many as Bob (as you will discover in the next two chapters); and while his last recording is a fitting swan song, it is by no means a lament. On the contrary, it's a joy! The musical world has not lost Bob. He is in every note of his music, as a composer, arranger, and as a damn fine valve trombonist and pianist. As a friend of mine once said, "Don't cry because it's over; smile because it happened."

Chapter 6

Inside Voices, Shining Lights

Introduction: Doctor Brookmeyer

A bit of background: Bob and Jan moved to Holland in 1990 and returned to Hanover, New Hampshire, four years later. While in Rotterdam he fulfilled a number of commissions and planned to seek funding for a new, innovative music school. Unfortunately, things did not go as planned.

Bob explained the fiasco to Dave Rivello as follows: "I had a commission for an opera and I was going to start a new school. So, we moved to Holland, but I picked the wrong partner for the school. I should've gone to Copenhagen and we'd have made it work, but my partner was a bomb and I couldn't get along with the opera people. The director yes, but nobody else. So after four years we came back and [subsequently] I began teaching at the New England Conservatory."[1]

Bob's eminence as an iconic musician, composer, arranger, and teacher made him an excellent addition to the jazz faculty, and he thrived at NEC for ten years, from 1997 until 2007. As you will read further in subsequent chapters, Bob was revered by many of his

Doctor Brookmeyer at work. Photo courtesy of Ann Corbett.

students, some of whom have gone on to achieve eminence of their own on both a national and global scale.

It's no secret among many who know and are drawn to Bob's musical genius as a composer, arranger, and, of course, legendary instrumentalist that he was an exemplary teacher as well. This chapter offers multiple "portraits of the artist" by some very gifted musicians who studied with Bob over the years, either in an educational setting or in performance or both.

Fortunately, those in academia recognized and were inspired by his eminence. It goes without saying that Bob brought a wealth of experience to the table as a composer, arranger, and as a player. Couple these gifts with his unique and challenging instructional methods—and his innate love of teaching and his students—and you have a clear picture of who Bob became in the latter years of his life. Three years before his passing in 2011, Bob was awarded an honorary doctorate from the NEC in honor of his decades-long multidimensional musical career and his ten years of service to the conservatory and especially to his many students.

This from the *NEC Publication* website:

> Bob had a huge impact on an entire generation of NEC students. He was one of the greatest player/composers in the history of jazz. He improvised with the same seemingly effortless grace and logic that characterized his writing. His voice was unmistakable. And he will be sorely missed.
> —Ken Schaphorst, Chair Jazz Studies, NEC[2]

> Bob was a beautiful person, a great teacher, and an even greater musician and composer. His boundary-crossing music spoke to our time in general and to NEC's vision in particular.
> —Michael Gandolfi, Chair, Composition Department, NEC[3]

Even though Bob's reputation as a teacher preceded him, he never rested on his laurels. I've been told that he was as hard on himself as he oftentimes was with his students. And yet, demanding as he was and as intimidating as he could be, he was dedicated to helping them find their paths. This chapter and the next offers the words and feelings of many of those whose lives he touched.

An Opening Retrospective: Darcy James Argue

One such person is Darcy James Argue, a graduate of the NEC and one of Bob's most notable students. Considered by many to be one of the most imaginative (and, I might add, innovative) big band composers and bandleaders of his generation, Darcy leads a critically acclaimed eighteen-piece ensemble called The Secret Society. In addition, Darcy has been the recipient of a Guggenheim Fellowship, a Doris Duke Artist Award, and multiple grants, fellowships, and commissions. As you read on, you will see that having Bob as a guiding light, both in and out of the classroom, helped Darcy find his voice. I think that his remembrance here, extracted from his December 23, 2011, article for Music Box USA, is a great way to begin this very special chapter, as it is a gateway to the many lovely voices that follow.

Darcy James Argue. Photo courtesy of Lindsay Beyerstein.

From the Inside/Out

Bob turned out to be the most exceptional teacher I've ever encountered. Lots of jazz musicians take teaching gigs because they need the money, or they enjoy basking in the admiration of young people. He did not take up the mantle of educator lightly—he was as serious about teaching as he was about composing or playing. He had developed a repertoire of assignments, which he gave to all of his students . . . but as he learned what a student required, he would tailor his approach to each individual. He didn't do anything by rote, and he judged everyone's work by the same impossible standards he set for himself.

It's funny, though. During our first several months together, Bob played his cards uncharacteristically close to the vest. I remember my fellow composition majors trading stories about how mercilessly he would dissect their work. But whenever I would bring in the chart I was plugging away at, Bob wouldn't say much of anything! He would listen attentively to the recording and perform a detailed examination of the score, but declined to offer any kind of feedback, other than, "Okay, what comes next?" I began to fear that Bob considered my work so thoroughly unremarkable that he could not even be bothered to voice a critique!

Finally, as we neared the end of the semester and I had completed the piece—a thirteen-minute blowout called "Lizard Brain"—and Bob saw the double bar line at the end, then the dissection began. (It was gloriously merciless.) Bob later told me, "I could see that you were pushing yourself to do something different, something you didn't exactly know how to do. But the wheels seemed to be turning okay on their own. I didn't want to stop the bus before you got to wherever it was that you were headed."

It's impossible to imagine what my life would've been like without Bob. Certainly, I would never have had the guts or the wherewithal to move to New York or start my own big band!

After I left Boston, we kept in intermittent contact. I wasn't as close to him as some, but I tried to keep him abreast of whatever I had going on. I have a treasure trove of concise but unfailingly encouraging correspondence from Bob:

"Congratulations! Very pleased that you are making a dent in the big city."

"Good News, my friend!!! Keep it up."

"I have been meaning to congratulate on the commission—read about it and am proud as always."

During his 80th birthday celebration concert at Eastman, I got to sit next to him as the students played their hearts out on perilously difficult material like "The Nasty Dance" and "Say Ah." I'd catch little sidelong glimpses of him beaming with admiration. It's one of my favorite memories.

The most important lesson Bob taught me, the one I hope will last me a lifetime, is the importance of patience. You've got to give each musical idea time and space, not just to be heard, but to be appreciated. Bob's best music is full of moments of tremendous power that are only possible because he's set them up so patiently.

In life Bob was not always an entirely patient man, and he was not always fully appreciated. He never really got his due; his music is not widely known outside of a small community of devotees, but among musicians, his status is properly legendary.

Bob packed several lifetimes' worth of music in almost eighty-two years of living. Now the rest of us have the rest of our lives to catch up to where he left off.[4]

Jim McNeely. Photo courtesy of Gerhard Richter.

Jim McNeely

Jim McNeely's reputation as a composer/arranger and conductor for large jazz bands continues to flourish and has earned him twelve Grammy nominations. He won a Grammy for his work on the Vanguard Jazz Orchestra's *Monday Night Live at the Village Vanguard* (Planet Arts). His work in Europe has been extensive and has included projects in the Netherlands, Denmark, Germany, and Switzerland. At this writing Jim is the composer-in-residence with the Frankfurt Radio Big Band.

Another dimension of Jim's work is his dedication as a teacher, which has also played an important role in his professional and personal life. He is professor emeritus in jazz composition at Manhattan School of Music and, in addition, has held positions at William Paterson University and New York University. He was also involved with the BMI (Broadcast Music Incorporated) Jazz Composers Workshop for twenty-four years, including sixteen years as musical director. He has appeared at numerous college jazz festivals in the United States as performer and clinician and has held major residencies at dozens of institutions in the States, Canada, Europe, Japan, China, Australia, New Zealand, and Egypt.

As a pianist Jim has recorded numerous albums under his leadership and has also appeared as a sideman on multiple recordings led by such stellar figures as Thad Jones, Mel Lewis, Bob Brookmeyer, Stan Getz, and Phil Woods. At this writing Jim is a member of a most unusual trio featuring bassist Martin Wind and trombonist Ed Neumeister. Drummers not allowed! Their initial recording is called *Counterpoint*, and I must confess, it is a true delight.

It seems as though Jim McNeely has crowded three lifetimes' worth of music composition, performance, and teaching into one. Yet even so, Jim—like the other contributors to this chapter—has a way with words that makes it all seems so effortless. Of course, the guy they are all writing about was no slouch in the wordsmithing department either.

What follows here is Jim's paean to Bob, originally published in the March 12, 2012, edition of *JazzTimes* magazine:

Remembering Bob Brookmeyer

In *Music Is My Mistress*, Duke Ellington invokes the image of himself as a young boy leaving his home and embarking on a journey. At certain points, standing on a street corner, unable to decide which way to go, a kind adult takes him, turns him in a particular direction and says, "Here—go this way." In my journey the most important "kind adult" was Bob Brookmeyer.

Bob played a number of roles in my life. The most important was that of mentor. The freelance world typically does not have the built-in mentoring system that more structured professions offer. I was very lucky that this generous man saw something in me and challenged me to develop what he saw as my talent. Whatever reputation I enjoy today as a composer/arranger/conductor can be traced back to early 1979, when I was the pianist with the Thad Jones/Mel Lewis Orchestra. Thad had left to assume the chief conductor's job with the Danish Radio Big Band. Mel took over leadership of the band and brought Bob in as musical director. He'd had his ups and downs in the '70s but came into Mel's band ready to enter the next, great chapter of his life. I remember when he brought in his now-classic arrangement of "Skylark." Before we played it at the Vanguard for the first time, he told me, "If this doesn't work, I'm not gonna bother with anything else." As I played the final phrase, absolutely stunned, I thought, "Damn, I guess he'll be writing some more!"

Bob encouraged my efforts as a writer; he brought me to Cologne as a soloist (along with Mel) for his WDR projects; he hired me to do some of the writing, and he helped set up my first project there, which led to many years of working and learning with them and many other European groups, including the Danish Radio. Which led to writing for the Carnegie Hall Jazz Band. Which led to my rejoining the Vanguard Jazz Orchestra and writing two CDs for them. Which led to my current position as chief conductor of the HR (Frankfurt) Big Band. All the time being encouraged and cheered on by "The New Hampshire Flash," as he called himself.

But our relationship was even more layered than that. Compositionally Bob had a huge impact. The music in the second album he wrote for Mel's band, containing "Make Me Smile" and "Nasty Dance," opened my ears and head to a huge new vista as a jazz composer. At this point in his career he could have just rested on his laurels as the "Bobby Brookmeyer" who people remembered from the '60s. But he kept pushing himself and exploring.

We never engaged in formal lessons. But we had many discussions on bus rides during tours with Mel's band. He would show me scores, introducing me to white chocolate in the process! And there were many times when I'd drive up to his house in Goshen, New York, on a Sunday. We'd listen to some music, talk about mutes, watch a New York Giants game on TV, get a bite to eat, listen to more music. Those were good days.

Bob was a great improviser, and it was an exciting challenge to play with him and support what he did without getting in the way. A lot of his younger fans have little if any awareness of Bob's early career as a player. Coming from Kansas City, he knew about the power of the quarter note. Boom-boom-boom-boom: right in the pocket. His trombone playing was at times incredibly lyrical, but at other times wonderfully gruff and rough. And don't forget his ability as a pianist. There's The Ivory Hunters, where he met Bill Evans in a duo piano setting. And his own Blues Suite from 1959, where he blends influences like Monk and Ellington into some of the most wonderfully cranky piano playing you'll ever hear!

These were all very important musical relationships. But I think that the most important role Bob played in my life was that of friend. More than that. He was my very hip uncle. We'd talk about life, politics, music, and love. When Marie and I got married, we had our rehearsal dinner at his place in Brooklyn (back when I called him "Brooklyn Bob"). The next morning his rocket-fuel coffee had me hyperventilating on the altar! And then Bob found Jan; well, that was a match made in heaven.

I'm going to miss his friendship, his support, his laugh. His musical legacy lives on, with me, Maria Schneider, John Hollenbeck, and so many others. Thank you, Bob, for being that "kind adult." I've learned my way around the neighborhood pretty well, but sometimes still find myself asking, "What would Bob do here?"[5]

John Hollenbeck

A six-time Grammy nominee, John is the recipient of a Guggenheim Fellowship, the ASCAP Jazz Vanguard Award, and a Doris Duke Performing Artist Award. He has also been the recipient of many commissions, both stateside and abroad. John humanizes the word "oblique." When listening to his music, one should expect the unexpected! It has a way of sneaking up on you and giving you a jolt when you least expect it.

John Hollenbeck. Photo courtesy of Lena Semmelhoggen.

In addition to being a gifted and wildly inventive composer and drummer/percussionist, John—like his mentor, Bob Brookmeyer—takes the road less traveled. He is the leader of the critically acclaimed Claudia Quintet and the adventurous John Hollenbeck Large Ensemble. You may remember from the previous chapter that John was the recurring musical thread that ran through each of the New Art Orchestra recordings. His authoritative and musical drumming is truly a sound and feeling to behold. Here is an edited version of our conversation:

John, would you please introduce yourself to readers who've not had the pleasure of meeting you and experiencing your many recorded works and concert performances before? Would you include a little bit about your early background?
I'm from Binghamton, New York (home of Rod Serling and Slam Stewart)! My brother Pat got me into this mess. I was lucky enough to grow up with Steve Davis, Dena DeRose, Kris Jensen, Tom Dempsey, and Tony Kadleck. All are now successful jazz musicians. I went to Eastman, moved to New York City, and lived there for fifteen years, then lived in Berlin for five, and now Montreal.

How did you come to meet Brookmeyer?
Al Hamme, the local jazz teacher, brought great artists in for summer workshops at SUNY Binghamton. The first band was Woody Herman and the next year it was a Brookmeyer small group for five days and five nights. I was 12 and had just had an emergency appendectomy, so I did not participate fully, but went to some workshops and gigs with the doctor's ok. I cherish my cassette bootlegs of those gigs! I remember the workshop big band played "Hello and Goodbye," so I think that was the first big band piece I ever heard live of Bob's. I remember he was wearing very comfortable, spiffy clothing and he was trying to get the workshop musicians to play freer, looser, and more outside.

I then met him again at Eastman when I was a freshman. We played the music from *Dreams*. I played percussion, including a washtub, which Bob approved of. The drummer in the band asked if the feel of a piece was straight or swung and Bob said, it is like "Zooba-dooba."

I applied for his World Jazz School in Rotterdam, so I think that recorded audition was the first time he heard me play the drums. I remembered he liked this acid jazz version of "Freedom Jazz Dance" we did, and he said this gave him the idea to ask me if I wanted to play in the Schleswig-Holstein Musik Festival Big Band, which became the New Art Orchestra.

What personal and philosophical/aesthetic qualities did he have that interested you from the outset?
Bob was forward looking, which was unique for a jazz musician of his age and experience. He was interested in the ephemeral and did not care about style as much as most. He mostly talked about composers like Ligeti and Lutoslawski. That gave me the confidence that I could work from that branch of jazz composition.

For our readers who are not musicians, could you describe what qualities in Bob's music (as a player and as a composer/arranger) influenced your own playing and orchestral compositions?
Unpredictable long forms where the improvisation is either an integral part of the form or it is not there at all! The groove always has to be solid.

I've noticed that the state of our country, our planet, and life in general has found its way into your music. Was that a result of Bob's influence? In what way? Would you elaborate on that a bit?

I think that I was naturally inclined to integrate topics that interested me and that I wanted to explore through music, but Bob certainly appreciated those early efforts and gave me confidence to continue on that path. This confidence was a gift from Bob. His support for me as a drummer and composer really helped me in my "lean" NYC years, a city with hundreds of incredible drummers and composers.

He would tell people like Manny Albam and Burt Korall about me, and they immediately accepted and liked me because of his endorsement. That probably helped me more than I even know!

The act of really listening to music seems equally important to the art of composing, arranging, and playing it. In your opinion what are some of the ways we can approach the act of listening to your music—or, for that matter, to any music? Had you ever spoken with Bob about these kinds of things?

Try to let go of categories and labels and listen with an open heart and an open mind. Bob was always listening and searching out new music. He was the oldest musician I met who was still open and searching. Remaining open and flexible is difficult as you get older it seems. I wrote a piece once based on a Joni Mitchell quote where she is speaking about that: "Can you get through this life with a good heart?"

For listeners who've never experienced your music, what recording(s) would you recommend they begin with? Also, which of your recordings with Bob stand out as favorites? Why?

I see my recordings as parents see their children, so there are no favorites!

But if I narrow it down to two I think I would start with *I, Claudia* [the Claudia Quintet's second recording] and *Eternal Interlude* [the John Hollenbeck Large Ensemble's second recording].

The reason I picked two second recordings is I think it is relatively easy to do the first album or work. I know comedians speak of this too. The first work is really something you have been working on since the day you were born. Then as soon as it is released someone will ask, when is the next album coming out? That is the first big artistic challenge. I think the second recording is much more difficult and more of an achievement and often more true to what an artist is.

With Bob, I'm very proud of the small group recording with Kenny Wheeler. I was happy to just be a fly on the wall for that meeting of two of my favorite musicians.

And the NAO record that I like the best is *Waltzing with Zoe*. It was the most difficult recording to make and has many flaws, but I simply loved the variety in the repertoire! And it contains my favorite Brookmeyer composition, "KP '94," which I'm proud to say others and I persuaded Bob to record!

Finally, if you could speak to Bob Brookmeyer this very minute, what would you say to him?
I love you, Bob, and miss you deeply! Thank you for what you are still giving me and many others.[6]

Dave Rivello

A member of the faculty at the Eastman School of Music, Dave Rivello is a composer, arranger, conductor, and bandleader working primarily in jazz, contemporary media, and modern classical idioms. His music has been widely performed throughout the United States, Germany, and Spain. He apprenticed with Bob Brookmeyer, Manny Albam, Bill Holman, and other notable composers and arrangers. Dave's personal relationship with Bob began as a copyist, then as a student, and finally as a close friend—all of which led to his book *Bob Brookmeyer in Conversation with Dave Rivello* (ArtistShare, 2019), which was the result of three days of conversations with Bob that focused upon such diverse topics as composing, conducting, bandleading, and teaching—a veritable treasure trove of wisdom, pedagogy, and, of course, the legendary Brookmeyer candor.

Bob with Dave Rivello, author of *Bob Brookmeyer in Conversation with Dave Rivello* (2019). Photo courtesy of Roland Paolucci.

"My Time with a Master"

My story with Bob Brookmeyer actually begins from my undergraduate days at Youngstown State University in Youngstown, Ohio. A fellow student in the jazz program caught me after big band rehearsal one day and told me to go the local record store and buy the album *Bob Brookmeyer, Composer, Arranger: Mel Lewis and The Jazz Orchestra*. I went over that day and picked it up. When I got home I put it on the turntable, and as the first notes of "Ding Dong Ding" rang out, my whole world changed. Up until then I had listened to a lot of big band music—Thad Jones, Basie, Woody Herman, Stan Kenton, Maynard Ferguson, Buddy Rich and others—but I never heard anything like what I was hearing at that moment. I wore this record out, I played it so much, and when the next album with Bob and Mel came out, *Make Me Smile & Other New Works*, I wore that album out, too.

(We sometimes jokingly refer to *Make Me Smile & Other New Works* as the "Brookmeyer White Album" because of its original LP cover.) This recording further expanded my sonic horizons and made me want to be a composer even more, and to be one more than anything else. Every time I listened to these two recordings, I thought to myself, "I wonder what it would be like to meet Bob Brookmeyer?" and "I wonder if that could happen someday?"

Well, not only did I get to meet him, but I got to spend fifteen amazing years working with him, first as his copyist, then as his student, and ultimately as his friend. Every time I visited, even in the later years when I'd go just to hang out for a weekend, he always continued to slip in a lesson, and they were always exactly what I needed to hear at that moment to further my work. But again, I jumped ahead, so let me go back and catch up with the story.

In the mid-1990s Fred Sturm (then chair of the Eastman School of Music Jazz and Contemporary Media program), told me that there was a new Brookmeyer recording called *Electricity*, but that it was only available in Europe. He suggested I call Bob to get a copy, and he gave me Bob's phone number in New Hampshire. When I finally got up the nerve to make the call, I dialed, hoping that I would get his answer machine and that I could just leave a message, but Bob answered the phone. I was a bit nervous, but after only a few minutes' conversation, Bob put me right at ease.

As it turned out, he knew my name from Manny Albam. He and Manny were coteaching the BMI Jazz Composer Workshop in New York City. I knew Manny from the Arranger's Holiday summer program at Eastman, headed by Rayburn Wright. Bob and I talked for a few minutes about his new CD, and then he asked me what else I did besides composing. I told him I had also worked as a professional copyist for years. This was right on the edge of Finale [the software] coming in and he asked me if I copied by hand or on the computer. I told him I did both but preferred copying by hand. He told me he might need me some day, and also that he would send me his *Electricity* CD. I hung up and thought, "Brookmeyer is so progressive, he probably wants computer copying and I probably just messed that one up."

A couple of weeks later, though, I got a call from Bob. He said, "Dave, it's Brookmeyer—I need you!" He told me he was very behind on writing a four-movement suite for Clark Terry's 75th birthday concert and wanted to know if I could copy it. Then he stated, "And I want hand copying."

I, of course, said yes. I couldn't believe my luck—that I would get to see a Brookmeyer piece before anyone else and get to study it . . . but there was no time for studying at that point. Bob wasn't joking when he said he was behind. I got to know the Fed-Ex guy by his first name. Every day more pages arrived. I hired two proofreaders so that one of them was always in my house. I wish I would have taken a picture of the stack of parts before I sent them to Germany. The pieces I copied were "Silver Lining," "Gwen," "Glide," and "Blue Devils." During this time, when I would call Bob with note questions, I said I would love to take a lesson with him. He said that we would find a time for that.

Shortly after the Clark Terry project was done, Bob called and gave me a date for the lesson. He told me to bring some of my work and that I could decide if I wanted to work with him, and that he would decide if he wanted to work with me. I knew the answer to my half of this equation, but thought that if he said, "No, sorry kid"—well, thankfully that didn't happen, and he took me on as his student.

As many who knew him will tell you, Bob was incredibly generous. He knew that I couldn't afford to pay for the lessons, so [. . .] our agreement was that we would barter copy work for the lessons, but somehow every time I copied for him, there was a "budget" for copying from whoever was commissioning the music. In other words, he never let me pay. Along with this, he always made me call collect for our phone lessons. So when he turned 80, I wanted to do something special for him. I organized an 80th birthday concert at the Eastman School of Music. We played two hours of his music programmed chronologically and then, as an extra, I asked Bill Holman, Jim McNeely, John Hollenbeck, and Ryan Truesdell to each write a one-minute tribute to Bob on "Happy Birthday." I also wrote one. I interspersed these commissions throughout the program. After the concert we had a reception upstairs, outside the Kilbourn Hall doors. I have a great picture of Bob blowing out the candles on the birthday cake we got for the occasion. I felt that it was a small thank you on my part for all he had given me. He wrote about it afterward and was clearly moved by the evening.

The other thing that I did around this time was take a page from his playbook. He once told me that later in Bill Finegan's life (Bill was Bob's hero), he called Bill once a week, always asking if his pencil was moving. I started doing the same thing every week with Bob; I don't know if he ever connected it.

From my first lesson on April 16, 1996, Bob changed my life. The compositional exercises and the Three-Pitch Module Approach to composition that he developed are what I have been teaching at the Eastman School of Music for the past several years and are life-changing for all of the students who go through them. These exercises certainly changed and shaped my own writing. I realized then that the only way to get these unique exercises and the Three-Pitch Module Approach was to study with Bob, or to study with someone who studied with Bob.

A few years into working with Bob, I started thinking that I would like to write a book about him and his compositional processes so that this information would be available to all. We both shared a love of books and particularly books of composers in conversation. There were several that we would often talk about: *Conversations with Witold Lutoslawski*, *Ligeti In Conversation*, *Conversations with Nadia Boulanger*, *Conversations with Iannis Xenakis*, *Morton Feldman Says*, and *Flawed Words and Stubborn Sounds: A Conversation with Elliott Carter*. So that is where I began my project from, and *Bob Brookmeyer in Conversation with Dave Rivello* is the result.

After Bob and I discussed the idea of the book and decided on a time we could sit down and talk, he had me come to his house for a few days in February 2010. It was during that weekend visit that I recorded over ten hours of Bob answering my questions, with his answers often making me think of new questions to ask. During those three days, we recorded the interviews that would eventually become the book, and then late into the nights we would listen to—and talk about—music. It was a magical time.[7]

John Mosca

A native New Yorker and Juilliard graduate, John Mosca has performed with Pierre Boulez and the Metropolitan Opera as well as with Dizzy Gillespie, Sarah Vaughn, Joe Williams, and Stan Getz, to name a few. He is one of the most respected instrumentalists in the world, a brilliant soloist, and one of the best jazz trombonists to ever grace the scene. John has played with the Grammy-nominated Vanguard Jazz Orchestra, formerly the Thad Jones/Mel Lewis Orchestra, since 1975 and has also performed with the Carnegie Hall Jazz Band. As an educator John has served on the faculty of the Manhattan School of Music, the New England Conservatory, and the University of Connecticut, among others. And as you will see below, he is also a fine writer.

Brookmeyer: Music and Humanity

F. Scott Fitzgerald is often quoted as having said there are no second acts in American lives. I believe he got that one wrong, and as proof offer the life and work of Bob Brookmeyer. It was at the beginning of his amazingly productive second act, in 1979, that I first met him. Bob's decision to return to life, New York, and active playing and writing coincided almost exactly (some would call this fate) with Thad Jones's departure from the helm of the band he started with drummer Mel Lewis to pursue

John Mosca. Photo courtesy of Mark Landenson.

opportunities in Europe. As a member of that band, I had been playing the great charts he contributed during his tenure as first trombonist in the late '60s. Of course his reputation was well established among musicians and fans for all his small group records—the great quintet with Clark Terry, the experimental trio with Jimmy Giuffre and Jim Hall, the writing and playing with Gerry Mulligan and the great big band record *Gloomy Sunday and Other Bright Moments*. As that title suggests, Bob had a unique sense of humor and irony, along with a predilection for telling the truth. When asked what it was like returning to the scene after ten years out West he said, "The guys who were playing sharp when I left are still playing sharp."

It was a natural mistake to assume he would bring in charts that resembled the ones we knew. The new things were for the most part through composed, meaning much less rest for the brass and less space for soloists. He explained, "At this point, I'm not turning my career over to a tenor player." That is unless he decided to write for you, in which case you got acres of space, changes, cadenzas, vamps—the whole gamut. As a result, the band was slow to accept the new music. We had to get hipper to get better. Al Porcino told me long ago that no matter how good your band was, when Brookmeyer walked in, it was better. We had a long way to go, but Bob was incredibly patient with us. There were personnel changes to be sure, but mainly there was rehearsing—every Monday afternoon for quite a while culminating in two live records at the Vanguard.

His confidence at least partially restored, Bob hit his stride, reuniting with Jim Hall, forming a number of different small groups, and touring with Mel and the band. He also was a natural teacher, a walking jazz history course, and with his great friend Manny Albam formed the BMI composers workshop. His dictum on copying: "It should be clear to an intoxicated 10 year old." It soon became evident that even New York (that is to say, America) couldn't contain and certainly wouldn't pay for all he had to give. So with plans for a new conservatory in Rotterdam, and considerable disgust with America's declining political culture, he went to Europe. The conservatory didn't work out, but a wonderful group of musicians coalesced around Bob. They are the New Arts Orchestra and for fifteen years had been his principal outlet. He also wrote and recorded CDs with nearly every major big band across Holland, Germany, Sweden, and Denmark.

Returning to settle in rural New Hampshire with his wonderful wife Jan, he headed the jazz composition department at NEC and was piling up frequent flier miles conducting his work in Europe. Through all this work, he managed to make time for his friends and to help any number of people to get sober. Bill Finnegan said Bob had called every day for months while his wife was ill, and several musicians have said that they got calls every day while quitting alcohol. On one of our quasi-regular calls, he asked what I thought of the new work, and I said I envied every page. He then allowed that it might be time to do something together again, and with a grant through We Always Swing, in Columbia, Missouri, we were able to get the project going. His and the band's longtime friend, producer John Snyder, filmed rehearsals and the premier concert, so we will have something out this year [2012]. My favorite moment came when we snapped off a passage and Bob pulled us up short with this: "That's how a hot jazz band plays it—we're not looking for that here." Still growing us thirty years later.

I treasure every moment spent with him, as they were invariably filled with music and humanity. I believe his influence will grow as time goes by and that there are musicians not yet born who are indebted to him.[8]

Jim Hall (1930—2013)

I can't imagine having a casual conversation with someone about jazz guitarists without mentioning Jim Hall first and foremost. What a sound: deep and pure, mellow yet articulate. Jim is a member of a pantheon of jazz guitarists who elevate the instrument to an unabashedly lyrical landscape, swinging all the while.

Jim and Bob began playing together as participants in the New York jazz loft scene in the 1950s, along with talented musicians such as guitarist Jimmy Raney; saxophonists Zoot Sims, Phil Woods, and Charlie Rouse; pianists Bill Evans and Thelonius Monk; bassists Charles Mingus and Bill Crow; and drummers Ronnie Free, Roy Haynes, and Art Taylor. Bob and Jim and Jimmy Raney had a natural affinity for one another and recorded some lovely records, which began Bob's close association with Jim Hall, one that gave listeners those innovative trio recordings made with multireed player Jimmy Giuffre, and numerous guitar quartets with Hall and/or Raney (as well as one quintet recording with both guitarists).

Jim offered this simple but eloquent remembrance at Bob's Memorial in April 2012:

Jim Hall. Copyright and courtesy of David Korchin.

"We Did a Lot of Playing Together"

In New York in the '50s, the scene was pretty amazing, especially around Greenwich Village. There were jam sessions at artists' lofts hosted by painters like Ray Parker, Willem De Kooning. . . . Gil Evans was around, and George Russell, Jimmy Raney, Bill Crow. That's where I really got to know Bob. We did a lot of playing together at those late-night sessions, with all different configurations of instruments.

Somehow, the trio with Giuffre seemed pretty normal to me. Bobby just could fit in anywhere; it was very easy making music with him, actually, in a duet or a trio or anything. In Giuffre's trio we went through several different bass players, but then we got to hanging out with Bob, and it worked so easily that it just seemed natural to get him in the trio.

[On Brookmeyer's Guitar Concerto] I had never fooled around with any foot pedals on the guitar. I sort of stayed away from those, but Bob had it written in my part that he wanted this effect and that effect, so he broadened my feeling about the guitar. That's the kind of musician Bob was: if there was something there to be done, he'd find a way to do it. And it was really a thrill to play with a symphony orchestra.

He was an incredibly bright, inventive, creative guy, with a great sense of humor, really. In a way, I think of the painters from those loft parties: Parker, De Kooning . . . an artist needn't get just frozen in one place. I'm sure that's kind of the way Bob felt about it. It certainly is the way I do as well.[9]

Clark Terry (1920—2015)

I had a friend named John Heard, one of jazz's all-time great acoustic bassists who was of the opinion that you could have a great jazz group on stage, but if the chemistry on and off the bandstand wasn't happening for one or more of the members, the group wouldn't "click" and chances are that the magic wouldn't happen. I could be wrong, but I think that the strong bond of friendship between Clark and Bob, as well as their musical affinity for each other, is what made the Clark Terry–Bob Brookmeyer quintet so well received by listeners and critics alike. It was a happy band, and the music radiated that feeling. In fact, the title of one of their recordings altered the famous Noman Vincent Peale book title *The Power of Positive Thinking* to *The Power of Positive Swinging*.

I remember picking them up at the airport in LA to get them to some gig or other. Regrettably, I have zero recollection of any further details; however, what I do remember is that their horns were safely tucked into the front passenger seat of my Chevy Blazer, and the luggage in the back cargo hold; Clark and Bob sat in the back seat, where the jokes and stories ran rampant for the length of the trip!

It was so clear to me how much these guys loved and respected each other. You will be able to witness a classic example of their shenanigans about eight minutes into the twenty-three-minute YouTube video ("The Life and Music of Bob Brookmeyer") noted at the end of this book.

A not-so-serious photo of "Mumbles" (Clark Terry) and "Grumbles" (Bob) from one of their mid-'60s quintet gigs in New York City. Copyright Raymond Ross, courtesy of Archives/CTSIMAGES.

The following is excerpted from Clark Terry's 2011 autobiography, *Clark*. I spoke to his wife, Gwen, who felt it was fine for me to include Clark's words here:

> Bob Brookmeyer and I had a "mutual admiration society," loved playing together, so much so that we got a little group together in the early '60s. We named it the Clark Terry/Bob Brookmeyer Quintet and got a nice gig going at the Half Note—Eddie Costa on piano, Osie Johnson on drums, and Joe Benjamin on bass. It was one of the best groups ever. [Later, it was Roger Kellaway (piano) Bill Crow (bass), and Dave Bailey (drums).]
>
> The harmony that Bob and I had was super. I was digging the valve trombone that Bob played because that was the first instrument I was given in high school, but the way its sound married with my flugelhorn sound was something special. We could feel each other's next moves and enjoyed the way we managed to play simultaneously throughout the changes. We called it "noodling."

Usually one player wants to outshine the other, but we had a way of blending together that allowed both of us to shine. We really tried to make each other sound beautiful.[10]

I could hear that love in the music they made together. Clark and Bob were true soul brothers.

I regret not knowing Clark, except via his music, although I had the opportunity to play a couple of nights with him in the mid-'70s at Blues Alley in DC. I do remember that once Clark counted off the first tune, I knew I was in the presence of a gracious, inspirational human being and a hell of a great musician.

Scott Robinson

One of today's most wide-ranging instrumentalists, Scott has been heard on tenor sax with Buck Clayton's band, on trumpet with Lionel Hampton's quintet, on alto clarinet with Paquito D'Rivera's clarinet quartet, and on bass sax with the New York City Opera. He has been heard with a cross-section of jazz's greats, representing nearly every imaginable style of the music, and has arrived at his own musical voice.

"Still Full of Surprises"

I couldn't believe it was actually Bob Brookmeyer calling me on the phone, out of the blue . . . asking me about being the baritone soloist for a recording of a suite he'd originally written for Gerry Mulligan. I had never met Bob or seen him play in person . . . but of course I had been listening to his music (his work with Mulligan in particular) since high school, if not before. It was a part of my upbringing.

Bob's importance to our music is not easy to fully assess. It runs through so many streams, so many avenues of creative expression: playing, improvising, teaching, mentoring, arranging, and of course composing. In each of these he was a giant, with a truly lasting legacy. Each could have been his all. Taken together, they constitute a breadth and depth of achievement that few in our music can claim.

Scott Robinson. Photo courtesy of Jeff Dunn.

These words would have annoyed Bob, because he was a no-nonsense person, not given to hyperbole—but I'm sorry, it's the truth!

Bob was possessed of a beautiful sound and an easy-flowing lyricism on his instrument. His was a sound not easily forgotten once you heard it. Bob was a fearless and principled improvisor, dedicated to the principle that each moment matters in music and should be addressed on its own terms. He was not a lick player, or a mechanical dispenser of worked-out patterns and ideas designed to impress or excite. Bob disliked insincerity in music. Every sound had to mean something. One of his pet peeves was the way so many trumpet players flick a valve before any held note, producing a quick approach tone from below . . . a thing the instrument easily lends itself to. This drove Bob crazy. Why? Because it was generally not done for the musical needs of the moment, but out of *habit*. Habits need to be broken, Bob believed, for real improvising to take place.

Bob's teaching legacy is well-known, from his work at Manhattan School of Music, New England Conservatory, and elsewhere. Less recognized, perhaps, is the important mentoring he did *outside* of the formal classroom: personal relationships that touched some of the important figures in our music today, Maria Schneider being a notable example.

As an arranger, Bob had a special gift. Like a lover with their partner, he had a way of bringing out some special, beautiful quality in the song that no one knew was there. He would find the personality hidden in the song and encourage it to come out and grow. "Willow Tree," "Skylark," and "Love for Sale" are great examples of this.

And as a composer, Brookmeyer's achievement is truly vast, spanning the worlds of jazz and concert music: orchestral and chamber works, music for jazz groups large and small, solo performance pieces—an astonishing variety of works, some still waiting to be discovered by the public.

Bob's phone call came in early 1997, when I'd been living in New York for about twelve years. He'd heard about me, he said, and he asked me to send him a cassette tape of some examples of my playing. What to send Bob Brookmeyer? I decided to go ahead and give him a pretty wide-ranging sample rather than just pick what I presumed he might like. So I included a few bass sax things, some traditional jazz stuff, and some crazy out-there music, along with examples of my baritone playing.

He called back after a couple of weeks, said I had taken him through every possible emotion, and asked me to do the recording. "I like you," he said, "because you're not a method player." So on July 23, 1997, after finishing up a European tour, I traveled to Stuttgart and met Bob for the first time the night before the recording. I was excited but also intimidated, and as we chatted in his hotel room, it became apparent that Bob held some very strong opinions and wasn't shy about expressing them. He was pretty tough on some people that I respected. My nervousness grew, and I wondered: What am I in for?

The next morning we assembled in the studio with his New Art Orchestra, which had already been rehearsing the piece. They had a short run-through with me, to touch on most of the tricky spots, and then he began to work just with the band on a section of the music.

I was beginning to relax and feel more confident, but I was also a bit exhausted from travel and lack of sleep. So after a while, while they were working, I lay down on the floor and soon fell asleep. After some time I heard Bob calling my name through the fog. "Scott!" He was looking down at me, grinning. "We're ready!"

I stood up, blinking the sleep from my eyes, and put the horn to my mouth. This is great, I thought. No time to get nervous. Bob raised his hands to start the piece. "It'll be great," he said with a smile. Then he suddenly looked at me. "Just play the changes!" and then gave the downbeat.

To this day I'm not sure if he meant to throw me, or if he was just kidding, or what. He had expressed every confidence that I was the guy for this, and then suddenly laid that on me right before the downbeat. I have to say it rattled me a bit. "What does he mean by *that*?" Looking back, I think he was probably just kidding me. Or maybe he really did want to shake me out of my complacency, I really don't know. Either way I suppose he got the result he wanted. I think it was a successful recording, and it remains among the few albums of which I am most proud. This amazing experience marked the beginning of a beautiful relationship with Bob (and his much-loved wife Jan) that lasted until his death.

I would like to say something about Bob's character. Bob had a strong sense of right and wrong. He cared about a lot of things and spoke up about them. Bob had made many mistakes in his life, and he owned up to them and took steps to correct them and make positive changes. Giving up drinking was one such move. Finding Jan was another. And I can give a personal example that made a real impression on me: Bob had called and hired me for a concert in California some months away, and I was looking forward to it. As the date approached and I hadn't heard from him about the travel, I called to ask how we were getting there. "Oh no," he said. "I didn't tell you? That date was canceled."

Naturally I was disappointed. But it didn't end there. Bob insisted on knowing if I had turned down work, which I had—a weeklong project, in fact. He was absolutely insistent on paying me for that whole week. "Come on, Bob, it was just a mistake. You don't have to do that."

"No, no," he said, "it's bad enough that I have to pay for my mistakes. I won't have other people paying for them too."

I never forgot that. To me, that showed true character. Bob Brookmeyer was honorable, in life and in music.

Toward the end of Bob's life I made an attempt to get him into my ScienSonic Laboratory to record some freewheeling improvised duo music. I know it would have been great! But as so often happens, I was too late. Bob wasn't feeling well enough or strong enough on his instrument to do that. He said he hoped to get his chops back up to speed, and maybe then. "Look," he said, "I'm not saying no!" But alas, it never happened.

One of my hopes, though, is that ScienSonic will soon issue authorized releases of some of the amazing, unheard music that Bob either mailed to me or played for me in the basement of his Grantham, New Hampshire, home. There are some real treasures—some startling stuff—that almost nobody has heard. Years after his passing, Bob Brookmeyer is still full of surprises.[11]

Kris Goessens (1967—2013)
"They Believed Us"

He [Bob]was an incredibly intelligent man, able to express and grab the essence of things in just a couple of words, just as he did with his music. I'll never forget the time we were playing duo for a week in La Villa in Paris. One of those nights, we ended the concert with "In Your Own Sweet Way." As we never planned anything in advance, we ended up playing single lines together for about six, seven minutes, or maybe even longer, as an outro. We were skating, a very nice blend in sound, time, and contour of the melodic lines. When we finished, it was clear by the audience's reaction that they had just experienced what we had. As we got off stage Brookmeyer turned and said, "They believed us."

Kris Goessens. Photo courtesy of Lena Semmelhoggen.

I was lucky to have spent time with Bob and his amazing life companion, Jan, while they were living in Rotterdam. We spent a couple of years playing in duo for hours at my home, three times a week, listening to and talking about music and life, to always end up playing chess.

During that period he founded his New Art Orchestra, for which he wanted to engage young musicians. He knew exactly which ingredients he needed for his band. One could apply to audition by sending a recording, and I remember that Bob would know in a few seconds who he wanted, why, and on which chair in the band. Hardly any changes have been made ever since. Playing his music with these musicians is like playing in a large ensemble with the feeling of a small ensemble.

I know Bob loved Jan a lot. His words were, "It's hard not to," and this I can only confirm. I think Bob and the guys would allow me to say that she is an important member of the band. The lady who breathes love. Without Jan it would have been very difficult to keep the band going and make the recordings and concerts we did.[12]

Paul Heller

In his liner notes to his third New Art Orchestra album, *Get Well Soon*, Bob introduces us to German saxophonist Paul Heller in glowing terms. And rightfully so! From the top of the horn to the bottom and all points in between, Paul not only exhibits his broad knowledge of and respect for past masters of the instrument but also does so in a very personal and organic way.

Paul's extensive knowledge of the jazz art is partly due to the fact that both his father and mother were musicians, as well as his older brother, Ingmar, who happens to have been a member of NAO and has played bass on many of Paul's recordings.

Paul continues to be one of Europe's leading saxophonists today and is well represented on many videos, and a variety of record labels such as Challenge Records (Holland) and Mons Records (Germany).

Paul Heller. Photo courtesy of Gerhard Richter.

A Voice from Germany

Me and my older brother, bass player Ingmar Heller, knew Bob Brookmeyer since our childhood from all the beautiful records—for instance *The Blues, Hot and Cold, Gloomy Sunday, Back Again,* and *Bob Brookmeyer and Friends*—that my dad played for us, because he was a big Brookmeyer fan. I literally grew up with Bob's sound.

In the beginning of the '90s, the renowned classical music festival the Schleswig-Holstein Musik Festival opened up to jazz and asked Bob Brookmeyer to put together a Festival Big Band as a masterclass for young jazz musicians. It was possible to audition for that band with a tape that you could send to him, which I didn't do, but I was on a recording of someone who sent his demo tape, and Bob wanted the tenor player on that recording, which was obviously me.

One day the telephone rang and the deep, impressive voice said, "Hello, Paul, this is Bob Brookmeyer," and it felt like I got a call from God!

Working with him and the band was, for everybody in the band, the most special, deepest, and most memorable experience of our musical lives and still is such an important and unforgettable part of our musical DNA. He worked hours with us to get the right blend in the horns and balance with the rhythm section, and he made us really listen and feel all together the same phrasing and timing up to a level of togetherness that nobody experienced ever since or again. He was a magician and perhaps the greatest conductor of all time. I never saw someone who was able to make musicians play exactly what he wanted to hear from them only by his magical way of conducting, besides creating music that was and still is so unique and outstanding, incomparable, inimitable, touching, heartbreaking, beautiful, and deep.

 The fantastic thing about Bob was also that he wasn't just this untouchable genius in writing, conducting, and playing, but he was such a warm, interested, and giving human being. I was so fortunate that we wrote a lot of emails to each another, just talking and exchanging thoughts and opinions about music and life. Also, we talked quite regularly on the phone about the same topics and because he was such a beautiful personality, I wasn't at all as intimidated anymore as I was with our first telephone call!

 In 1994 Bob started with us as the Schleswig-Holstein Musik Festival Big Band, playing concerts with guests like Gerry Mulligan, Mike Brecker, and Clark Terry until 1997, when Bob wanted to go on with us as his band, which then became the New Art Orchestra.

 In 2008 I played with the New Art Orchestra at the North Sea Jazz Festival in Rotterdam, and my wife, jazz singer Fay Claassen, also performed at the festival and luckily could make it to listen to our concert. She had just released an album with all Cole Porter repertoire arranged by Michael Abene, and since Bob was always very interested in what we were doing, I gave him that album. A short time after he listened to the album, he called us and since he was planning to make an all-standard album with the New Art Orchestra, he said, "I have always looked for a singer who could sing my arrangements—now I found her!" It started with three songs he wanted Fay to sing on the album, but within the next days he came up almost every day with an idea for another song, and it ended up to be then that the whole album, with the only exception being his classic instrumental arrangement of "Willow Weep For Me," featured Fay's vocals.

"Detour Ahead" and "How Deep Is the Ocean" were the last arrangements he ever wrote in his life, and they are again masterpieces. One day, luckily, Fay and I weren't at home when Bob called to talk about the general idea of the "How Deep Is the Ocean" chart, so he talked and played on the answering machine, which is of course a super special treasure for us. The *Brookmeyer/Standards* album was the first time Fay worked again after the birth of our daughter Inga, and since my brother Ingmar was the bass player in the band from the beginning, we had the full family affair on that last album, which was Bob's last.

I am more than forever thankful and grateful for the love, the music, and the experience we got from Bob—something we could all share with one another and the world.[13]

Danny Gottlieb

When I put the two words "versatility" and "virtuosity" together in the same sentence, you can be sure that I will easily be referring to all of the drummers mentioned in this book. Mel Lewis, John Hollenbeck, John Riley, Adam Nussbaum, Dave Bailey, and of course, Danny Gottlieb, who has graced these pages about Bob Brookmeyer with the same energy that he infuses into his drumming and teaching.

However, I must admit that until recently, I was not very well acquainted with Danny's playing. I am now! He is, by all accounts, a fantastic musician, an exemplary teacher, and a very warm and engaging guy. If you asked me who he's played with, I would answer by saying, "Who hasn't he played with?" Check out his website and you'll see what I mean.

I'll let Danny tell you about his relationship with Bob, and about Bob's compassionate generosity and support, which were such valuable assets to Danny's development as a master musician and teacher.

Danny Gottlieb. Photo courtesy of Danny Gottlieb.

Bob Brookmeyer was so important in my life! He played an incredible role and provided so much inspiration as a mentor, teacher, second father, and best friend. I loved him so much, as did so many!

I first heard Bob during the late '60s, performing with the Thad Jones/ Mel Lewis Orchestra at their steady Monday night gigs at the Village Vanguard. Our inspirational Union NJ High School music teacher, Mr. Geist, would bring many of us high school jazz students to hear the band, and like everyone else, I was so in awe of everyone in the band. Through Joe Morello, my main drum set teacher, I eventually met Mel Lewis, and with my teacher's urging, Mel agreed to get together with me and give me lessons. I spent many days with Mel, and he would generously leave my name at the Vanguard door so I could hear the band frequently.

I don't remember the exact chronology, but after Thad Jones left the band, and Mel became the sole leader—sometime during the 1980s— Mel started using me as one of the subs when he would go out of town.

Bob liked my playing, and in 1988 he and Manny Albam, along with author, jazz authority, and BMI leader Burt Korall, started the BMI Jazz Composer Orchestra. I remember Bob and Manny asking me to split the drum chair with Mel. It was an unbelievable honor! I remember Mel saying, "I'll play everything in 4/4 and you play anything that is not in 4."

Tragically, Mel took ill and passed away just a few short years later, in 1990. It was an awful blow to all of us. For many years Mel and Bob had been going to Europe frequently to do projects with a variety of European Radio bands, and now Bob had no one for a bandmate. Amazingly, after Mel passed, Bob approached me and asked me, with Mel's absence, would I like to start traveling with him to Europe to play and record on some upcoming projects? I was floored, and so honored!

He started bringing me to Koln, Germany, to perform and record with the WDR big band (which at the time did not have a steady drummer), and it was unbelievable. I remember playing and recording with the band for the album *Electricity*, and it was a chance to play with both legendary guitarist John Abercrombie and German bassist Deiter Ilg. I remember the music being very adventurous, and Bob loved it when John and I would really improvise in a fusion-oriented way. Because I had the opportunity to play in John Mclaughlin's Mahavishnu Orchestra for a couple of years in the '80s, it was a normal way to improvise, but for Bob it was really something special!

I knew how important Bob was to the world of music (and to me!), and I had just started using video cameras. So I decided to video tape every rehearsal I could with Bob, and I have over fifty hours of video of Bob in concert and in rehearsal with the WDR big band. I also have a wonderful video of Bob being interviewed by a radio station.

Musically, my strongest memory was that he always wanted me to play where the band "didn't play." When I would double band figures, maybe more like the way Buddy Rich might have played, he felt that for him and his approach, it made the band figures feel stiff. He wanted me to play in the holes, which was pretty much the way Mel played.

Mel called it the "rub-a-dub" way of filling in, where you played eighth-note fills in between the figures. That way the band always knew where the time was and there was no guess work about phrase entrances. Hearing him describe that is now forever ingrained in my playing.

The greatest moments were of course the music itself and also the time spent together with Bob. Hearing his approach to life, music, and what he felt was important were such precious experiences. And being with him, and his positive belief in my playing ability, gave me such confidence. I loved every moment with him.[14]

John Riley

By now it's no secret that Bob loved drummers. And he seemed always to make it known to those of us whom he felt gave our all to his music. If you were a drummer and Bob liked your playing, that would've been a real feather in your cap. Brookmeyer was not one to hand out false praise. And to know John Riley's skillfully adaptive drumming is to understand why Bob felt that way.

I first heard John years ago with guitarist John Scofield's trio and was impressed by his empathy and creativity in that intimate setting. Shortly after that I saw John again on a DVD with Scofield and saxophonist Joe Lovano. Then in 1999 I saw him again at the Village Vanguard with the Vanguard Jazz Orchestra for Bob's 70th birthday bash and enjoyed his playing again. Great grooves, great touch.

John has also won accolades for his ability as an educator. His academic relationships with the Manhattan School of Music and Kutztown University of Pennsylvania, and his numerous publications with Alfred Publishers, bear witness to his teaching and pedagogical skills.

A Phone Call from Bob

I first became aware of Bob years ago on the recordings of Gerry Mulligan's Concert Jazz Band. His playing was both swinging and soulful, but I also heard a somewhat abstract element in his writing.

John Riley. Copyright the Percussive Arts Society.

I loved his contributions to the original Thad and Mel band and really studied his writing, and Mel's playing, on the two recordings' worth of compositions he contributed as musical director of the Mel Lewis Jazz Orchestra in the early 1980s. As a longtime member of the Vanguard Jazz Orchestra, we still play everything Bob contributed to the book from day one.

My first direct contact with Bob was in the Netherlands when he was developing his concept for a music conservatory with a faculty consisting of a rotating faculty of world-class players. This was a unique idea and ahead of its time. Bob was prescient, as several schools have successfully explored Bob's approach in recent years.

My most intimate work with Bob was when he presented and rehearsed the music he wrote for the VJO's recording "Overtime" between 2009 and 2011. We had several rehearsals with Bob, and he was extremely clear on how he wanted the music to sound. At times his criticism of particular phrasing was super pointed and direct and took some of the players aback. At the same time, Bob was very enthusiastic when things were flowing as he'd designed them to be.

After one of our rehearsals I was surprised to receive a phone call, the one and only time we spoke on the phone, from Bob where he mentioned how happy he was with the way the music was coming together and my contribution to that end. I'm proud of the band's efforts and results on Bob's last compositions.

I consider myself one of the fortunate musicians to have spent time with someone considered one of the true visionary thinkers in this music we call jazz.

Thank you, Bob, for creating so many unique soundscapes for us to explore and enjoy.[15]

Rob Hudson

Rob Hudson is the assistant director of the Carnegie Hall Rose Archives, where he works to ensure discoverability and access to Carnegie Hall's archival resources and collections that tell the story of the musicians, politicians, and world figures who have appeared in more than fifty-six thousand events at the hall since its beginning in 1891.

Rob is also a trombonist, composer, and arranger, author of *Evolution: The Improvisational Style of Bob Brookmeyer*, and has composed numerous books of short instrumental pieces, all published by Universal Edition. As a trombonist he has performed with the Grammy-nominated John Hollenbeck Large Ensemble and toured with the Tommy Dorsey Orchestra, among others. He has also taught jazz history and jazz arranging, and has directed jazz ensembles at the University of New Hampshire, the University of Connecticut, and the Eastman School of Music.

Evolution: A Day with Bob Brookmeyer

The culmination of my graduate work at the Eastman School of Music was an in-depth study of the trombone playing of Bob Brookmeyer through transcription and analysis of his solos, tracing the development of his improvisational style from the early 1950s through the late 1980s. This was 1989; Bob's work as a composer was starting to gain major

Rob Hudson. Photo courtesy of Rob Hudson.

traction and acclaim, but few seemed to be paying much attention to his trombone playing. While I didn't have any illusions regarding the potential reach or influence of my small project, I knew that Bob's great artistry as a trombonist deserved serious and careful study.

In the early 2000s, a serendipitous and extremely lucky encounter with a fellow Eastman alum brought me a publisher for my analysis of Bob's trombone style. Thankfully, the intervening decade and a suggestion from the publisher helped me realize there needed to be much more, and I expanded the original seven transcriptions to twenty-one, completely rethinking my analysis in the process. In September 2002 Bob and his wife Jan welcomed me to their home in Grantham,

New Hampshire, and together Bob and I spent a single, long, intense day discussing the book and conducting a lengthy interview. You'd better believe I was extremely nervous walking into the home of one of my greatest musical idols. Who was I to have the temerity to analyze *his* work? Yet from the beginning, Bob was extremely warm and gracious toward me, and, most notably, he took me seriously and treated me as an equal. At that moment we were so focused on the discussion and the work that I didn't understand it was happening, but I later realized he'd put me completely at ease, something I know he did for several generations of his students.

Bob was remarkably clear-eyed about his earlier work. While he winced at a few solos he clearly didn't like, he was confident enough to acknowledge what he felt was good work. Great artists are seekers, and that level of self-awareness is very difficult for most, since they're continually focused on finding something new and better, on searching for an overarching truth in their art. Bob possessed these qualities in great measure, but I think he was genuinely proud of his progression and didn't mind hearing some of the earlier recordings—almost like taking a favorite old book off the shelf, one you haven't read in years, and discovering you still like it, but then you put it back and move on.

When it came time to discuss a title for the book, Bob asked me what I wanted to call it. When it began its life as my grad school project, I'd called it "The Power of Positive Swinging," after the title of one of his quintet sessions with Clark Terry from 1964. When I asked him what title he'd like, Bob pivoted gently, saying "What about 'Evolution'?" I'd been clinging to my (perhaps too) clever, adequate title, but in a flash Bob suggested the perfect one; if you were forced to pick a single word to describe him as an artist, "evolution" would be it. Bob was never one to gaze in the rearview mirror; he was always seeking something new. In describing his approach to improvising, he'd often say he liked to poke around in the corners, see what was under the rug, to go "shopping for the right wrong note." That joyful sense of a treasure hunt always came across in his playing.

Bob remarked many times that, particularly as he got older, he viewed himself as merely a conduit for music that was already out there, just waiting to be amplified through his trombone. You can't force it any more than you can change the weather; music will happen according to a logic of its own, as long as you are ready and have developed the tools to receive it. He told me a wonderful story that illustrates this concept perfectly (his quartet with Mel Lewis, Marc Johnson, and Kenny Werner was part of an Ellington tribute tour organized by Gunther Schuller; also on the tour was saxophonist Michael Brecker's group):

> So, we were playing Tokyo near the end of the tour, and I look over, and there's Brecker [at the edge of] the bandstand watching, so I said, "Okay, tonight I'm gonna be chromatic like a motherfucker!" And I stood up, and I just fell right apart. It was terrible—couldn't do anything. And I realized that I was trying to be someone I wasn't that night. You know, we can't *be* anybody when we stand up and it's time to play. If it's tonal, fine. If you're out of the key, and just staying there, deliberately, making people uncomfortable, fine. As long as that's the way it is by natural inclination. Young musicians say, "How do I do it?" I say, "Play a note." "What do I do?" "Play another note."[16]

Terry Teachout (1956—2022)

The late Terry Teachout was a man who in his lifetime wore many impressive hats. He authored four biographies (including one each that focused upon the lives of Louis Armstrong and Duke Ellington, respectively), two books of memoirs, and a volume of shorter pieces that dealt with a variety of subjects. He was also a playwright, librettist, stage director, and a writer who wore two more hats: as a drama critic and as an arts columnist for *The Wall Street Journal*.

Teachout met Bob shortly before the latter's 70th birthday party and celebratory concert by the Vanguard Jazz Orchestra at the Village Vanguard in New York City. It was around that time that the two men formed a solid friendship via frequent emails and phone conversations. I remember Janet saying how much Bob enjoyed their rapport.

Terry Teachout. Self-portrait courtesy of Terry Teachout and Creative Commons ShareAlike 4.0, https://creativecommons.org/licenses/by-sa/4.0/.

The following is Terry Teachout's presentation at Bob's memorial. He posted these remarks on Doug Ramsey's *Rifftides* blog several days after the event.

"I Think He Was a Genius"

I suspect a lot of people who either went to the Brookmeyer memorial service or would have liked to do so will read this post, so I'm putting up a copy of the brief remarks that I delivered there:

New York is a tough place to live, but if you come here, and you're lucky, you can meet people you've admired your whole life long and get to know them. I claim no intimacy with Bob. I'm sure that half the people in this room knew him much longer, and far better. And by the time I met him, he was—by the calendar—an old man. But only in years. I met him just before his 70th birthday, and he had the creativity and imagination of a man half his age, and the wisdom of a man twice his age.

I don't need to belabor what you all know perfectly well, and what will be demonstrated many times over tonight. Bob was one of the giants of jazz: a great valve trombonist, a composer of the first rank, an astonishingly gifted teacher. He was even a pretty damned good piano player! I think he was a genius—and I don't use that word casually.

He was also, as everyone here knows, a man of ear-shattering candor who liked nothing better than saying whatever was on his mind at any given moment, especially when he knew it would give offense. Yet unlikely as it may sound, Bob was genuinely lovable—unless you happened to be on the receiving end of one of his diatribes, and sometimes even then—and I adored him.

What drew the sting of his candor, other than the fact that he was usually right, was that he was as candid about himself as he was about everybody and everything else. When I first met him, I had the nerve to ask him about his drinking days, and this is what he told me: "I didn't think I'd see 30. I almost didn't make 45. My major accomplishment back then was not falling down more than, oh, ten times a day."

I also asked Bob about his music, and he said this: "There's another place waiting for me. I don't know where it is yet, but it's where I have to move." That was in 1999. He got there, and he let the rest of us come along for the ride.

In the last years of Bob's life, he was searching for—and finding—ultimate essences, just like Matisse and Bartók did in the last years of their lives. He had become the greatest living jazz composer. How very, very lucky we were to watch it happen.

Now he belongs to the ages. I can't imagine a world without him.[17]

Bob with Maria Schneider in Cologne, Germany. Courtesy of WDR, cologne/communication/multimedia.

Ninety Minutes with Maria Schneider

It was a lovely spring day here in the Poconos and I was driving through the Pennsylvania woods, enjoying the mild weather. Several days earlier I had received a copy of Maria's Grammy-winning recording *The Thompson Fields*, and I felt that the best time to give it a first listen would be while driving through the delightfully bucolic surroundings on the back roads to Bartonsville.

The first track of the recording was titled "Walking by Flashlight." About one minute into the piece, I was compelled to find a place to pull over to the side of the road and give my full attention to the music. Some compositions, no matter the genre, just hit you that way. Maria's feeling for the natural world, and for all it has to offer, yielded the kind of quiet power that can only happen when you stop whatever you're doing and pay attention. It's always been a spiritual moment for me when music is that powerfully resonant. Sitting there on the side of the road, I realized that Bob gave the kind of support to Maria that enabled her to find her true voice. "Walking by Flashlight" exemplified the beauty of that voice for me.

It would be easy to fill an entire volume about composer, conductor, and orchestra leader Maria Schneider. Her accomplishments include, but are not limited to, fourteen nominations and seven Grammy awards, *DownBeat* and *Jazz Times* Critics' and Readers' Polls, an honorary doctorate from her alma mater, the University of Minnesota, and America's highest honor in jazz, the NEA Jazz Master Fellowship, bestowed in 2019 by the National Endowment for the Arts. Maria's many compositions have also garnered a variety of awards, including a finalist for the Pulitzer Prize in Music for her incredible 2021 masterwork *Data Lords*.

While all of her well-earned accomplishments taken together seem almost overwhelming, Maria is one of the most approachable musical artists I have ever known. Thanks to Zoom technology, we spent almost an hour and a half engaged in friendly conversation about a variety of subjects. Bob always spoke of Maria in glowing terms, and their relationship as mentor and mentee was certainly a productive and inspiring one.

I have abridged the following, highlighting Maria's thoughts regarding her growth as a composer, most notably during her time spent studying with Bob.

Some Beginnings

One of the reasons I think I really gravitated to the world of jazz is because in the classical world it was, at that time, "If it's not atonal, you're out of the club." And in jazz it could be everything from David Sanborn to Cecil Taylor to what Miles was doing. There were a thousand different things—traditional, or whatever—and I felt it to be so inviting, because I've always loved melody. I love songs. I love the things that harmony does to the soul.

And so suddenly I discovered the world of jazz. And what I became so attracted to—and I remember the first time I listened to *Make Me Smile*, that album, so I was listening a lot to Gil Evans—and what I loved about Gil Evans was there was this melding of the classical world: the color, the nuance, the emotion. It had so many elements of classical music, but then it had all the elements of jazz and rhythm and improvisation. Then I heard *Make Me Smile*. And *Make Me Smile* showed me that jazz can have unique form. . . . And I loved it. Because now, suddenly, it felt like the modernism that they were talking about in my classical studies, which I felt so oppressed by, entered into that music in a context that had the emotion and the lyricism and the openness of jazz and the visceral impact of what jazz has. And I just said, Oh, my god.

Meeting Bob

There was no jazz program at school in Minnesota; there was only a big band. But what was so great is that I could go and watch that band rehearse, and with the music I was hearing, I was just an open slate, and I would just flail about and try things; and a kid in the band gave me some lessons in writing for big band—you know, just some basic stuff that got me going. But I basically was just groping, finding my own unorthodox ways of doing things.

I reached out to Bob in summer of '85, I guess. I was graduating from Eastman School of Music Master's program. And back then the National Endowment for the Arts had these wonderful apprenticeship grants, where you could get a grant to study with a teacher, but you had to be approved by the teacher. So I called Bob out of the blue. He'd never heard of me. And on the phone he was so—you know how Bob could be kind of intimidating—so when I told him I'd like to study with him, he said, "What's your burn?" And it was such a weird thing, and I wasn't even sure if I'd understood him right. I said, "What's my *what*?" "Your burn!" I said, "I'm sorry, I don't know what you mean." He said, "What is it you want to do?" And I said, "Well, I just want to be a better composer."

It's like, okay—I don't know what answer he was looking for, but it was very scary, and I thought, I don't know that I like this—this is kind of horrible. But I proceeded, and I went to Brooklyn where he was living, and dropped off some scores. I was not living in New York yet, but I guess I went down there for a weekend, probably just because of that, and dropped off some scores and a cassette tape of my music, and then he said that he would give me lessons. And so when I moved to New York I started studying with him.

He taught at Manhattan School of Music, and so we would do our lessons up there in his room . . . and we really spaced the lessons out. I was working full-time and beyond as a copyist, and he pretty quickly then hired me as a copyist, so sometimes I was really busy copying for him. So this thing that should have maybe been over in the course of the year we started stretched over a longer period of time, and it never really ended. It was good.

People like Bob, you hear and you know so quickly it's Bob, George Russell, you know it's George Russell, you hear it and it's got something in it. Gil Evans, Thad Jones—all of them—Ellington, Monk, everybody, and what am I? Do I have anything unique to say? I'm this girl who grew up among cornfields in Minnesota. What do I have to say? And maybe I don't. And that's what I feared.

At our first lesson, when I brought in a rather traditional thing, he crossed his arms and asked rather gruffly, "Why is there a solo there?" I couldn't really answer, except to say, "Well, it's jazz." He responded, saying, "A solo can only happen when the only thing that can happen is a solo." And I just said, "Oh, okay. Okay, uh-huh." And I nodded my head, and inside I was thinking, *Oh, my god, I'm so scared of you, and I have no idea what you're talking about, but I better pretend I do.*

He went on asking me about every aspect of the music that way; for instance, "Why is the bass player playing the chords of the tune on the solo? There are endless other choices." Over time it got me thinking about what *I* wanted, rather trying to fit into the big band mold. What Bob basically did with me was to break down these walls and say, "Every aspect of the music, it can be anything." By me starting to consider that, all of a sudden, my music became my own unique voice somehow, because I started putting my own ideas into each aspect about the music and what that could be. And not just filling in the blanks of a prefab house.

And so, you know, I said to Bob one day, "You were the one who helped me find my voice." And it was because he made me ask those questions. So that was a powerful thing.

[At this point in the conversation, I interjected, "So Bob was the gardener and you were the garden . . . and he helped you. He showed you where the sun was. And as a result, you were able to blossom."]

Definitely. He was super supportive. And then, over time, I would go to him when I was in crisis mode and stuck on some piece and didn't know where it was going, and feeling lost. And it's funny—sometimes just going up to New Hampshire where he lived with Jan, sitting there next to him and showing him my music and talking it through . . . I knew what he was going to say—all these things you weren't honest with about yourself, you could just *feel* him and his dissatisfaction, which was something.[18]

Sort of a Coda

We covered so much ground in the ninety-plus minutes we Zoomed! In retrospect, what began as an interview wound up feeling like a lively conversation between two friends. That afternoon, in addition to all things Brookmeyer, we veered off into the realms of musical pedagogy, aesthetic philosophy, politics, ethics, gardening, and the virtues of using deer repellent when trying to sustain plant life.

However, here are a few thoughts that Maria shared that I find intriguing:

On Lyricism

I think lyricism—maybe you could think of lyricism sort of like language that speaks in a way that communicates directly. Lyricism maybe almost feels somehow like speech, as opposed to music maybe that's not lyrical is like a deconstructing speech, and putting it together as like some sort of montage and it's sort of like a musique concrète with language or something, as opposed to just the way something naturally speaks. To me lyricism speaks in a natural way.

On Melody

Melody is not just about melody, but melody is what are those notes in relationship to what's underneath that creates a tension and whole different meaning for what that melody does. And for me, that's the whole intrigue and the love of music. And without that, I don't want to be a composer.

On Becoming a Composer

I wanted to be a composer, honestly, since I was young. But I felt very intimidated to even make that a dream I would tell somebody. It was a private dream. I listened to Aaron Copland. I was in love with Aaron Copland. I was in love with Chopin. I was in love with songwriters—Cole Porter. When I got to college and the only reason I dared to say I wanted to become a composer was because a student teacher heard something I wrote in a theory class and said, "That was really good; you should consider adding composition to your major. "That gave me permission to do it, because I didn't have the guts to say that to myself.

On Brookmeyer as Soloist and Composer

Bob's motivic development as a soloist carries into his writing. When you listen to Bob play and then you listen to his writing, it's the same aesthetic and brilliance and what would I say . . . just intelligence, too. It's so smart. His last album he made, the *Brookmeyer/Standards* album—the introduction on, I think it's "How Deep Is the Ocean" that just keeps going and going and going and going, and it just sets up expectations. It just plays with you in that same kind of way that he does as a soloist. It's so brilliant. It's just amazing. I feel like everything about Bob's personality comes out. Everything from his kindness, his generosity, to his supremely acute intelligence, to his intensity and his boldness and it's just all there. Everything . . .

Chapter 7

...And Other Bright Moments

Bob's reaction to his 70th birthday cake in NYC. "Break out the fire extinguisher just in case!" From author's collection.

Introduction

The late Jake Hanna, one of the most consistently swinging big and small band drummers on the jazz scene for four decades beginning in the 1950s, was not one to mince words when it came to storytelling. Even though Jake was born a Bostonian, when he was in story mode, he sounded just like a character in one of Damon Runyon's Duffy's Tavern stories. If you were lucky enough to be in his presence at the Professional Drum Shop in LA on any given day, or one of the southland's legendary jazz clubs like Donte's, Carmelo's, or Pasquale's, you might have had the chance to hear Jake pontificate about any number of funny recollections involving the foibles of well-known musicians and entertainers. Even though Jake could be artfully hilarious while eviscerating some hapless show biz character, he chose his words carefully when complimenting someone he admired. One night at Carmelo's when I told Jake that I'd be working at the club with Bob Brookmeyer in the near future, he smiled and said something reverential like, "Brookmeyer is the Bach of the trombone."

I never forgot Jake's perceptive comment, because I knew what an apt description it was. The sad thing was, I don't think I ever shared it with Bob.

Sharing that wee bit of jazz history seems like a good opener to this chapter whose vignettes are often as image rich as some of the longer pieces that grace the pages of the preceding chapter. Most are based upon personal experiences that, despite their brevity, are heartfelt and generous, and often quite funny (see bassist Bill Crow's contribution as well as Bill Holman's dryly oblique narrative as examples).

On and Off the Bandstand

This is a sampling of voices from a diverse group of people, including some of Bob's oldest friends and musical associates, to one person who happened into Brook's Memorial accidentally at

St. Peter's Cathedral that evening. Each of these vignettes shine brightly, with memorable moments often filled with both affection and humor.

Bill Crow: Bassist, Recording Artist, Author

Gerry [Mulligan] continued to work with his quartet: Brookmeyer, Mel Lewis, and me. We appeared on Mike Wallace's television show during the time that Wallace was in the process of building a reputation as an investigative reporter. Wallace's television interviews were popular partly because of his prosecutorial style.

At the rehearsal Wallace was courteous and low-key. He asked questions that had been prepared by his staff, and Gerry answered frankly about his career, his experiences with drugs and the law, and other aspects of his life. On the air, Wallace's tone became more contentious. . . . Gerry managed to field Wallace's questions with his usual aplomb, but he found himself at a loss when Wallace asked him, "I notice there are no Black musicians in your group. Is this accidental or by design?"

Actually, it was the first time in many years that, by happenstance, there were no Black musicians in Gerry's quartet, but any short answer to that question would have sounded lame. As Gerry considered how best to respond, Bob Brookmeyer glared at Wallace, jerked a thumb at Mel Lewis and said frostily, "We've got a Jewish drummer. Will that help?"

Wallace dropped the subject.

Bill Holman: Composer, Arranger, Multiple Grammy Winner

The term "highly evolved person" is being thrown about a lot lately, but no one personified it more than Brookmeyer.

I met him in 1957 when, after reading in a record review that his playing was "erudite," and wanting to meet such a person, I introduced myself at the Lighthouse in LA. Fifteen minutes later we were at a liquor store buying a jug of Scotch. I imagine that he paid; he was always a tab grabber.

Intelligence, humor, honesty (brutal), enthusiasm, patience, care, and most of all, love. These are a few of the words that come to mind, though there are probably others that haven't been coined yet.

Bob had a way with words as well as with music; he could have been a literary writer. When he was living in LA, he made a few rehearsals with my band, and one day I asked him what he thought of a chart that I had brought in and rehearsed. His answer: "Glad you did, wish you hadn't."

That was a friend.

Joe Lovano: Saxophonist, Composer, Recording Artist, Grammy Winner

Long before I was in Bob Brookmeyer's audience, he was a major influence on my approach as an improviser and composer. Bob was an amazing soloist, accompanist, composer, and orchestrator of the highest order. He embraced all things in the world of music and expressed them in his personal approach.

Listening to Maestro Brookmeyer growing up in some of the hippest collaborations in jazz taught me about what could be created when there is an egoless collective exchange of ideas within the music and the ensemble you're in. This is well-documented in his work along with Clark Terry, Stan Getz, Gerry Mulligan, Jimmy Giuffre, Jim Hall, Bill Evans, and the Thad Jones/Mel Lewis Jazz Orchestra among others.

In 1980 I joined the Mel Lewis Jazz Orchestra at the moment when Thad moved to Copenhagen and Bob came back to New York and became musical director of sorts with the band. Bob toured Europe with us and started contributing new music to the classic book within the band's library; he was a founding member of the band from its inception in 1966. His early contributions of "Willow Weep for Me," "St. Louis Blues," "ABC Blues," "Willow Tree," and "Samba Con Getchu" were classics that were also in contrast to Thad's music. That was inspiring.

For me, all of a sudden having Bob's embrace as a musician and friend was a pivotal point in my life. He was a joyous, positive, creative spirit that was inspired and inspiring. We also played together in a sextet with Dick Oatts, Jim McNeely, Michael Moore, and Adam Nussbaum; that was one of the hippest bands I've ever been a part of because of the way Bob led and opened the door for us to lead as well.

Sharing the space: this is a universal concept about living life. I will be forever grateful to Bob Brookmeyer for his influence on and off the bandstand. I am a better musician and human being for having known him.

Kenny Werner: Pianist, Composer, Author, Recording Artist

Bob Brookmeyer was a mentor of mine, no question. In more ways than one. He had gone through some life tests that I was going through, and at a crucial time he assured me that I would "get my brains back" somewhere within the next five years.

All the while I was simultaneously aware that he had changed the face of "big bands" to truly earn the moniker "jazz orchestra." His extended forms can now be heard in every major jazz orchestral composer on the scene today. It was my great privilege to play some of his music every Monday night in the Vanguard Jazz Orchestra and, before that, the Mel Lewis Jazz Orchestra.

Bob and I didn't play together that much, perhaps a dozen times. But he played with so much clarity that you could still hear him composing. It's very rare that a player can be in that kind of control of his voice. Adding an even rarer ability after achieving such intellectual victory—truly intelligent music, unlike others of similar intellectual ability—every note from his horn came straight from the heart and went straight into my heart.

What else can you say about such a great being? Was he a cuddly teddy bear of a person? Certainly not. He could be quite caustic and as he got older more and more resentful that his music didn't leave the kind of footprint it deserved (i.e. the awareness of people beyond our little universe of musicians). But the width and breath of his spirit, his heart in his music, spoke for itself. He increasingly found no need to express it any other way.

David Liebman: Saxophonist, Author, NEA Jazz Master, Recording Artist

Bob was one of a kind. The valve trombone, seemingly hidden from view, became his chosen instrument . . . smooth as silk played with a great sense of control and good taste. But Bob was a triple threat. Besides being the master of the valve trombone, he was a fine pianist and was, above all, a great composer and arranger in any musical construct. He influenced composers and arrangers who became famous in their own right. I was honored that Brookmeyer wanted to spend some time with me looking over my *Chromatic Approach* book. He was intensely curious toward developing other ways of writing that would be memorable. No question. Bob was the consummate artist and a powerful mentor—one of the greatest musicians in the history of jazz.

Dick Oatts: Saxophonist, Composer, Educator, Recording Artist

A common dream most musicians have when they move to a large city is to get the opportunity to perform and record great music by seasoned composers and arrangers. More than any material or personal career advancement, having a chance to play great music is what propels and encourages us to improve, find our voice, and continue the tradition of great music played by dedicated musicians who will encourage young musicians to do the same. Whatever I have learned (and will continue to learn), I owe to Bob Brookmeyer and other past, present, and future composers with Bob's intensity.

Brookmeyer's art can provocatively entertain you, but at the same time, his intention was meant to challenge you. . . . Like Picasso, there will never be another like Brookmeyer.

Doug Ramsey

With Bob, jazz was never a "Last Chance." No matter what the "Bracket," no matter what "The Wrinkle," even when he was "In a Rotten Mood" over "Big City Life," for Brookmeyer, music was always "Open Country." (Song titles by Bob Brookmeyer. Context created by Ramsey for the Brookmeyer memorial.)

Joe LaBarbera: Drummer, Recording Artist, Author, Educator

My first exposure to Bob Brookmeyer was the same as Michael's. It was on the 1960 Verve recording of the Gerry Mulligan Concert Jazz Band live from the Village Vanguard. This downsized powerhouse big band boasted several outstanding soloists, all of whom had an individual sound and a personal style, including Gerry on baritone sax, Clark Terry on trumpet, Jim Reider on tenor sax, and Bob on valve trombone. Bob put so much personality into each solo, including growls and shouts, which I had never heard anyone else do before. The first time I heard him live was in 1967 at the Jazz Workshop in Boston in a quintet that also included Clark Terry. It was the same experience for me hearing him live as it was on record. His sound on trombone is easily as recognizable as any of the other giants of trombone like Joe "Tricky Sam" Nanton or J. J. Johnson. Bob's writing was also catching my attention. He contributed the very first arrangement to the Mulligan book: "Manoir de Mes Rêves (Django's Castle)."

When we recorded together on the album *Live at Sandy's Jazz Revival*, the producer asked me for a quote for the liner notes, and that quote sums up my feelings about this unique artist: "Playing with Bob was a great pleasure and an opportunity to work with one of jazz music's original stylists."

John Scofield: Guitarist, Multiple Grammy Winner, Educator

When Bob moved back East from LA in the late '70s, I got to play with him a bit, which was exciting for me. I'd heard him on records and loved his sound. The first time we played was as a duo on a Dutch TV show. Jim Hall had been scheduled to play but had to cancel at the last minute. The organizers of the show found out I was in Europe on tour and invited me to fill in. I was quite nervous, it being TV and all, but Bob, whom I'd never met, was kind and supportive. He called me again to play with his group for a week at the Blue Note in NYC with a great band—Mel Lewis, Jim McNeely, and George Mraz. It was the first week the club was open, so unfortunately attendance was light, but it was a great musical experience playing Bob's music.

I also remember a gig with Marc Johnson and Bob at a club in New Jersey called Struggles. He asked me to bring some of my tunes, and I loved the way he played them. I wish I had gotten to play more with Bob, but those were the only times. As I heard more of his work I realized that he was a true master as both player and writer. I remember guesting once with the Vanguard Orchestra and getting to play Bob's arrangement of "Willow Weep for Me." That piece is exceptionally beautiful. I feel lucky for the little bit of playing and hanging I got to do with Bob.

Larry Koonse: Guitarist, Recording Artist, Composer, Educator

My relationship with Bob Brookmeyer was initiated by our mutual friend Michael Stephans. I had worked with Michael in a number of different bands throughout the years, and we both had similar notions about not letting tradition limit where the musical moment might take us. Sensing that I might be able to operate on the same wavelength as Bob, he welcomed me into what was to become a huge learning experience for me as a developing improviser. Throughout the years I probably played with Bob about a dozen times when he would visit Los Angeles, and I always felt so honored to be up on the stage with one of my heroes.

This all culminated with the recording *Stay Out of the Sun*. I forget exactly how it was determined that we were going to record "Blue in Green" in a duo format, but nevertheless I found myself dealing with a healthy dose of insecurity sitting across from the great master while getting ready for our first take. Nothing was really discussed other than Bob's request that I set it up in a solo context. I remember the first take being a little stiff on my part as I started to anticipate what my next move should be rather than let the moment happen. Sensing my unease Bob offered this in his most fatherly tone: "I love your playing. Remember none of us are psychic, I don't know what you are going to do next and vice versa. Just go on the journey and accept what happens. Don't second guess yourself for a second." Whatever icy resistance was there just completely dissolved as he offered this warm invitation. The second take just spilled out of my hands and heart, and that is what ended up on the recording.

This brief moment was to become one of the five major learning experiences in my life. To give yourself permission to move forward and accept the harmony, dissonance, resonance, friction, agreement, disagreement, and the ensuing beauty that comes from letting things be all while being present to witness their magical alchemy. From that moment on, there was a shift in me, a letting go in getting beyond self-criticism and preconception. All of this because this brilliant, warm, and insightful creative genius offered me that powerful bit of wisdom that took all of sixty seconds to impart.

Scott Reeves: Trombones, Alto Fluegelhorn, Composer, Arranger, Educator, Recording Artist

I regret not knowing Bob Brookmeyer better and studying with him both as a composer and trombonist. By the time I finally moved to New York, he had largely moved on to Europe and, later, New Hampshire. Much of what I do know about Bob is through studying and playing his scores, playing though transcriptions of his solos, and studying with his protege, Jim McNeely, in the BMI Jazz Composers Workshop, of which Bob was one of the founders. But I do have a couple firsthand encounters to share:

When I was teaching in Maine, I contacted him for his permission to publish a four- trombone and rhythm section arrangement of his seminal modal composition "Hum," which included my harmonization of Clark Terry's solo. Not only was he gracious enough to give me a license, but nearly two decades later he called me to tell me that he was playing my arrangement at the Blue Note with a four-trombone ensemble, which, if my memory is correct, included Steve Turre, Douglas Purviance, and Slide Hampton. He invited me to come hear it, which I did. What a thrill! I couldn't believe he still remembered that chart.

Another moment was hearing him speak at Manny Albam's memorial at St. Peter's Church in Manhattan. Bob talked about how difficult it was for him to get studio work because he played valve trombone instead of slide trombone. So Manny had him play first, second, and third chair on different tunes on the date and then asked the people who hired the sidemen to listen to each trombone track. None of them could identify which track was the valve trombone. Bob said it opened up a lot of work for him and how grateful he was to Manny.

As someone who doubles on slide and valves, I could identify with this dismissive attitude toward valved low brass. Many trombonists consider valves as "cheating" or not having the expressive qualities of the slide. Yet Bob had an incredibly warm, lyrical, and compositional approach to the valve trombone, complete with a wide range of nuance and expressive devices. I found inspiration in his remarks.

Theo Saunders: Pianist, Composer, Recording Artist

I first began playing with Bob in the late '70s before he made the move back to NYC. It was usually in a quartet setting with Putter Smith or John Gianelli on bass and Michael Stephans on drums. On occasion we were joined by Bill Stapleton on trumpet and flugelhorn. We played local LA gigs around town at clubs such as Carmelo's and Donte's.

Of course I had heard Bob on classic recordings most of my adult life, but after getting to know him, I was struck by how closely his music paired with his personality—dry and sardonic but always polite and direct. In addition, those Bach-like flowing and weaving phrases for which he was so famous reflected in no small way his manner of speech.

When he returned to the West Coast for a visit in 1980, he lined up a short tour in Arizona (Phoenix, Yuma, Prescott) for the quartet. I have fond memories of that time and to this day still have his handwritten charts (in pencil) from that tour. Lots of great tunes: "Tootsie Samba," "Hum," "Milo's Other Samba," "Hot Tune," and "Oslo," to name a few.

Speaking of Oslo, Bob got in touch with me in 1986 to record an album that eventually became a Concord recording of the same name. I had moved to Ojai by that time and, unfortunately for me, had a losing battle with a lawn mower that prevented me from participating. However, in 1987 we connected again for a concert at the NOS jazz festival in Amsterdam (the group at that time included Eric Von Essen on bass). We arrived shortly after Chet Baker's untimely passing and coincidentally wound up staying on the same canal street where he died. I believe the last time Bob and I played together was in 1989 at Wheeler Hot Springs in Ojai, California.

Bob was an utterly unique and brilliant talent whose development from the preeminent bebop valve trombonist to an orchestral composer of twentieth-century classical music was unprecedented.

We will never see his like again!

Michael Patterson: Pianist, Grammy and Emmy Award Winner, Composer, Arranger, Educator, Recording Artist

When I think of Bob Brookmeyer, I think of the Robert Frost poem, "Acquainted with the Night," which begins:

> I have been one acquainted with the night.
> I have walked out in rain—and back in
> rain. I have outwalked the furthest city
> light . . .

It always seems to me that Bob was on a true hero's journey. He went way beyond the normal careerist path and confronted his demons and came back to teach us about that. First through his work as a performer and composer, which displays a stunning level of creativity and innovation. But I think, perhaps, most significantly through the acquired knowledge he shared with the musical community as a teacher.

Putter Smith: Bassist, Composer, Recording Artist

[Bassist] Red Mitchell's "Happy Minors" and Oscar Pettiford's "Volume Two" were favorites of mine in 1955. I listened to them for years and got to know Brookmeyer that way. Bob, a no-nonsense player, always satisfied. When Mike called me to do a tour with Bob, I was thrilled. Playing with him felt like home and he was a great friend ever after.

Edith Farrar, Impromptu Attendee

Jazz is not where I have any musical genes, or experience. I did not know of Bob Brookmeyer before this memorial service, nor was I aware of his career. On the recommendation of a dear friend who now lives here on the west coast, I had stopped by the church to experience the Louise Nevelson sculpture in the chapel. My quiet meditation was overcome by the hubbub downstairs . . . and I decided to stay after seeing the music stands set up in the sanctuary. What an honor it was to be part of the gathering to honor the life of this musician, teacher, mentor, composer, father, friend. I understood very quickly that I was in the presence of greatness, and goodness, incredible music making, and someone who was well loved. The words and the music were so moving. It was especially my honor to come home and share the evening with my friend, Frank Laico, who was a recording engineer at the Thirtieth Street Studio for many years. "So Frank," I said, "Did you know this guy?" Frank said, "Oh yes. Fabulous trombone. Great guy." Please accept my sympathy for what was clearly a very great loss to many people.[1]

Musical Tributes

We continue with two special "love letters"—special in that they take the form of two distinct recordings of musical compositions. The first by the Vanguard Jazz Orchestra, which pays tribute to Brookmeyer in memoriam by recording some of his never-before recorded pieces; and the second, conceived by bass trombonist Ed Partyka, consists of eight original commissioned compositions dedicated to Bob by colleagues and former students in honor of his 70th birthday. An added bonus here is that the maestro himself is the featured soloist on all tracks.

Also of note are two recordings that, while distinctly different from each other, offer us two more examples of Bob's extraordinary creative gifts, first as an arranger and then as a composer of classical orchestral music.

The chapter comes to a close with "Family Memories," stepson Greg Bahora's lovely narrative, which offers glimpses of Bob's transition from "Who's this guy?" status to member of the Bahora family; and an evocative poem called "With Bob," written by another son, Ben, who is very good at mixing laconic humor with a bit of pathos—which shows us yet another side of Bob.

Over Time: A Tribute from the Vanguard Jazz Orchestra (2014)

I

At this writing, the amazing Vanguard Jazz Orchestra (VJO) continues upholding the fifty-plus-year legacy of its two predecessors, the Thad Jones/Mel Lewis Jazz Orchestra and the Mel Lewis Jazz Orchestra. As you know from chapter 4, Bob Brookmeyer was an integral part of both of these ensembles, initially as a charter member of the Jones/Lewis Orchestra and, soon after Thad's departure, as a two-year stint as the musical director of the Mel Lewis Jazz Orchestra.

When Mel passed in 1990, the band recorded a tribute album called *To You* later that year, their last as the Mel Lewis Jazz Orchestra. No recordings were made for the next half dozen years. However, thanks to the ongoing efforts of pianist/composer/arranger Jim McNeely, trombonists John Mosca and Doug Purviance, saxophonist Dick Oatts, and others, the Vanguard Jazz Orchestra was born officially in 1997 with the release of its first album, *Lickety Split: Music of Jim McNeely* (New World Records). Since that time the VJO have recorded over a half dozen albums before getting to number eight: *Over Time: The Music of Bob Brookmeyer.*

II

> When the VJO comes together to record, it feels like a family reunion. The vibe is intense yet relaxed. As the sessions continued, the depth and beauty of Bob's writing became clearer. By the end, we felt like we had done something very special this recording is about Bob. His writing, his leadership, and his spirit continue, and will continue, to inspire us all.
> —Jim McNeely, liner notes for *Over Time*

The recording's copious liner notes for *Over Time* were written not only by Jim McNeely but also by band members John Mosca, Douglas Purviance, and Dick Oatts. Taken together their contributions offer a complete picture of how this special recording came to be.

Bringing an idea from the drawing board into a reality can be a real challenge, especially when the idea involves well over a dozen musicians plus recording engineers, producers, consultants, art designers, and, of course, the best studio in which to record. And if Bob were here right now, he would probably say, "It ain't exactly cheap."

Ultimately, with the aid of a commission, he was able to secure some monetary support, which enabled him to write a three-part suite called *Suite for Three*, which featured Dick Oatts, Scott Wendholt, and Rich Perry on alto saxophone, fluegelhorn, and tenor saxophone, respectively.

Of the other five tracks, three were Bob's early 1980s originals written for Mel's band ("The Big Time," "XYZ," and "Sad Song"), one was written in 2010 ("At the Corner of Ralph and Gary"), and the remaining track was a welcome return to Bob's beautiful arrangement of "Skylark," which was the very first piece he brought in when he became musical director of the VJO after Mel's passing. The soloist back in 1980 was Dick Oatts, who reprised that role brilliantly thirty-four years later in this 2014 recording.

Over Time is a paean to the memory of Bob Brookmeyer—his genius, his generosity, and his undying commitment to the jazz art.

Madly Loving You: The Ed Partyka Jazz Orchestra (2000)

The idea for this truly unique recording was conceptualized and developed by composer/arranger/bass trombonist Ed Partyka, who invited seven composers to join him by writing a piece that would honor Bob on the occasion of his 70th birthday. Each accepted the invitation, and the result became *Madly Loving You*, which was recorded in the fall of 1999 and released in late 2000 by Challenge Records.

Partyka's exposure to Bob's music and, ultimately, their fifty-plus-year friendship expanded his aesthetic as a musician and composer significantly. Ed was a member of Bob's composers workshop in Cologne, Germany, and a member of the brass sections of the Schleswig-Holstein Musik Festival Big Band and its offspring, the New Art Orchestra.

In addition to an original composition by Partyka, the roster of composer invitees was (and still is) quite impressive: one of Bob's role models, colleagues, and close friends, Bill Holman was one of the first to be invited, followed thereafter by Jim McNeely and Maria Schneider. Famed composer Manny Albam heard about the project and made it known that he wished to be a part of it as well. Other invitees included the American drummer/composer John Hollenbeck, Austrian reedman Marko Lackner, and German saxophonist Frank Reinshagen.

In the recording's liner notes, Ed suggests that we avoid listening to all eight compositions nonstop, and instead that we spend time experiencing each composition in a way that would enable us to savor the *musique du moment* without moving right away to the next track, which allows us little or no time to think about what we just heard.

To me that would be overdosing and not appreciating each composition on its own merits.

Eight compositions, eight perceptions, eight voices. One of the important things to remember is that while Brookmeyer's influence can be heard here and there, it is by no means all-pervasive. None of these composers is consciously trying to imitate Bob's approaches to composition. The opening track, Bill Holman's "Septuagenary Revels," is proof positive of that. Each track stands alone stylistically, and that's one of the beauties of *Madly Loving You*. Another is that you will have the opportunity to enjoy his valve trombone solos throughout the recording. Finally, there is a wonderful surprise on one of the tracks; your challenge is to find it!

Two Sui Generis Brookmeyer Recording Projects

Impulsive! Eliane Elias, Bob Brookmeyer, & the Danish Radio Jazz Orchestra Play the Music of Eliane Elias (1997)

I've included this totally unique recording here for a number of reasons. First, Bob had never written arrangements for an entire album that would highlight the compositions and playing of another musician. Peter Larsen, head of the Jazz Department and Danish Radio Big Band, was one of the executive producers of *Impulsive!* who knew Brazilian pianist/composer Eliane Elias and suggested that she consider the possibility of doing a project with the Danish Radio Jazz Orchestra (DRJO). Eliane, a brilliant pianist and composer (and eventually a multiple Grammy winner) whose playing and composing were beginning to garner attention from the global jazz community, was receptive and they began to hammer out the details.

At that time, Bob was the chief conductor of the DRJO and had already established himself as an innovative composer and arranger, so it was only natural that Larsen would want to connect Eliane and Bob (who had never heard of Eliane or her music). As it turned out, Larsen's intuition and efforts paid off. The result was six of Eliane's songs arranged by Brookmeyer and performed beautifully by the DRJO. Great solos throughout by Eliane, members of the orchestra, and Bob, who offers his warm, lyrical valve trombone voice on two tracks.

I have also included *Impulsive!* for another reason: to bring it into the light. It truly is a bright moment in both Bob's and Eliane's careers! And it deserves far more recognition than it has received.

In the 1990s Eliane recorded nine albums, including *Impulsive!*, and from the beginning of the millennium through 2022, she recorded twenty albums, roughly one a year, for a variety of labels including Blue Note, Candid, Bluebird, and Concord. Interestingly enough, on Blue Note's website, the Elias/Brookmeyer pairing elicited the following comment: "It was 2000s [actually 1997s] *Impulsive!* that proved one of the largest surprises in her career as she collaborated with conductor and arranger Bob Brookmeyer leading the Danish Radio Jazz Orchestra."[2]

The project was recorded and released by the Danish jazz label Stunt Records, a subsidiary of Sundance (a.k.a. the Scandinavian Music Company). To my knowledge there was never a rerelease by a stateside label. Consequently, given the plethora of Eliane's subsequent releases, it seems as though *Impulsive!* got lost in the shuffle, making it difficult to find. Looking at Eliane's extensive discography, it's easy to see how that may have been the case. Once in a while Amazon offers a few copies, and there are also individual sellers who may have some as well; however, if you enjoy the thrill of a good treasure hunt, you may be able to find a copy. Believe me, it's worth the effort! It's also available to stream on multiple platforms.

Music for String Quartet and Orchestra: The Gustav Klimt String Quartet and the Metropole Orchestra (2003)

"This intriguing recording doesn't know what it wants to be!" was my first giddy thought. My second thought was, "What a stupid thing to say!"

Sure, it's not jazz ala Brookmeyer, nor does it seem to fall completely into any one categorical period of classical music. Romantic?

Impressionistic? Postmodern? All of the above? We dive into the deep end of the pool when we attempt to compartmentalize one type of music or another, in *any* genre, because each has its own subgenres; so before long it's not unusual for readers to lift up their hands to the heavens and say, "Enough! I'll just listen to the music and I don't really need to know all the particulars." But then if, once we listen, we *are* attracted to what we've heard, we might want to explore the history of that music and its inception.

So back to my original opening sentence.

One of the things that makes this recording intriguing for me as listener is that I can only surmise how Bob set out to compose a piece of music. He spoke several times in interviews about his belief in "the Music God," which many of us in our respective aesthetic endeavors might call our "muse." In any case, when inspiration arrived, Bob seemed to see that as a mystical event. This from his liner notes: "'American Beauty' [one of the compositions on this recording] came to me on the wings of the Music God. I really have no idea who wrote it, and I still hear it with the pleasure of a consumer, not a maker."[3]

And so with blank score paper and a dozen pencils with multicolored rubber erasers, he began the journey. And if he was either satisfied or intrigued with his initial results, he might just keep going, which he did for this challenging project.

Ultimately, the people who awarded Bob the commission requested a composition for string quartet and orchestra. Bob's response: "It was both challenging and scary, a delicious package. That's a lot for me. I set to work and wound up with over 50 pages of sketches. I began to write the score."[4]

Immersing myself in Bob's large ensemble recordings, beginning with his first efforts in the mid-fifties through his final recordings with the New Art Orchestra in 2011, I tried initially to write about what those stylistic changes in Bob's compositions and arrangements actually were. However, I think that my first attempts were too technical in nature, and quite frankly, too far off the mark. So "write, revise, rewrite," became my mantra.

Bob's large ensemble recordings, including those in which he gradually began to abandon the more conventional style of the postwar big band jazz playbook, which was the order of the day. For me those shifts away from convention began ever so slightly with the unique instrumentations of the various ensembles in his first outing in 1956 (*Brookmeyer*) and more than a few of the tracks on 1960s *Portrait of the Artist*—notably the haunting ballad "Mellow Drama" and Bob's atmospheric "Blues Suite," which conjures 1930s Kansas City in an affectionate, sepia-toned musical portrait. Around that same time came Bob's version of a song by guitarist Django Reinhardt, the beautiful "Manoir Des Mes Rêves," one of Bob's initial arrangements for the Gerry Mulligan Concert Jazz Band. His drifting soundscapes on that arrangement for the band's first recording were a preview of what was to come as Bob continued to expand his studies into other melodic, harmonic, and rhythmic realms.

What did come shortly thereafter in 1961 were Bob's elegant orchestrations for *Gloomy Sunday and Other Bright Moments*, and four years later there were the things he wrote for the Thad Jones/ Mel Lewis Jazz Orchestra, and soon after for Mel's Orchestra, which I think is when the pot really started to boil. And after two compositionally adventurous albums with Mel, Bob decided that it was time for him to move on to the next phase of his musical life.

We know from previous chapters that the path to having his own large ensemble was beginning to widen. His stepping-stones forward were his standalone orchestral recordings such as *Dreams*, *Electricity*, and *Impulsive!*. The New Art Orchestra lay just around the bend. In retrospect, under Bob's direction the NAO became a powerful musical force in the global jazz community. As we know, it was a dream come true for its conductor as well as his musicians.

However, *Music for String Quartet and Orchestra* no doubt threw jazz fans for a loop. Recorded in 2003 and released by Challenge Records five years later in 2008, this is a four-part classical piece devoid of any improvisation or swinging passages. My suggestion is this: If you listen to one or more of Bob's New Art Orchestra recordings first, then you allow yourself some quiet time afterward, when you begin to spend time with this classical recording, you may hear some very identifiable "Brookmeyer-isms," such as his predilections for

1. brass and woodwind fanfares
2. spritely jigs, waltzes, frolics, folk elements
3. streams of flowing, fluid passages
4. staccato accents that often land in unpredictable places
5. drifting somber, yet melodic soundscapes

Ken Dryden, a highly regarded jazz journalist, wrote a review of this recording that appeared in a number of jazz media outlets, including this one from *AllMusic*. I particularly like his brief descriptions of each of the four tracks:

> The opening track, "Fanfares and Folk Song," is a furious and exuberant number showcasing the full orchestra, then ending with just the string quartet and an unidentified pianist. The somber "American Beauty" initially sounds like a requiem, with its mournful feature for cello, though it blossoms into a tender tone poem. The complex yet joyous "A Frolic and a Tune" is full of surprising twists, while the tense "Wood Dance" provides a dramatic closing. Arguments may ensue among listeners as to how to label this enticing music, but Duke Ellington's favorite description of works he enjoyed hearing as "beyond category" is more than sufficient.[5]

Ken's final sentence above brings us full circle to the beginning of this section and my brief admonition to avoid putting this work into a specific stylistic box. I think that such labeling is too often unfair to the composer, the artists, and especially so to those who've not yet experienced it.

It would have been interesting to see where Bob was headed, what conceptual avenues he would traverse. Indeed, as noted in Dave Rivello's valuable book, there is a treasure trove of Brookmeyer compositions that have never reached the public arena. We can only hope that someday in the not-too-distant future they will see the light of day. Stay tuned!

One of the many gifts Jan brought to Bob is that of family life, A kind of stability that I don't believe he'd ever known before. This next section bears witness to that. Here are Greg and Ben Bahora's affirmations:

Family Memories

Greg Bahora, one of Bob's four stepsons, spoke on behalf of his brothers at Bob's memorial at St. Peter's Church on April 12, 2012. He was an eloquent speaker, and his offering provided one of the many memorable moments of the evening.

Greg is a mechanical engineer and hails originally from St. Louis, Missouri. In the mid-1990s Greg relocated to Asia, where he is currently a regional manager for an engineering and construction company based out of Singapore. Here he offers us a unique and intimate portrait of Brookmeyer at home, and his assimilation into family life.

Greg Bahora

We four brothers—Ben, Scott, Cary, and I—met Bob in 1987 while we were in our mid-20s. Like most young adults in that age group, we thought we knew everything while we were in the midst of finding our way and how we fit into the world. Bob's arrival in our lives at the time brought a host of fresh, unexpected, and positive influences, as well as a few surprises.

When we first met Bob, we were impressed by his easygoing, amiable demeanor and his seeming ease with himself and others. We said to ourselves at that time, "Who is this cool cat, and where did he get it from?" And as any son might wonder, "Is he the real deal for my mom?" It was time to look into who this guy truly was!

The Bahora brothers (*left to right*), Ben, Greg, Cary, Scott, and Bob (Goshen, NY, 1988). Photo courtesy of Jan Brookmeyer.

But discovering the real Bob Brookmeyer wasn't so easy at first. However, this had a lot to do with Bob being quite humble. He never talked himself up or let on that he was somehow a jazz legend. It was only through questioning our mom and random interactions with others that we began to learn of his reputation and influence.

One such encounter was when, upon learning our dad was Bob Brookmeyer, my bass guitar instructor excitedly explained "Wow, his music is so intricate and cerebral. You are a really fortunate guy." Bob's ability and influence were evident in my instructor's enthusiastic and passionate response.

But even more crucially, we were given a front-row ticket to Bob's life. We got our first view of the true Bob Brookmeyer in his living space in Goshen, New York, and later in New Hampshire, thanks to Bob's open house policy—and it was incredible!

Through the simple things he did, we quickly learned of his real caring and kindness. He always greeted you with a hug when you first met him. He'd inquire as to how you were and compliment you. He would sincerely listen to and engage in your response after asking what was going on in your life.

We also found him to be inquisitive and amusing. He loved sitting around the kitchen table with everyone and talking about life and nearly everything under the sun. His laugh, honesty, and candor were contagious. We learned wonderful stories of his sneaking into clubs as a minor to play with some of the early jazz greats. He talked about his boredom and challenging days in New York as a house musician on the Merv Griffin Show and about his years in California. His insights into his long relationships with numerous jazz greats throughout his career—including Stan Getz, Gerry Mulligan, Jim Hall, Clark Terry, and a slew of others—were legendary.

Bob, as many of us knew, was also passionate about politics, so there were some lively debates at the dinner table. Regardless of the topic or intensity, however, the discussions were always respectful and open, resulting in everyone being better off as a result of the new insights obtained.

As we learned more about Bob, we realized that one of the reasons he was so calm and wise was because he had conquered so many obstacles in his life. He was the physical embodiment of the pearl analogy, in which the pearl emerges polished and sparkling brightly for all to see after years of irritation and roughness.

Finally, knowing how much Bob had won over our mother's heart was the icing on the cake. His wit, charm, caring, and openness drew people in like a magnet, and our mom was no exception. Everyone could see how happy they were and how much they treasured their days together.

Bob had a huge and positive influence on us four brothers without a doubt. We miss him dearly, and it gives us tremendous joy to see his spirit continue to live on via his music and the countless people he touched and continues to inspire over his long, fruitful, and meaningful life.

Of the four brothers, Ben Bahora is the resident poet. One of my poet/mentors always said that a poem shouldn't tell us something, it should show us something. And Ben's poem here does exactly that, with both Ben's dryly laconic humor and pathos.

Ben Bahora: "With Bob"

I.

driving to NYC he would play

his crazy music super L O U D
in the fast lane like a madman
refused to shift out of third gear
hit the brakes
for no apparent reason

the car lurching down the road
down the road
crazy music screeching !

i finally had it "shift or i'll kill you"

bob liked that
from then on i drove

II.

bob loved football toward the end, it was

the couch and the big screen bob was always bigger than life
when he was low
i would take his hand
and we would talk that would refresh him
then it was back to the game

... And Other Bright Moments 223

"We'll have no gum chewing or bubble blowing on the bandstand! And while I'm at it, no loud rim shots on the bass solos either!" (Thank goodness, this was only a posed photo!) Arizona, 1980. Photo courtesy of Theo Saunders.

A Place Called Home

Music has the power to bring people together. We often create and nurture friendships based initially upon our mutual interest in the kind of music we favor as either musicians or fans. The possibility of building long-term relationships this way may seem far-fetched but is, in fact, quite doable.

Bob and I were friends for decades, and our relationship grew from casual to familial, beginning almost fifty years ago. Witness Kathleen's and my wedding pictures in this book. Others I know feel the same way about him and Jan as Kathleen and I do—even though earthbound Bob is no longer here. Bob liked calling me his younger brother on occasion and was always there to literally or figuratively place his arm around my shoulder at various times in my life either

At home in New Hampshire: Jan holding Fern, Bob with a very disgruntled-looking Sally. Photo by Ann Corbett.

with advice or a joke. For example, here's a typical (but semifictional) exchange when I was feeling pretty low:

Me: I'm feeling really bad about life right about now.
Bob: Well kid, if anything, it'll help you play the blues better.

- During one visit to New Hampshire, Bob offered Kathleen and me his beloved Camaro to drive to Vermont to visit a cousin. It was "four-on-the-floor" all the way and the sheer power of the car scared the hell out of the Honda driver in me! That year we actually brought him a sign to hang in the garage: "No Parking Except for Bob." Jan still has the sign hanging in the house.
- One Thanksgiving we were visiting Jan and Bob and were invited to a holiday feast that their friends were hosting (about twenty people all told). We were all seated at long tables that extended in two rooms. Bob and Jan sat across from Kathleen and me, and Bob looked kind of bored. Once the food arrived and we all were

Relaxin' on the veranda: "Ahhh. It doesn't get any better."
From author's collection.

Left to right: Kathleen; Bob, holding camera-shy, uncooperative Sally; and Jan. From author's collection.

eating, I noticed Bob eyeing Jan's plate. When Jan was engaged in conversation with someone to her right, Bob was stealing food from her plate quite nonchalantly until Jan finally caught him in the act. I wish I could've captured the look on his face. All I could think of was what might've transpired in Kansas City in 1941 at the Brookmeyer dinner table.

- When Bob laughed, his voice dropped an octave and became very sinister and guttural sounding. I still do my impression of him, whereupon Jan immediately joins in with her own version and cracks both of us up.

Kathleen and I always felt at home with Bob and Jan on Allen's Drive. There was a lot of love in their house and a cozy, relaxed feeling that permeated the place. Of course, Bob and I spent much of the time in his studio, talking about everything from music to his short-lived infatuation with Western wear, which found us going shopping at three or

Kathleen and the maestro at one of our last visits with Bob and Jan (2010). From author's collection.

four "authentic" Western clothing shops while we were gigging years ago in Arizona. Lots of laughter then and a continued closeness for which I will always be grateful.

Included on these pages are some glimpses of the Brookmeyers at home in New Hampshire.

Kathleen and I have remained good friends with Jan over the years and make the trek annually to New England to spend time with her. By the way, Jan marveled at the huge smile on Bob's face in the photo of him and Kathleen. I also seem to remember that it was a very happy day for Bob. I know now that that's the way I'll always remember him.

Chapter 8

Goodbye, World

"Minuet Circa '61": Last Words, Last Song

Due to ill health, the last few years of Bob's life were difficult for him and Jan. He told me once around that time that he was more interested in composing music for his large European ensemble—the New Art Orchestra—than he was in playing. He expressed this succinctly in the following email to me: "Sorry to be so brief last call, but I have too many worries . . . getting some real sleep would help. I'm having to cancel a commission and hope I make Sweden OK in a month. Also, with what I learn about the 'real world,' a few nights in a jazz club doesn't do much against Martial Law. I just don't have the interest in being a jazz musician anymore."[1]

Bob hated what was happening in the world, especially here at home during the George W. Bush presidency. He wrote any number of blog entries for the "Currents" portion of his website that excoriated Bush and other higher-ups in government positions, and was thinking seriously of moving to Vancouver, British Columbia. There were times I remembered when Kathleen and I would visit Bob and Jan in New Hampshire and find Bob "raging against the machine"; and it seemed clear to us that his passionate cynicism was close to becoming somewhat obsessive. Around that time I also remember responding to one of his lamentations of utter hopelessness, by saying, "I think the best thing you can do to avoid making yourself ill is to sit at the piano and use your compositional gifts to write the first four bars of a new piece—at least immerse yourself in the process. And If you like those, try for four more. Bring what beauty into the world you can. There's enough anger out there already. A little music goes a long way." I'm not sure Bob was listening, and we were worried that he was on a toxic merry-go-round spinning out of control.

Like so many others do, I have the feeling that the light at the end of the tunnel was Jan, and that her loving presence and compassion provided a sort of metaphysical balm for Bob. In our late conversations, he spoke about his *Brookmeyer/Standards* recording project, his proposed composition book, and his desire to record a "solo-duo-trio" project with bassist Scott Colley and me, which, sadly, never came to be, due to Bob's weakening health condition.

In what was perhaps our final phone conversation, I mentioned to Bob that his solos reminded me at times of those of tenor saxophonist Lester Young, in that both he and Prez were linear storytellers due to their unabashed lyricism and the way they were able to get inside a song's lyrics and portray the feeling of those lyrics in their improvisations. "Besides," I said, "both you and Prez played solos that sounded like little melodies unto themselves. They were singable."

Silence at the other end of the line . . . and my first thought was that I may have just put my foot in my mouth. Then he replied: "That's one of the nicest things anyone ever said to me about my playing."

"I didn't say that to be nice. I said it because it's true."

Bob Brookmeyer passed peacefully from this life in December of 2011, just shy of his 82nd birthday. As mentioned earlier, there was a memorial for him at St. Peter's Cathedral in New York City that featured musical performances, impromptu and prepared reminisces, and the video montage mentioned at the end of this book. The cathedral was packed with musicians, writers, poets, and fans. Bob was certainly well-loved by so many people, young and old. Regrettably, years after Bob's passing, upon interviewing the legendary saxophonist Sonny Rollins for my Ornette Coleman book, when Bob's name came up, Sonny said how much he admired Bob's playing and how he would've liked to have recorded a song with Bob called "The Things We Did Last Summer." I know that Bob was an admirer of Sonny's playing and spirit and that he would've been thrilled to hear that Sonny felt the same way about him.

Like Sonny, Bob was and will always be a legend and an icon whose music, wisdom, humor, and inspiration will continue to be his legacy for generations to come. And he was my lifelong friend, to whom I owe so much for being such an important part of both my musical and personal life. Elsewhere in this book, Bob gifted me by saying that I was his "younger brother—in music and in life."

On the Way to the Sky is my gift to him . . . and to you.

"Brookmeyer at the Half-Note, 1965"

You step up to the mic   turn to Jones: e-flat   one . . . two . . .

Piano arpeggios shimmering like blue lights on 48th and 8th
Crow hugs the wood   notes ring like dark glass bells

Bailey's snare swishes and swirls, lush carpet of orbiting whispers
    Skylark   *have you anything*
    to say   *to me?*

(Frank stops pouring and Sonny comes out of the kitchen)

You dig deep gruff and tender   Kansas City Still Life (1954)
Gray dawn under a street lamp   some hooch   a broken heart
    Won't you tell me   *where*
    my love   *can be?*

Burry sound   plaintive song   to someone or somewhere
in the night sky   on the shoulders of   melody

You play to the floor then in a sweeping arc   to the stars
above Hudson & Canal   above Manhattan   above all
an out-of-whack Gabriel filling our void   telling your story

no one moves   speaks   doubts   that   love
            is
    in a meadow   *in the mist,*
     someone waiting
      to be kissed.[2]

—Michael Stephans

In the moment. Stock photo.

"Minuet Circa '61"

The setting sun was making way for dusk as I walked through a little grove of trees behind your house on Allen's Drive, until I came to the small clearing where your memorial stone was. After a moment of silence, and with the last sunbeams casting their streaks of gold and copper onto the leafy floor, I sang note-for-note your solo on "Minuet Circa '61," after which I turned and walked back to the house in dusky silence . . . without saying goodbye, because I knew that you would always be there.

Selected Discography

As a Leader

The Modernity of Bob Brookmeyer: The 1954 Quartets. Fresh Sound Records, 1958.

The Dual Role of Bob Brookmeyer. Prestige, 1956.

Brookmeyer. Vik, 1957.

Traditionalism Revisited. World Pacific, 1957.

The Street Swingers. World Pacific, 1958.

Kansas City Revisited. United Artists, 1959.

The Ivory Hunters, with Bill Evans. United Artists, 1959.

Jazz Is a Kick. Mercury, 1960.

Portrait of the Artist. Atlantic, 1960.

The Blues Hot and Cold. Verve, 1960.

Gloomy Sunday and Other Bright Moments. Verve, 1961.

7 x Wilder. Verve, 1961.

Trombone Jazz Samba. Verve, 1962.

Bob Brookmeyer and Friends. Columbia, 1965.

The Bob Brookmeyer Small Band. Gryphon, 1978.

Back Again. Sonet, 1979.

Through a Looking Glass. Finesse, 1981.

Oslo. Concord Jazz, 1987.

Dreams, with the Stockholm Radio Orchestra. Dragon Records, 1989.

Electricity. ACT, 1994.

Paris Suite. Challenge, 1995.

Out of This World, with Metropole Orchestra. Koch Jazz, 1998.

Old Friends. Storyville, 1998.

New Works Celebration, with The New Art Orchestra. Challenge, 1999.

Together with Mads Vinding. Challenge, 1999.

Holiday. Challenge, 2001.

Madly Loving You, with the Ed Partyka Jazz Orchestra. Challenge, 2001.

Waltzing with Zoe, with The New Art Orchestra. Challenge 2002.

Stay Out of the Sun, with Michael Stephans. Challenge, 2003.
Get Well Soon, with The New Art Orchestra. Challenge, 2003.
Island, with Kenny Wheeler. Artists House, 2003.
Spirit Music, with The New Art Orchestra. ArtistShare, 2006.
Brookmeyer/Standards, with The New Art Orchestra, featuring Fay Claasen. ArtistShare, 2011.
On the Way to the Sky. WDR: Cologne Broadcasts, Jazzline, 2016.

As a Co-leader
With Al Cohn
The Al Cohn Quintet Featuring Bobby Brookmeyer. Coral, 1957.

With Stan Getz
Complete 1953–54 Quintet Recordings with Stan Getz. Definitive Records, 2004.
Stan Getz at the Shrine. Verve. 2009.
Recorded Fall 1961. Verve, 1961.

With Jimmy Giuffre
Trav'lin' Light. Atlantic, 1958.
Western Suite. Atlantic, 1960.

With Jim Hall
Live at the North Sea Jazz Festival. Challenge, 1999.

With Gerry Mulligan
Paris Concert. Pacific Jazz, 1955.
The Concert Jazz Band. Verve, 1960.
Gerry Mulligan and the Concert Jazz Band at the Village Vanguard. Verve, 1961.
Gerry Mulligan Presents a Concert in Jazz. Verve, 1961.
Gerry Mulligan and the Concert Jazz Band on Tour. Verve, 1962.
The Gerry Mulligan Quartet. Verve, 1962.

With Zoot Sims

Tonite's Music Today. Storyville, 1956.
Zoot Sims–Bob Brookmeyer Octet: Stretching Out. United Artists, 1959.
Morning Fun. Black Lion, 1989.

With Clark Terry

The Power of Positive Swinging. Mainstream, 1965.
Tonight. Mainstream, 1965.
Gingerbread Men. Mainstream, 1966.
Previously Unreleased Recordings. Verve, 1973.
Gingerbread Gal. Mainstream, 1974.
What'd He Say. Mainstream, 1974.

Selected Videography

Brookmeyer, Bob, and Jim Hall. "I Should Care." 1987 Bath Music Festival, UK. YouTube, April 25, 2020. 3:25. https://youtu.be/vsvan-Q7mww.

Brookmeyer, Bob, and John Scofield. "Moonlight in Vermont." YouTube, April 27, 2008. 3:50. https://youtu.be/7o-pi8rs1Jk.

Gerry Mulligan Quartet. *Ralph J. Gleason's Jazz Casual*. DVD. San Francisco: Idem Home Video, 2001.

Horowitz, Murray, prod. *The Making of a Song* (1981), ABC Video Enterprises, Inc., courtesy of the Mel Lewis Estate / Lori Lowell. YouTube, December 30, 2022, by Michael Stephans. 26:20. https://youtu.be/LuMsLyJvZqg.

Le Claire, Marie, Marie Schneider, Ryan Truesdell. "The Life and Music of Bob Brookmeyer (2012)." YouTube, June 10, 2012. 23:10. https://youtu.be/juJF5WWmEGE.

Metropol Orkest and Bob Brookmeyer. *American Beauty* recording session. Hilversum, Holland: MetropolVideo, 1999. 20:33. https://youtu.be/ylCr0dCCbCo.

Metropol Orkest and Bob Brookmeyer. *Fanfares and Folk Song* recording session. Hilversum, Holland: MetropolVideo, 1999. 10:03. https://youtu.be/fdlsfucTQHk.

Metropol Orkest. "Stella by Starlight," Bob Brookmeyer, soloist (1981). Hilversum, Holland: MetropolVideo, May 23, 2011. 3:47. https://youtu.be/ylCr0dCCbCo.

"Suite for Three": A Documentary on Bob Brookmeyer's Compositions. Columbia, MO: ArtistsHouseMusic, 2009. 47:55. https://youtu.be/e52y4zUOs2A.

Terry, Clark, and Bob Brookmeyer Quintet. *Jazz 625*. DVD. London: Impro Jazz, 2007. 31:50.

Thad Jones/Mel Lewis Jazz Orchestra, *Ralph J. Gleason's Jazz Casual*. DVD. San Francisco: Idem Home Video, 2001.

Acknowledgments

As lamented elsewhere, it is often truly difficult to put into words what we're hearing when we listen to music—in this case jazz—either in real time or on a recording. The writers who really did it well in the past included Whitney Balliett (in his fabled column in *The New Yorker*), Nat Hentoff, A. B. Spellman, Burt Korall, Dan Morgenstern, Stanley Crouch, Val Wilmer, and Martin Williams (in their respective books and magazine articles). Among the musicians who were also accomplished wordsmiths were trumpeters Kenny Dorham and Rex Stewart, reedman Buddy Collette, and drummer Art Taylor, and, of course, Bob Brookmeyer. Among the current crew of adept jazz musicians who also know how to turn a phrase are reedmen Dave Liebman and Bill Kirchner; pianists Kenny Werner and Jim McNeely; drummers Joe LaBarbera, Charles Levin, and Chris Smith; and especially venerable bassist Bill Crow, who is a fine musician and writer who manages to bring jazz and its creators into the light with great empathy, warmth, and more than a dollop of humor. All have one thing in common: they listened deeply and wrote about the music and musicians perceptively and with great insight.

I would also like to offer my gratitude, first and foremost, to Janet Brookmeyer for her generosity, wisdom, and patience. She was Bob's raison d'être. Love and thanks also to my wife Kathleen for her input, wise counsel, and compassion every step of the way. Without her this would've indeed been a lonely journey.

Big thank yous are in order for the many wonderful people who contributed to each chapter. Special kudos to Dave Rivello, Maria Schneider, Jim McNeely, John Hollenbeck, John Mosca, Lori Lowell, Adam Nussbaum, Bill Holman, Bill Crow, Paul Heller, Scott Robinson, John Riley, Ryan Truesdell, Theo Saunders, Danny Gottlieb, Rob Hudson, and Bob's stepsons Greg and Ben Bahora. *On the Way to the Sky* would not have been nearly as memorable without your contributions and those of the many others who paid tribute to Bob in chapters 6 and 7.

Finally, none of this would've been possible without the guidance of Ron Chrisman, Amy Maddox, and others on the UNT Press staff for bringing this book into the light; and for the assistance of David Peter Coppen, archivist from the Sibley Music Library at the Eastman School of Music, for access to the many fine photographs from the Brookmeyer Special Collection. Finally, deepest gratitude to journalist Cameron Kiszla and master designer Chris Drukker for their wisdom and truly Herculean organizational skills in helping to keep me on track.

In Memoriam

"The Life and Music of Bob Brookmeyer," a twenty-three-minute video montage conceived and produced by Maria Schneider, Ryan Truesdell, and Marie Le Claire. St. Peter's Church, April 11, 2012, https://www.youtube.com/watch?v=juJF5WWmEGE&t=3s.

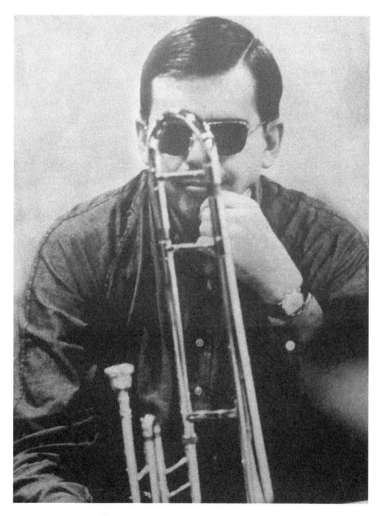

Photo from author's collection.

Endnotes

Notes for the Preface
1. Norman Ferguson, T. Hee, and Wilfred Jackson, dirs., *Pinocchio* (Walt Disney Productions, 1940).
2. William Shakespeare, *The Tragedy of Hamlet, Prince of Denmark.*

Notes for Chapter 1
1. David Ware, "Bob Brookmeyer—Doin' It His Way," *Jazz Education Journal* 36, no. 2 (2003): 42.
2. Ware, "Bob Brookmeyer."
3. Brookmeyer in Rob Hudson, *Evolution: The Improvisational Style of Bob Brookmeyer for Trombone* (New York: Universal Edition, 2003), iv.
4. Brookmeyer, liner notes for *Traditionalism Revisited* (World Pacific Records, 1957).
5. Brookmeyer, *Traditionalism Revisited.*
6. Nat Hentoff, liner notes for Brookmeyer, *Traditionalism Revisited.*
7. Nat Hentoff, *Jazz Is* (New York: Limelight, 1976).
8. Charlie Parker, quoted in Nat Shapiro and Nat Hentoff, *Hear Me Talkin' to Ya: The Story of Jazz as Told by the Men Who Made It* (Mineola, NY: Dover Publications, 1955).
9. Mort Fega, liner notes for *Samba Para Dos*, by Lalo Schifrin and Bob Brookmeyer (Verve Records, 1963).
10. Ware, "Bob Brookmeyer."
11. Bob Brookmeyer and Dave Rivello, *Bob Brookmeyer in Conversation with Dave Rivello* (New York: ArtistShare, 2019).
12. Bob Brookmeyer and Michael Stephans, liner notes for *Stay Out of the Sun* (Challenge Records, 2003).
13. Bob Brookmeyer, note published on author's website, 2006.

Notes for Chapter 2
1. "Mental Illness and Alcoholism Plagued Buzz Aldrin," *PACE Recovery Center*, July 23, 2019, https://www.pacerecoverycenter.com/mental-illness-alcoholism-buzz-aldrin/.
2. The Bob Brookmeyer Small Band, *Recorded "Live" at Sandy's Jazz Revival*, CD (Norman Schwartz, 1978).
3. Herb Ellis, Lou Carter, and John Frigo, "Detour Ahead" (Soft Winds, 1948).

4. Marc Myers, "Interview: Bob Brookmeyer (Part 5)," *JazzWax* (blog), June 26, 2009, https://www.jazzwax.com/2009/06/interview-bob-brookmeyer-part-5.html.
5. Marc Myers, "Interview: Bob Brookmeyer (Part 4)," *JazzWax* (blog), June 25, 2009, https://www.jazzwax.com/2009/06/interview-bob-brookmeyer-part-4.html.
6. Elizabeth Spires, "Two Shadows," *New Criterion* 3, no. 8 (1985): 43, https://newcriterion.com/issues/1985/4/two-shadows.

Notes for Chapter 3

1. Loren Schoenberg, "Reissuing *Recorded Fall 1961*," liner notes for *Recorded Fall 1961*, by Stan Getz and Bob Brookmeyer (Verve Records, 2000).
2. Brookmeyer and Rivello, *Brookmeyer in Conversation*, 118.
3. Brookmeyer and Rivello, *Brookmeyer in Conversation*, 125.
4. Ed Dix, liner notes for *Full Circle*, by Bob Brookmeyer and Ed Dix, CD (CD Baby, 2002).
5. Bob Brookmeyer, liner notes for Brookmeyer and Dix, *Full Circle*.

Notes for Chapter 4

1. Marc Myers, "Interview: Bob Brookmeyer (Part 1)," *JazzWax* (blog), June 22, 2009, https://www.jazzwax.com/2009/06/interview-bob-brookmeyer-part-1.html.
2. Marc Myers, "Interview: Bob Brookmeyer (Part 3)," *JazzWax* (blog), June 24, 2009, https://www.jazzwax.com/2009/06/interview-bob-brookmeyer-part-1.html.
3. Gordon Jack, *Fifties Jazz Talk: An Oral Retrospective* (Lanham, MD: Scarecrow Press, 2004), 42–43.
4. Wayne Enstice and Paul Rubin, *Jazz Spoken Here: Conversations with 22 Musicians* (New York City: Da Capo Press, 1994), 68.
5. Jerome Klinkowitz, *Listen: Gerry Mulligan: An Aural Narrative in Jazz* (New York: Schirmer Books, 1991), 126.
6. Bill Kirchner, liner notes for *The Complete Gerry Mulligan Concert Jazz Band Sessions*, CD (Mosaic Records, 2003).
7. Jack, *Fifties Jazz Talk*, 42–43.
8. Nat Hentoff, liner notes for *Portrait of the Artist*, by Bob Brookmeyer, Atlantic Records, 1960.
9. Bob Brookmeyer, liner notes for *Portrait of the Artist*.
10. Myers, "Brookmeyer (Part 3)."
11. Myers, "Brookmeyer (Part 4)."
12. Chris Smith, *The View from the Back of the Band: The Life and Music of Mel Lewis* (Denton: University of North Texas Press, 2014), 134.

13. Enstice and Rubin, *Jazz Spoken Here*, 62.
14. Jack, *Fifties Jazz Talk*, 48.
15. John Mosca, "A Life in Two Acts (or More): Remembering Bob Brookmeyer," *Allegro* 112, no. 2 (February 2012).
16. Smith, *View from the Back*, 30.
17. Smith, *View from the Back*, 68.
18. Smith, *View from the Back*, 206.
19. Jim McNeely, "Jim McNeely Remembers Bob Brookmeyer," *Jazz Times*, March 21, 2012.
20. Johnny Mercer and Hoagy Carmichael, "Skylark" (Frank & Simon Music, 1942).
21. "Mel Lewis – Bob Brookmeyer: *The Making of a Song*," YouTube, December 29, 2022, https://youtu.be/LuMsLyJvZqg?si=5fcv7VztzRr2PnGb.
22. Burt Korall, *Drummin' Men: The Heartbeat of Jazz—The Bebop Years* (New York: Oxford University Press, 2002), 248.
23. Jan Brookmeyer, conversation with the author, Manchester, Vermont, October 28, 2002.

Notes for Chapter 5

1. Myers, "Brookmeyer (Part 5)."
2. Roger Scruton, *Beauty*, (New York City: Oxford University Press, 2009), 120.
3. Scruton, *Beauty*, 124.
4. Scruton, *Beauty*, 167.
5. Leonard Feather, *The Book of Jazz from Then Till Now: A Guide to the Entire Field* (New York: Crown Publishing, 1976), quoted in Nat Shapiro, *An Encyclopedia of Quotations About Music*, (Garden City, NY: Doubleday, 1978).
6. Nat Hentoff, quoted in Shapiro, *Encyclopedia of Quotations*, 286.
7. Brookmeyer and Rivello, *Brookmeyer in Conversation*, 43.
8. Brookmeyer and Rivello, *Brookmeyer in Conversation*, 103.
9. Douglas Payne, "Bob Brookmeyer: *Electricity*," *AllAboutJazz*, May 1, 1997, https://www.allaboutjazz.com/electricity-bob-brookmeyer-act-music-review-by-douglas-payne.
10. Payne, "Brookmeyer: *Electricity*."
11. Payne, "Bob Brookmeyer: *Electricity*."
12. Payne, "Bob Brookmeyer: *Electricity*."
13. Payne, "Brookmeyer: *Electricity*."
14. Bob Brookmeyer, interview by Eric Nemeyer, *Jazz Inside NY*, 2009.
15. Bob Brookmeyer, liner notes for *New Works Celebration*, CD (Challenge, 1999).

16. Brookmeyer and Rivello, *Brookmeyer in Conversation*, 110.
17. John Hollenbeck, email to author, February 9, 2023.
18. Bob Brookmeyer, liner notes for *Waltzing With Zoe* (Challenge Records, 2002).
19. Brookmeyer and Rivello, *Brookmeyer in Conversation*, 107.
20. Hollenbeck, email to author, February 9, 2023.
21. Bob Brookmeyer, liner notes for *Get Well Soon* (Challenge Records, 2003).
22. Jack Bowers, "Bob Brookmeyer New Art Orchestra: *Get Well Soon*," *AllAboutJazz*, August 6, 2004, https://www.allaboutjazz.com/get-well-soon-bob-brookmeyer-challenge-records-review-by-jack-bowers.
23. Brookmeyer, liner notes for *Get Well Soon*.
24. Brookmeyer, liner notes for *Get Well Soon*.
25. Brookmeyer, liner notes for *Get Well Soon*.
26. Brookmeyer, liner notes for *Kansas City Revisited* (United Artists, 1959).
27. Jean Sibelius, quoted in Bengt de Törne, *Sibelius: A Close-up* (Boston: Houghton Mifflin, 1937).
28. David Franklin, "Bob Brookmeyer and the New Art Orchestra: *Spirit Music*," *AllAboutJazz*, April 1, 2007, updated April 25, 2019.
29. Sylvia Boorstein, *Don't Just Do Something, Sit There: A Mindfulness Retreat with Sylvia Boorstein* (New York: HarperCollins, 1996).
30. Bob Brookmeyer, liner notes for *Spirit Music* (ArtistShare, 2006).
31. Maria Schneider, liner notes for *Brookmeyer/Standards* (ArtistShare, 2011).

Notes for Chapter 6

1. Marc, "Brookmeyer (Part 4)."
2. Ken Schaphorst, "Bob Brookmeyer Stories," *New England Conservatory*, December 2011, https://necmusic.edu/archives/bob-brookmeyer-stories.
3. Michael Gandolfi, "Bob Brookmeyer Stories," New England Conservatory, December 2011, https://necmusic.edu/archives/bob-brookmeyer-stories.
4. Darcy James Argue, "Celebration: Remembering—A Tribute to Bob Brookmeyer," *NewMusicBox*, December 23, 2011, https://newmusicusa.org/nmbx/celebration-remembering-a-tribute-to-bob-brookmeyer.
5. McNeely, "McNeely Remembers."
6. John Hollenbeck, email to author, January 21, 2022.
7. Dave Rivello, "My Time with a Master," *International Society of Jazz Arrangers and Composers*, January 1, 2020, https://isjac.org/artist-blog/dave-rivello-my-time-with-a-master.

8. Mosca, "Life in Two Acts."
9. Jim Hall quoted in Argue, "Celebration."
10. Clark Terry quoted in Argue, "Celebration."
11. Scott Robinson, email to author, September 5, 2022.
12. Kris Goessens quoted in Argue, "Celebration."
13. Paul Heller, email to author, March 31, 2023.
14. Danny Gottlieb, email to author, April 5, 2023.
15. John Riley, email to author, January 19, 2023.
16. Rob Hudson, email to author, August 21, 2022.
17. Terry Teachout, "They Said Goodbye To Brookmeyer," *Rifftides: Doug Ramsay on Jazz and Other Matters*, ArtsJournal, April 13, 2012, https://www.artsjournal.com/rifftides/2012/04/they-said-goodbye-to-brookmeyer.html.
18. Maria Schneider, interview by author, August 25, 2022.

Notes for Chapter 7

1. Teachout, "They Said Goodbye."
2. Craig Harris and Thom Jurek, "Eliane Elias," *Bluenote*, accessed April 20, 2023, https://www.bluenote.com/artist/eliane-elias.
3. Bob Brookmeyer, liner notes for *Music for String Quartet and Orchestra* by the Gustav Klimt String Quartet and Metropole Orchestra (Challenge Records, 2008).
4. Brookmeyer, liner notes for *Music for String Quartet and Orchestra*.
5. Ken Dryden, review, *Music for String Quartet and Orchestra*, allmusic.com, December 3, 2008.

Notes for Chapter 8

1. Bob Brookmeyer, email to author.
2. Michael Stephans, "Brookmeyer at the Half-Note, 1965," in *The Color of Stones* (Red Dancefloor Press, 1997). Johnny Mercer and Hoagy Carmichael, "Skylark" (Frank & Simon Music, 1942).

Bibliography

Archives

Bob Brookmeyer Special Collection. Sibley Music Library, Eastman School of Music, University of Rochester, NY.

Albums

The Bob Brookmeyer Small Band. *Recorded "Live" at Sandy's Jazz Revival*. Norman Schwartz, 1978.

Brookmeyer, Bob. Concert handout for *On the Way to the Sky*. WDR Studios, 1989.

Brookmeyer, Bob. Liner notes for *Electricity*. ACT Records, 1994.

Brookmeyer, Bob, and Ed Dix. Liner notes for *Full Circle*. CD Baby, 2002.

Brookmeyer, Bob. Liner notes for *Get Well Soon*. Challenge Records, 2003.

Brookmeyer, Bob. Liner notes for *Kansas City Revisited*. United Artists, 1959.

Bob Brookmeyer, liner notes for *Music for String Quartet and Orchestra*, by the Gustav Klimt String Quartet and Metropole Orchestra. Challenge Records, 2008.

Brookmeyer, Bob. Liner notes for *New Works Celebration*. Challenge Records, 1999.

Brookmeyer, Bob. Liner notes for *Portrait of the Artist*. Atlantic Records, 1960

Brookmeyer, Bob. Liner notes for *Spirit Music*. ArtistShare, 2006.

Brookmeyer, Bob. Liner notes for *Traditionalism Revisited*. World Pacific Records, 1957.

Brookmeyer, Bob. Liner notes for *Waltzing with Zoe*. Challenge Records, 2002.

Brookmeyer, Bob, and Michael Stephans. Liner notes for *Stay Out of the Sun*. Challenge Records, 2003.

Dix, Ed. Liner notes for Brookmeyer and Dix, *Full Circle*.

Ellis, Herb, Lou Carter, and John Frigo. "Detour Ahead." Soft Winds, 1948.

Fega, Mort. Liner notes for *Samba Para Dos*, by Lalo Schifrin and Bob Brookmeyer. Verve Records, 1963.

Gitler, Ira. Liner notes for *The Ivory Hunters*, by Bob Brookmeyer and Bill Evans. United Artists Records, 1959.

Hentoff, Nat. Liner notes for Brookmeyer, *Portrait of the Artist*.

Hentoff, Nat. Liner notes for Brookmeyer, *Traditionalism Revisited*.

Kirchner, Bill. Liner notes for *The Complete Gerry Mulligan Concert Jazz Band Sessions*. Mosaic Records, 2003.

Schneider, Maria. Liner notes for *Brookmeyer/Standards*, by Bob Brookmeyer. ArtistShare, 2011.

Schoenberg, Loren. "Reissuing *Recorded Fall 1961*." Liner notes for *Recorded Fall 1961*, by Stan Getz and Bob Brookmeyer. Verve Records, 2000.

Other Sources

Argue, Darcy James. "Celebration: Remembering—A Tribute to Bob Brookmeyer." *NewMusicBox*, December 23, 2011. https://newmusicusa.org/nmbx/celebration-remembering-a-tribute-to-bob-brookmeyer/.

Boorstein, Sylvia. *Don't Just Do Something, Sit There: A Mindfulness Retreat with Sylvia Boorstein*. New York: HarperCollins, 1996.

Bourdain, Anthony. *The Nasty Bits*. New York: Bloomsbury, 2006.

Bowers, Jack. "Bob Brookmeyer New Art Orchestra: *Get Well Soon*." *AllAboutJazz*, August 6, 2004. https://www.allaboutjazz.com/get-well-soon-bob-brookmeyer-challenge-records-review-by-jack-bowers.

Brookmeyer, Bob, interview by Eric Nemeyer. *Jazz Inside NY*, December 2009.

Brookmeyer, Bob, and Dave Rivello. *Bob Brookmeyer in Conversation with Dave Rivello*. New York: ArtistShare, 2019.

Coss, Bill. "Bob Brookmeyer: Strength and Simplicity." *DownBeat*, January 19, 1961.

de Lint, Charles. *Greenmantle*. New York: TOR Publishing, 1992.

de Törne, Bengt. *Sibelius: A Close-up*. Boston: Houghton Mifflin, 1937.

Enstice, Wayne, and Paul Rubin. *Jazz Spoken Here: Conversations with 22 Musicians*. New York City: Da Capo Press, 1994.

Feather, Leonard. *The Book of Jazz from Then Till Now: A Guide to the Entire Field*. New York: Crown Publishing, 1976.

Ferguson, Norman, T. Hee, and Wilfred Jackson, dirs. *Pinocchio*. Walt Disney Productions, 1940.

Franklin, David. "Bob Brookmeyer and the New Art Orchestra: *Spirit Music*." *AllAboutJazz*, April 1, 2007, updated April 25, 2019.

Gelatt, Tim, Ray Hooper, and Bill Quinn. *About John Coltrane*. New York: National Jazz Museum in Harlem, 1974.

Hentoff, Nat. *Jazz Is*. New York: Limelight, 1976.

Hudson, Rob. *Evolution: The Improvisational Style of Bob Brookmeyer for Trombone*. New York: Universal Edition, 2003.

Jack, Gordon. *Fifties Jazz Talk: An Oral Retrospective*. Lanham, MD: Scarecrow Press, 2004.

Klinkowitz, Jerome. *Listen: Gerry Mulligan: An Aural Narrative in Jazz*. New York: Schirmer Books, 1991.

Korall, Burt. *Drummin' Men: The Heartbeat of Jazz—The Bebop Years*. New York: Oxford University Press, 2002.

Lisik, Dave and Eric Allen. *50 Years at the Village Vanguard: Thad Jones, Mel Lewis, and the Vanguard Orchestra*. Chicago: SkyDeck Music, 2017.

"The Making of a Song, Bob Brookmeyer, Mel Lewis and The Jazz Orchestra." ABC Arts, August 1, 1981.

McNeely, Jim. "Jim McNeely Remembers Bob Brookmeyer." *Jazz Times*, March 21, 2012.

Morgenstern, Dan. "Bob Brookmeyer—Master of the Brass Stepchild." *DownBeat*, January 26, 1967.

Mosca, John. "A Life in Two Acts (or More): Remembering Bob Brookmeyer." *Allegro* 112, no. 1 (February 2012).

Myers, Marc. "Interview: Bob Brookmeyer (Part 1)." *JazzWax* (blog), June 22, 2009. https://www.jazzwax.com/2009/06/interview-bob-brookmeyer-part-1.html.

Myers, Marc. "Interview: Bob Brookmeyer (Part 3)." *JazzWax* (blog), June 24, 2009. https://www.jazzwax.com/2009/06/interview-bob-brookmeyer-part-3.html.

Myers, Marc. "Interview: Bob Brookmeyer (Part 4)." *JazzWax* (blog), June 25, 2009. https://www.jazzwax.com/2009/06/interview-bob-brookmeyer-part-4.html.

Myers, Marc. "Interview: Bob Brookmeyer (Part 5)." *JazzWax* (blog), June 26, 2009. https://www.jazzwax.com/2009/06/interview-bob-brookmeyer-part-5.html.

Payne, Douglas. "Bob Brookmeyer: *Electricity*." *AllAboutJazz*, May 1, 1997. https://www.allaboutjazz.com/electricity-bob-brookmeyer-act-music-review-by- douglas-payne.

Scruton, Roger. *Beauty*. New York: Oxford University Press, 2009.

Shakespeare, William. *The Tragedy of Hamlet, Prince of Denmark*.

Shapiro, Nat. *An Encyclopedia of Quotations About Music*. Garden City, NY: Doubleday, 1978.

Shapiro, Nat, and Nat Hentoff. *Hear Me Talkin' to Ya: The Story of Jazz as Told by the Men Who Made It*. Mineola, NY: Dover Publications, 1955.

Smith, Chris. *The View from the Back of the Band: The Life and Music of Mel Lewis*. Denton: University of North Texas Press, 2014.

Spires, Elizabeth. "Two Shadows." *New Criterion* 3, no. 8 (1985): 43. https://newcriterion.com/issues/1985/4/two-shadows.

Stephans, Michael. "Brookmeyer at the Half-Note, 1965." In *The Color of Stones*. Red Dancefloor Press, 1997.

Stephans, Michael. *Experiencing Ornette Coleman: A Listener's Companion*. Lanham, MD: Rowman & Littlefield Publishers, 2017.

Terry, Clark. *Clark: The Autobiography of Clark Terry*. Oakland: University of California Press, 2011.

Truesdell, Ryan. "Study Scores: On the Way to the Sky (Complete)." *ArtistShare*, July 29, 2006. https://www.artistshare.com/Projects/OfferDetails/22/136/2575/1/6.

Ware, David. "Bob Brookmeyer—Doin' It His Way." *Jazz Education Journal* 36, no. 2 (2003): 42–44, 46, 48.

Index

7 x Wilder, 54–55

A

"ABC Blues," 26, 90–91, 203
Abercrombie John, 120–21, 184
"Airport Song," 38
Albam, Manny, 51, 76, 104, 108, 160–61, 163, 168, 184, 208, 213
AllAboutJazz, 12, 119–20, 134, 140
Argue, Darcy James, 151–52

B

Back Again, 61–62, 180
Bahora, Ben, 211, 219–20, 222
Bahora, Greg, 211, 219–20
Bailey, Dave, 18, 50, 60, 172, 182, 232
Basie, Count, 51, 66, 74, 79, 81, 84, 92, 108, 145
bass, 34–35, 37–39, 49–50, 55, 71–73, 77, 91–92, 170, 172, 180, 182, 196, 208–10
bassoon, 85, 87
Bennett, Tony, 59
"Blue in Green," 10, 38, 207
Blue Note (New York City), 206, 208, 215
The Blues Hot and Cold, 11, 52–53, 55, 72, 180
"Blues Suite," 80–81, 97, 217
BMI Jazz Composers Workshop, 155, 163, 168, 184, 207
Bob Brookmeyer, Composer, Arranger: Mel Lewis and The Jazz Orchestra, 98, 162
Bob Brookmeyer in Conversation with Dave Rivello, 21, 98, 120, 161–62, 166
Bob Brookmeyer and Friends, 58–59, 180
The Bob Brookmeyer Small Band, 62
Bowers, Jack, 134, 140
Braff, Ruby, 12

253

brass, 15, 18, 73, 77, 79, 81, 87–88, 94, 96, 122–23, 132–33, 213, 218
Broadbent, Alan, 30, 35, 37, 48
Brönner, Till, 134–36
Brookmeyer, Janet "Jan," 39, 42–45, 130, 179, 188, 190, 197, 220, 223–24, 226–27, 229–30
Brookmeyer/Standards, 143, 146–48, 182, 198, 230
"Bruise," 5, 41
Brüninghaus, Rainer, 121

C

"Cameo," 128–29
Carnegie Hall, x, 131, 187
Carnegie Hall Jazz Band, 156, 166
Celebration Suite, 124–25, 129
Challenge Records, 37, 40, 52, 64, 118, 179, 213, 217
Claassen, Fay, 14, 143, 181
clarinet, 3–4, 50, 73, 77, 80, 85, 173
Clark Terry–Bob Brookmeyer Quintet, 54, 61, 172
Cohn, Al, 49–51, 70, 77, 79–81, 84–85, 87, 95, 104
Columbia Records, 12, 58
The Concert Jazz Band, 5, 22, 26, 54, 57, 69, 71–74, 76, 83, 90, 97
Concert Jazz Band at the Village Vanguard, 54, 83
Concord Records, 32, 35
Conover, Willis, 110–11
Crow, Bill, 18, 50, 55, 60, 72, 140, 169–70, 172, 200–201, 232

D

Danish Radio Jazz Orchestra (DRJO), 93, 156, 214–15
Davis, Miles, 10, 54, 59, 137
"Detour Ahead," 36, 85–86, 113, 143, 146, 182
"Ding, Dong, Ding," 67, 162
Dix, Ed, 65–66
Dobson, Smith, 33
Dolphy, Eric, 8
Dreams, 111–12, 116, 159, 217
drums, 6, 15–19, 35, 37, 39, 49–50, 55, 57, 71–72, 77, 103, 127, 133, 159–60, 172

E

Eastman School of Music, x, 19, 68, 161, 165, 187
The Ed Partyka Jazz Orchestra, 213
Electricity, 111, 119–21, 163–64, 184, 217
"Elegy," 135, 137–38
Elias, Eliane, 214–15
Ellington, Duke, viii, 74–75, 79, 81, 84, 108, 144–46, 155, 157, 190, 196, 218
Evans, Bill, 4, 10–11, 36, 38, 51–52, 54, 57, 72, 78, 85–86, 137, 169–70
Evans, Gil, 14, 108, 135, 170, 195–96
Evolution: The Improvisational Style of Bob Brookmeyer, 5–6, 187

F

Finale (software), 164
Finnegan, Bill, 69, 84, 104, 108, 168
Fitzgerald, Ella, 145
flugelhorn, 30, 57, 59, 61, 65, 85, 124, 134–36, 172, 208
Franklin, David, 140
French horn, 17, 77, 79, 123
Full Circle, 65–66

G

Gandolfi, Michael, 151
Germany, 107, 109, 116, 123–24, 154, 161, 164, 168, 179–80, 184, 193
Gershwin, Ira, 128
Get Well Soon, 130, 134–35, 138–40, 179
Getz, Stan, 1–4, 14, 24, 26, 29, 48, 54, 56–58, 69, 71, 93, 155, 166, 202, 221
Gianelli, John, 30, 208
Gibbs, Terry, 18, 96
Giuffre, Jimmy, 26, 50–51, 55, 71, 167, 169–70, 202
"Gloomy Sunday," 84, 88–89, 102
Gloomy Sunday and Other Bright Moments, 26, 36, 54, 83–85, 88–89, 96–97, 102, 113, 167, 180, 217
Goessens, Kris, 64–65, 126, 130, 135–38, 147, 177–78
"Goodbye, World," 101, 103, 105
Gottlieb, Danny, 18, 120–21, 182–83
guitar, 6, 12, 38–39, 50, 55, 58, 73, 77, 117–18, 121, 169–70, 206

H

Hall, Jim, 4, 42, 50–51, 55, 58, 64, 71, 107, 117–18, 167–70, 202, 206, 221
Harrell, Tom, 62
"Have You Met Miss Jones?," 32
Haynes, Roy, 57, 169
Heard, John, 29, 171
Heller, Paul, 135, 138–39, 179–80
Hentoff, Nat, 7, 9, 80–81, 112, 140
Herman, Woody, 74–75, 108, 144, 159, 163
Holiday, Billie "Lady Day," 36–37, 52, 65, 85–86, 144–46, 163
Hollenbeck, John, 18, 65, 123–25, 127, 132, 135, 139, 142–43, 146, 157–58, 160, 165, 182, 213
Holman, Willis "Bill," 29, 61, 104, 108, 135, 161, 165, 200–201, 213–14
Hudson, Rob, x, 6, 187–88

I

Ilg, Deiter, 184
Impulsive!, 214–15, 217
Island, 65
The Ivory Hunters, 51, 157

J

"Janet Planet," 39
Johnson, Gus, 50
Johnson, Osie, 18, 51, 60, 172
Jones, Elvin, 18, 59
Jones, Hank, 50, 60, 88, 90–91
Jones, Thad, 14–15, 61–62, 76, 90–91, 93–94, 155–56, 163, 166, 196, 202, 211. *See also* Thad Jones/Mel Lewis Jazz Orchestra
Juris, Vic, 6

K

Kansas City, 3, 7, 17, 42, 51, 66, 74, 80, 101, 217, 226
Kansas City Revisited, 51, 72, 80
"Kathleen," 39
Kind of Blue, 10, 54
Kirchner, Bill, 74

Koonse, Larry, 5–6, 10–11, 30, 38–39, 41, 65, 206
Korall, Burt, 105, 160, 184
"KP 94," 131–33, 161
Kuhn, Steve, 56–57

L

LaBarbera, Joe, 18, 62
Lewis, Jack, 51–52
Lewis, Mel, 14, 18, 49, 53, 55, 61–62, 72–73, 88, 90–96, 101–5, 109, 117, 155–56, 182–85, 201. *See also* Mel Lewis Jazz Orchestra; Thad Jones/Mel Lewis Jazz Orchestra
Liebman, Dave, 140
Live at the Village Vanguard albums (various), 54, 96, 104, 108, 111–12
Lovano, Joe, 63, 104–5, 145, 185, 202

M

"Make Me Smile," 156
Make Me Smile & Other New Works, 98, 163, 195
Manhattan, 25, 30, 208, 232
Manhattan School of Music, 154, 166, 174, 185, 196
"Manoir Des Mes Rêves," 73, 205, 217
Maupin, Bennie, 8
McNeely, Jim, 62–63, 94, 98–99, 103, 154–55, 165, 203, 206–7, 212–13
Mel Lewis Jazz Orchestra, 101, 108, 111, 129, 131, 145, 186, 202–3, 211
Mingus, Charles, 7–8, 40, 102, 169
Monk, Thelonious, 25, 40, 54, 115–16, 157, 169, 196
Mosca, John, 94, 101, 166–67, 212
Moutin, Francois, 6
Mulligan, Gerry, 1–2, 4–5, 22, 26, 47, 54, 57, 69–76, 83, 90, 96, 124–27, 167, 173, 181, 201–2, 205, 221
Music for String Quartet and Orchestra, 215, 217
"My Funny Valentine," 98–101, 111, 131
Myers, Marc, 12, 38, 43, 68–69, 90, 109

N

"The Nasty Dance," 40, 104–5, 111, 145, 153
Nelson, Kathleen, 39, 43–45, 113–14, 223–24, 226–27, 229
Nemeyer, Eric, 122–23

Neves, John, 57
The New Art Orchestra (NAO), 107–8, 123–25, 128–29, 132, 134–35, 139, 142–43, 145–46, 175, 179, 181, 213, 216–17
New England Conservatory, 142, 149, 166, 174
New Hampshire, 43, 45, 136, 144, 149, 187, 189, 221, 224, 227, 229
The New Jazz Sounds of Showboat, 12
New Works Celebration, 124–25,
New York, 24–25, 42, 60–61, 92–93, 153, 156, 158, 166, 168, 170, 192, 196, 221
New York City, 25–26, 30, 51–52, 54, 68, 72, 76, 79, 158, 160, 163, 206, 208
A Night at the Village Vanguard, 54
Nussbaum, Adam, 18, 63, 182, 203

O

Oatts, Dick, 62–63, 94, 98–99, 102, 203–4, 212–13
"Old Man River," 12–13
Oles, Darek, 30
"On the Sunny Side of the Street," 11, 53
On the Way to the Sky, 111, 116–17, 119–20, 231
Oslo, 32, 35, 37, 48, 64, 209
Over Time: Music of Bob Brookmeyer, 212

P

Paris Suite, 38, 64–65, 136
Parker, Charlie, viii, 9, 171
Payne, Douglas, 119–21
Perry, Rich, 103, 212
piano, viii, 3–4, 10, 49, 51–52, 55–56, 58, 60–61, 65, 77, 79–82, 147, 172
Portrait of the Artist, 67, 72, 80, 82, 85, 97, 217
Pribeck, Gary, 103

R

Ramsey, Doug, 140, 191, 205
Raney, Jimmy, 49, 58, 169–70
Reinhardt, Django, 73, 217
rhythm section, 30, 32, 36, 49, 53, 55, 57, 60, 69, 72, 87–88, 99, 102
Rifftides, 191

Index 259

Riley, John, 18, 182, 185–86
Rivello, Dave, x, 19, 63, 98, 113, 117, 120, 131, 149, 161–62, 218
Robinson, Scott, 124–26, 173–74
Rollins, Sonny, 54, 137–38, 231
Rowles, Jimmy, 49, 53, 61

S

Samba Para Dos, 13, 58
Saunders, Theo, 22, 28, 30–33, 35, 208, 223
saxophone, 25, 49, 52, 72, 77, 103, 132–33, 138, 179, 202, 204
   alto, 12, 88, 98–99, 212
   baritone, 21, 26, 47, 50, 57, 70–72, 90, 124–27, 205
   bass, 173, 175
   soprano, 102
   tenor, 49, 51, 56, 63, 65, 91, 103, 138, 145, 205, 212
Schaphorst, Ken, 151
Schifrin, Lalo, 13–14, 58
Schleswig-Holstein Musik Festival, 125, 134, 180
   Big Band, 123–24, 159, 181, 213
Schneider, Maria, 130, 147, 157, 175, 193–94, 213
Schoenberg, Loren, 57
Scofield, John, 32, 185, 206
Scruton, Roger, 110–11
Sims, Zoot, 49, 131, 169
"Skylark," 61, 98–99, 143, 156, 175, 213, 232
slide trombone, 4, 7, 22–23, 208
Smith, Chris, 18, 90, 95–97
Smith, Putter, 30–31, 208, 210
Snyder, John, 169
Spires, Elizabeth, 44
Spirit Music, 130, 139–41, 143
St. Peter's Cathedral, 201, 208, 219, 230
Stan Getz–Bob Brookmeyer Recorded Fall 1961, 56
"Stay Out of the Sun," 40
Stay Out of the Sun, 5, 34, 37, 40, 65, 207
Stockholm Jazz Orchestra, 112, 115
Stravinsky, Igor, 104, 122
Sweden, 42, 107, 109, 168, 229

T

Tabackin, Lew, 28, 75
Teachout, Terry, 190–91
Terry, Clark, 1, 4, 8, 57, 59–60, 88, 124, 164, 167, 171–72, 202, 205, 208. *See also* Clark Terry–Bob Brookmeyer Quintet
Thad Jones/Mel Lewis Jazz Orchestra, 5, 14, 90, 108, 111, 146, 156, 166, 202, 211, 217
"Time After Time," 13
Traditionalism Revisited, 50, 56, 71–72
trombone, 3–4, 49, 52, 71–72, 77, 79–80, 102–4, 114, 127, 133, 135, 187–88, 190, 205, 207–8
Trombone Jazz Samba, 58
trumpet, 3–4, 7, 69, 71–72, 77–78, 80, 82, 88, 115, 117, 127–28, 133, 135, 173–74, 205
"Two Shadows," 44

U

Uchida, Mitsuko, 137

V

"Valentine," 100–101
valve trombone, viii, x, 3–4, 7–8, 11–13, 21, 23, 49, 52–53, 55–56, 58, 61, 77, 204–5, 208–9
Vanguard Jazz Orchestra (VJO), 116, 156, 166, 185–86, 190, 203, 211–13
Verve Records, 11, 13, 48, 53–54, 57–58, 72–73, 82–83, 89, 97, 129, 205
The View from the Back of the Band, 18, 90, 95
Village Vanguard (New York City), 36, 54, 98, 101, 112, 145, 183, 185, 190, 205
Von Essen, Eric, 32, 35, 38, 209

W

Waltzing with Zoe, 130, 132, 161
Warrington, Tom, 5, 30, 34, 38–39, 65
Werner, Kenny, 190, 203
Wheeler, Kenny, 65, 161, 209
"Where, Oh Where," 85, 87, 89
"Whooeee!," 49
"Willow Weep for Me," 14–15, 26, 90–91, 143, 146, 182, 203, 206
Woods, Phil, 12, 88, 155, 169